W9-AMY-344

ARTISTIC LICENSE

ARTISTIC LICENSE

Three Centuries of Good Writing and Bad Behavior

Brooke Allen

Ivan R. Dee
CHICAGO 2004

 For information, address: Ivan R. Dee, Publisher, 1332 North Halsted Street, Chicago 60622. Manufactured in the United States of America and printed on acid-free paper.

Library of Congress Cataloging-in-Publication Data:
Allen, Brooke.
Artistic license : three centuries of good writing and bad behavior / Brooke Allen.
p. cm.
ISBN 1-56663-595-0 (alk. paper)
1. Authors, English—Anecdotes. 2. Authors, American—Anecdotes. 3. Conduct of life—Anecdotes. 4. Authorship—Anecdotes. I. Title.
PR106.A55 2004
820.9—dc22

2004045537

To Lizzy, Evie, and Jay Jay

Acknowledgments

"Pepys's Indecent Familiarity," "The Unsentimental Journey of Laurence Sterne," "The Scholar of Scandal," "The Self-renewing Jane Austen," "The Tragic Life and Comic Art of William Makepeace Thackeray," "Wilkie Collins: An Enlightened Libertine," "Henty's Christian Gentlemen," "William Saroyan's Unchained Ego," and "The Dishonorable Schoolboy" first appeared in *The New Criterion.*

"Boswell: A Quivering Jelly" and "The Byronic Melodrama" first appeared in *The Hudson Review.*

"Hans Christian Andersen: A Fight for Love and Glory," "Hawthorne's Twilit Soul," "No Ladies' Man," "The Wizard Behind the Curtain," and "With the Murphys: What a Swell Party It Was" first appeared in the *New York Times Book Review.*

"Bram Stoker and Modern Myths" was first published as the introduction to the Barnes & Noble Classics edition of *Dracula*; "Main Street's Scourge" was first published as the introduction to *Main Street* under the same imprint.

I would like to express my thanks to the following people for their invaluable help: Roger Kimball, Hilton Kramer, Michael Anderson, Alida Becker, Charles McGrath, Paula Dietz, Frederick Morgan, Ron Koury, Jeffrey Broesche, George Stade, Myron Kolatch,

Barbara Shapiro, James Panero, Robert Messenger, Christopher Carduff, David Yezzi, and Evan Hughes.

B. A.

Hudson, New York
April 2004

Preface

Anyone who studies or writes about major authors must sometimes be surprised at the dysfunctional and apparently destructive nature of great talent. The Western literary tradition, it seems, has been dominated by a sorry collection of alcoholics, compulsive gamblers, manic-depressives, sexual predators, and various unfortunate combinations of two, three, or even all of the above. The occasional exception pops up: Jane Austen, for example, was a model citizen. But such birds are very rare, and only the habitual perversity of the pedagogue could have turned this rogues' gallery of weirdos into the dim procession of canonical "dead white males" that now sends college students to sleep: Dante, the Christian synthesist; Pope, the high priest of neoclassicism; Eliot, the reverent holdout for Tradition.

When artists do uphold order and tradition, it is usually as a desperate device for keeping the chaos in their own minds and hearts at bay, and Eliot is of course the supreme example of this principle. Contemporary iconoclasts, who reject "the canon" as a form of mental imprisonment imposed by an educational establishment, too seldom understand how very iconoclastic the canonical writers themselves were in their time, and how nearly all of them were in fact spiritual, intellectual, political, or artistic liberators. Incendiaries of the eighteenth and nineteenth centuries were, in real terms, far more daring and more disturbing to the moral and ideological systems of their time than is the modern mutineer, who has staged his rebellion within a social framework that condones, or at least pretends to condone, rebellion.

In the face of today's supposed moral tolerance and relativism, it is odd and disturbing that we now talk about and teach literature in simplistically moral terms. We don't think much of contemporary writers unless they toe the line of good manners established by our nervous consensus. Any author, for instance, who writes about racial issues with any degree of subtlety is suspected of being racist and artistically dismissed: one wonders how Faulkner or Twain would fare if they came along today, and indeed *Huckleberry Finn* is often castigated, absurdly, as a racist tract. John Updike and Philip Roth might be major talents—"but," say contemporary readers, conditioned by today's careful, polite sexual politics, "if only they weren't so sexist, such phallocrats!" A recent Updike novel had its hero spying on his luscious daughter-in-law as she sat on the toilet, a scene that enraged women critics. But why the rage? Aren't we all despicable creatures? Isn't it the artist's duty to portray the human being—the *whole* human being, including the despicable elements?

Huckleberry Finn is in fact a milestone in the liberal tradition; so is *The Scarlet Letter*, despite the fact that its author was a political conservative who refused to join the all-conquering abolitionist movement. So, for all we know, might be even *Portnoy's Complaint*. Personal rectitude never has been, and must not be today, a prerequisite for literary honor. For a writer, the only kind of rectitude that matters is the artistic variety.

What is surprising is that so many writers *have* held on to artistic rectitude in the face of all-but-insuperable personal failings. Henry James, so petty in his private life, banished pettiness from his great *oeuvre*. Hans Christian Andersen, an emotionally stunted narcissist, produced beautiful and terrible images of human cruelty, vanity, and doom. Sinclair Lewis and Richard Brinsley Sheridan, hopeless alcoholics, created sublime comedy. James Boswell and George Gordon, Lord Byron, who both suffered from bipolar disorder, were not only great writers but also, despite their faults and vicissitudes, beloved by their long-suffering friends.

Writers' lives are not always particularly interesting; knowledge of them does not necessarily add to one's enjoyment of the work. In some cases, though, such knowledge does enrich our understanding. To learn the tragic facts of Thackeray's life, for instance, is to be able to see beneath the brilliant comedy of *Vanity Fair* to its much sadder depths. To know about Bram Stoker's mutually parasitical friendship with the actor Henry Irving is to gain insight into Count Dracula's relations with his acolytes.

The writers in this book would seem to have little in common. They prove, if such proof again be needed, that there is no such thing as an "artistic temperament"; there never has been. There are only artists, infinitely variable and fascinating.

Contents

Acknowledgments	vii
Preface	ix
Pepys's Indecent Familiarity	3
The Unsentimental Journey of Laurence Sterne	20
Boswell: A Quivering Jelly	36
The Scholar of Scandal	49
The Self-renewing Jane Austen	65
Hans Christian Andersen: A Fight for Love and Glory	80
The Byronic Melodrama	87
Hawthorne's Twilit Soul	98
The Tragic Life and Comic Art of William Makepeace Thackeray	105
Wilkie Collins: An Enlightened Libertine	125
Henty's Christian Gentlemen	143
Bram Stoker and Modern Myths	153
No Ladies' Man	171
The Wizard Behind the Curtain	177
With the Murphys: What a Swell Party It Was	184
Main Street's Scourge	191
William Saroyan's Unchained Ego	210
The Dishonorable Schoolboy	219
Index	235

ARTISTIC LICENSE

Pepys's Indecent Familiarity

Samuel Pepys's *Diary* (1660–1669) is an extraordinary document in many ways, but its most extraordinary aspect is that Pepys seems to have had no model for it. In terms of informality and naked self-revelation, it was unprecedented; the only comparable writings to precede it were Montaigne's essays (1580–1588), but Montaigne wrote principally in the interests of philosophical inquiry, which Pepys did not—and in any case Pepys had not read Montaigne when he wrote the *Diary*. It is true that some of Pepys's contemporaries kept journals, the best-known being John Evelyn's, begun in the 1640s. But this was a decorous (not to say dull) chronicle of travel, politics, and public affairs, unlikely to shock anyone. Another of Pepys's friends, the famous scientist Robert Hooke, also wrote a journal, but it was dry and relatively impersonal. So that when the twenty-seven-year-old Pepys began his diary he was effectively creating a new genre.

Robert Louis Stevenson saw Pepys as an "unparalleled figure in the annals of mankind," for three reasons:

> first, because he was a man known to his contemporaries in a halo of almost historical pomp, and to his remote descendents with an indecent familiarity, like a tap-room comrade; second, because he has outstripped all competitors in the art of virtue of a conscious honesty

about himself; and, third, because, being in many ways a very ordinary person, he has yet placed himself before the public eye with such a fullness and such an intimacy of detail as might be envied by a genius like Montaigne.

What prompted this obscure but rising young clerk to undertake this odd project? Why did he write, and for whom? For himself alone? For posterity? Though he wrote it in shorthand and kept its existence a secret during his lifetime, he must have believed that the *Diary* would be read after his death, for he didn't destroy it, as he did many other papers and documents; indeed he took good care of its six volumes, binding them expensively and leaving them, along with his other books, to Magdalen College, Cambridge. How, then, does one account for an entry like the following:

> Thence away to the Strand to my bookseller's, and there stayed an hour and bought that idle, roguish book, *L'escholle des Filles*, which I have bought in plain binding (avoiding the buying of it better bound) because I resolve, as soon as I have read it, to burn it, that it may not stand in the list of books, nor among them, to disgrace them if it should be found.

He destroyed this lewd volume lest it disgrace his posthumous memory; yet at the same time he recorded his reading of the book, *and* its destruction, in the diary he so carefully preserved. As Stevenson asks, "to whom was he posing . . . and what, in the name of astonishment, was the nature of the pose?" His behavior is irrational, possibly hypocritical; but the wonderful thing about the *Diary* is its cheerful acceptance of the irrational and the hypocritical. Nothing human is alien to Pepys.

Pepys, middle class, striving, intelligent without being a genius, selfish, lecherous, greedy for life and all the good things it has to offer, is a classic Everyman, surely as recognizably human to readers in

China or Africa as he is to his compatriots. Yet he was also very much a man of his particular circumstances, and the remarkable nature of those circumstances has given his *Diary* historical as well as literary importance. Censorship during the 1660s ensured that only one newspaper was published in London, the government-controlled *London Gazette*. Pepys's vivid insider's account of the political turmoil of the Restoration, as well as his famous eyewitness reports of public events and panics such as the plague of 1665, the great fire of 1666, and the Dutch attack on the Medway in 1667, detailed and informative, have probably done more to shape our vision of Restoration London than the work of any other artist or writer of the period, including Marvell, Dryden, Milton, and the great court painter Lely.

Pepys lived for seventy years, perhaps the most interesting seventy-year span in British history; the *Diary* covers only nine. Claire Tomalin, the author of biographies of Jane Austen, Katherine Mansfield, and Mary Wollstonecraft, has provided us with a full biography of the diarist in *Samuel Pepys: The Unequalled Self*. The abrupt termination of the *Diary* has always frustrated readers: with failing eyesight and fearful that he was going blind, the thirty-seven-year-old Pepys reluctantly took a course which, as he put it, was "almost as much as to see myself go into my grave—for which, and all the discomforts that will accompany my being blind, the good God prepare me." His eyes soon recovered, but he never resumed the *Diary*, a sad loss for readers and historians. It would have been enlightening to have had his version of the next thirty years: the Test Acts, the Popish Plot, the Glorious Revolution were all events in which, as he rose ever higher in government administration, he was deeply involved; his friendly working relationship with Charles II and his far more intimate knowledge of James II would have made his account uniquely valuable. As Robert Latham, onetime curator of the Pepys Library at Magdalen College, commented, the Pepys *Diary* of the 1670s and '80s "must rank as one of the most interesting books never written."

The inevitable problem Tomalin has had to contend with is the richness and color of the material for the 1660s, and the thinness of the sources for the rest of Pepys's life. She has struggled somewhat under this handicap, not always with the greatest success. Pepys, so stunningly alive as a young man, abruptly disappears in 1669 and is replaced by an imposing, bewigged, middle-aged civil servant. As he ages he accrues honors and titles; but he becomes ever more distant from the crude youth we so enjoyed.

Pepys was one of the earliest examples, in England, of a self-made man, and as such he stood out as peculiarly modern in a society that still retained many feudal traits. Pepys benefited from this system in his youth, but his life, as it progressed, is emblematic of the erosion of aristocratic prerogative and the beginnings of a new meritocracy.

Pepys belonged to the bottom layer of the middle class: his parents were a tailor and a former washmaid. He possessed, though, an advantage over most of his peers in the form of an upper-class cousin, Edward Montagu, eight years his senior, who was willing to act as patron to this exceptionally bright boy and to drag him along on his own rather rocky road to the top. With the outbreak of the Civil War in 1642, Pepys was nine, Montagu seventeen years old, a passionate Parliamentarian and a friend of Cromwell's. Montagu joined the Parliamentary army, fought at Marston Moor and Naseby, and in the 1650s became a member of Cromwell's council of state and eventually the Commonwealth navy's sole general at sea.

Pepys was brought up as a Puritan and a Parliamentary sympathizer. He was educated at the very grammar school, in Huntingdon, where Cromwell had been a pupil, and later at St. Paul's, the most Puritan of the London schools. "St. Paul's," comments Tomalin, "was responsible for the education of two of the greatest writers of the century, Milton . . . and Pepys. The fact that both have been found shocking is in itself a tribute to the quality of the education they got there." As a schoolboy Pepys snuck out of St. Paul's to watch the execution of

Charles I, and remained staunchly unmoved upon that memorable scene; years later he remembered having told his school friends that if he were required to give a sermon on the event, he would take as his text "The memory of the wicked shall rot."

He would occasionally be embarrassed when, as a servant of the Restoration, he was reminded by former schoolfellows that he had been "a great roundhead" in his day, and certainly the Stuarts had few more loyal retainers than he. Still, and for all his pleasure-seeking and lechery, the early Puritan ideals never really died. In 1667 he was prompted to reflect on "the bad management of things now compared with what it was in the late rebellious times, when men, some for fear and some for religion, minded their business; which none do now, by being void of both"; a year later he found himself irritated at a performance of Jonson's *Bartholomew Fair*, remarking that "the business of abusing the puritans begins to grow stale, and of no use, they being the people that at last will be found the wisest."

This admiration for Puritanism was strictly secular. In the *Diary* he confessed to being a religious skeptic, and, as Tomalin says, "so little religious feeling did he possess that even at Cambridge [that is, when the Puritan government was in power] he took the sacrament only 'once or twice'—he was not sure which—and then not again for more than ten years." She also remarks on the extreme sparseness of biblical allusion in the *Diary*, unusual for a writer of his generation. He paid lip service of course, like all his contemporaries, to conventional Protestant dogma, but his formulaic thanks to God sound perfunctory except when he expresses gratitude for health or wealth, in which case the tone is more sincere.

It was the Puritan efficiency, what we would nowadays call the Puritan work ethic, that he admired, not Puritan theology. "For myself," he wrote in 1665, "chance without merit brought me in, and that diligence only keeps me so, and will, living as I do among so many lazy people, that the diligent man becomes necessary, that they cannot do anything without him." Diligence was his one and only key to further advancement, and he struggled mightily with its enemies: like Bridget Jones, he filled many diary pages with vows to lay off the booze, and with self-congratulations when he managed to do so. (In a wonderful Jonesian moment he falls happily off the wagon, justifying his behavior by claiming that his oath no longer holds, since his doctor, to whom it was made, has just died of the plague.)

During the 1650s Pepys lived in his cousin Montagu's household as an only slightly glorified servant, Figaro to Montagu's Almaviva. In 1655 he married Elizabeth Marchant de St. Michel, a fourteen-year-old French girl from an impoverished and rather seedy family, and for three years the temperamental young couple resided, uncomfortably and unhappily, in a garret above Montagu's offices in Whitehall; Pepys at this point was still such a lowly insect in the great scheme of things that he did not think of introducing his bride to his patron. In 1658 the couple procured a little house in Axe Yard, Westminster, along with their fourteen-year-old maid, Jane Birch. "A trio where they had been a duet," Tomalin says, "and perhaps the trio form suited them better. . . . And since tact was not the foremost quality of either Sam or Elizabeth, much was expected of Jane."

The political climate of the country was ominous. Cromwell died suddenly in September 1658; Edward Montagu sided with those who wished Richard Cromwell to succeed his father, rather than with the radical republicans. Richard duly took office but proved as unlike his father as it was possible to be: "The old Vulture died," as one chronicler put it, "and out of his ashes rose a Titmouse." After only a few months he retired, to be replaced by a republican government; but in the leadership vacuum the emotional tide of the country had definitively turned, and people at the top of government—Edward Montagu included—began to look toward Charles Stuart in his continental exile. In a secret correspondence, Charles offered Montagu rich rewards, an earldom and a fortune, in exchange for his support. It was a moment of tremendous delicacy for those in positions of power, most of whom were well aware that their careers and sometimes even their lives depended on their behavior at this juncture. Montagu knew that "he must judge exactly when to jettison [his] loyalty to the remnants of Cromwell's regime and to make [his] submission to the king, and then to make it so acceptably that he would reward [him] for it."

This is the moment at which the diary begins; it was a turning point in history, in some ways comparable, as Tomalin proposes, to 1989, when power brokers throughout the Soviet Empire began desperately re-placing bets and shifting alliances while the long pent-up force of the popular will changed their world with an irresistible momentum. In January the army of the kingmaker general, George Monck, crossed the border from Scotland and began marching toward the capital; his support would be critical for either king or parliament, but no one knew, even after he had arrived in London, which side he would give his weight to. With characteristic evenhandedness Pepys juxtaposes the dramatic—his first sight of the great army camped ominously in the streets—with the homely: ". . . went walking all over Whitehall, whither Gen. Monke was newly come and we saw all his forces march by in very good plight and stout officers. Thence to my house, where we dined; but with a great deal of patience, for the mutton came in raw and so we were fain to stay the stewing of it."

Monck, as it turned out, put himself at the service of Charles. So did Edward Montagu, who was responsible, as the newly appointed commander of the fleet, for fetching Charles from the Netherlands in a great warship—the *Naseby*, hastily renamed the *Royall Charles*—and bringing him home to England, a journey on which Pepys accompanied his master, describing his impressions memorably: at one point "the shore was so full of people to expect their coming as that it was black (which otherwise is white sand) as everyone would stand by one another"; three days later he shared a barge "with a dog that the King loved (which shit in the boat, which made us laugh and me think that a King and all that belongs to him are but just as others are").

This is a note that will creep into the *Diary* on many a subsequent occasion. Pepys was a royalist from policy rather than conviction. In 1665, for example, after a meeting with the king and his brother James, Duke of York (the Lord High Admiral, Pepys's ultimate boss at the Admiralty, and the future King James II), he finds himself, as usual, underwhelmed: "God forgive me, though I adore them with all the duty possible, yet the more a man considers and observes them, the less he finds of difference between them and other men, though (blessed be God) they are both princes of great noblenesse and spirits."

It is a magnificent example of damning with faint praise; elsewhere in the *Diary* Pepys is not so polite, and rails constantly against the luxury of the Court and the indolence and profligacy of the king. The monarchy, seen through Pepys's pragmatic eyes, appears merely a decorative, expensive necessity: necessary because the experiment in republicanism had broken down, and the ultimate post-1688 settlement of constitutional monarchy had not been conceived.

But Charles II looks better in retrospect than he did to sharp contemporaries like Pepys. His weaknesses were manifold, but it must be said that he was a great deal better than he could have been. He could have been stubborn and dogmatic, like his father, Charles I, and his brother, James II. Worse, he could have been a power-hungry absolutist, like his fearsome cousin Louis XIV. He was none of those things; he was flexible, canny, willing to work with Parliament. His clemency and utter lack of vindictiveness went far toward healing the dreadful rifts of the 1640s and '50s. Best of all, he was exceedingly tolerant, and if he had had his own way none of the laws against Catholics and Presbyterians passed by parliament during his reign would ever have been introduced. Like Pepys, he was a modern man, in many ways ahead of his time. His worst qualities were laziness and cynicism, and these are not the deadliest sins.

As a reward for his role in the Restoration, Montagu was now created Earl of Sandwich and was heaped with honors and titles: privy councillor, Treasury commissioner, master of Wardrobe, vice admiral of the navy under the Duke of York. He in turn rewarded his clever servant Pepys: "I will do you all the good Jobbs I can," he promised, and quickly got him a post as clerk of the acts with the Navy Board and a second job at the Privy Seal. Pepys, as Tomalin writes, "knew he owed every part of his good fortune to Lord Sandwich and rejoiced with him. How could he do otherwise? The world had turned over, and he had come out on top."

He was becoming, little by little, a gentleman. As early as March 1660 he received his first letter addressed to Samuel Pepys, *Esqr.*, "of which, God knows," he comments, "I was not a little proud." A year later he dined at the Tower in fine style and expressed his satisfaction fulsomely: "I was much contented to ride in such state into the towre and be received among such high company—while Mr. Mount, my Lady Duchesses gentleman-usher, stood waiting at table, whom I ever thought a man so much above me in all respects."

Pepys's social progress in the early 1660s was a bit like that of Molière's *bourgeois gentilhomme*: he took lessons in singing and dancing, more necessary to an English *gentilhomme* of the period than a French one, since dancing had been banned under the Commonwealth and Pepys, rather incredibly, had never danced in his life until 1661, when he was twenty-eight. He was self-conscious about his deficiencies—"I was forced to dance," he wrote after one shindig, "and did make an ugly shift"—and quickly set out to ameliorate the situation. Another new activity was playgoing: the theaters had been closed during the Puritan regime. Now they reopened with a vengeance, and, to add to the thrill, Restoration audiences witnessed "the astonishing first appearance on the English stage of women to play women." Pepys was addicted to the theater, though his taste was certainly not of the highest; he almost invariably praised ephemeral junk and rejected the best new plays like *The Rivals* ("the play not good") or *'Tis Pity She's a Whore* ("a simple play and ill acted") as well as the Shakespearean classics that he was seeing for the first time: "We saw *Midsummers nights dreame*, which I have never seen before, nor shall ever again, for it is the most insipid ridiculous play that ever I saw in my life."

Pepys's partner in this giddy social ascent was his wife, Elizabeth. Tomalin claims with a certain justice that the *Diary* gives

> as good an account of the married state as has ever been written, its struggles, its woes, its pleasures and its discontents. You might put the Diary into the hands of a Martian to explain the institution and its workings, at least as it existed for the middle classes for three centuries, from the seventeenth until the twentieth, when men held economic and intellectual sway over their wives; and in many aspects it is still perfectly relevant, because its great achievement is to map the tidal waters of marriage, where the waves of feeling ebb and flow from hour to hour and from month to month.

This is true, with the vital *caveat* that the account is entirely one-sided: not one single line of Elizabeth's writing has survived. Not that anyone could accuse Pepys of glossing over his faults or trying to justify them. He was always disarmingly fair-minded, if not in his actual dealings with his wife then at least in his written versions of their quarrels. There are some wonderful observations that anyone who has been a spouse will instantly recognize:

> I see that she is confirmed in it that all that I do is by design, and that my very keeping of the house in dirt [he was supervising some home improvements], and the doing of this and anything else in the house, is but to find her imployment to keep her within and from minding of her pleasure. In which, though I am sorry to see she minds it, is true enough in a great degree.

> We fell very foul; and I do find she doth keep very bad remembrances of my former unkindnesses to her, and doth mightily complain of her

> want of money and liberty; which I will rather hear and bear the complaint of then grant the contrary.

Pepys was a domestic bully, but Elizabeth gave as good as she got: she had a violent temper to match his own and never allowed herself to assume the victim's role. One of the very first entries in the *Diary* shows them indulging in a public *fracas* when Elizabeth makes known her resentment at being left at home: "My wife was very unwilling to let me go forth; but with some discontent, would go out if I did; and I going forth towards Whitehall, I saw she fallowed me, and so I stayed and took her round through Whitehall, and so carried her home angry." Physical violence broke out between them from time to time, and again, Elizabeth invariably fought back.

> I was very angry and begun to find fault with my wife for not commanding her servants as she ought. Thereupon, she giving me some cross answer, I did strike her over her left eye such a blow, as the poor wretch did cry out and was in great pain; but yet her spirit was such as to endeavor to bite and scratch me. But I cogging with her, made her leave crying, and sent for butter and parsley, and friends presently with one another; and I up, vexed at my heart to think what I had done, for she was forced to lay a poultice or something to her eye all day, and is black—and the people of the house observed it.

Pepys, as Tomalin points out, did not attempt to cast himself in the *beau rôle*. In 1663, as part of his campaign to educate and "finish" his wife (Stevenson described Elizabeth as vulgar, and though some have objected to the adjective I would say it is a reasonable one), Pepys hired a dancing master, a Mr. Pembleton. At first he was pleased by his Elizabeth's interest in her lessons; then he began to worry that she was a bit *too* interested, and got "a little angry with my wife for minding nothing now but the dancing-maister, having him come twice a day, which is folly." A few days later he found them alone, not dancing but walking! "Now, so deadly full of jealousy I am, that my heart and head did so cast about and fret, that I could not do any business possibly . . . and ready to chide at everything; and then suddenly to bed and could hardly sleep, yet durst not say anything."

The drama goes on and on, with Pepys skulking around the house, checking the bedsheets to see whether they have been mussed up, worrying to see Pembleton "leer upon" Elizabeth at church, and being made mock of by her. He openly voiced the classic male terror, usually unspoken: "I fear, without great discretion, I shall go near to lose too my command over her; and nothing doth it more then giving her this occasion of dancing and other pleasure, whereby her mind . . . finds other sweets besides pleasing of me, and so makes her that she begins not at all to take pleasure in me or study to please me as heretofore."

Both Pepys and his wife were conscious of the timeless double standard he practiced. "God knows, that I do not find honesty enough in my own mind but that upon a small temptation I could be false to her—but God pardon both my sin and my folly herein." The "God pardon" is strictly formulaic; he had no intention of curtailing his own activities, and as he ranted about his wife's friendly feelings for the dancing master he himself was availing himself of the complaisant Mrs. Betty Lane: "I did give her a Lobster and do so towse her and feel her all over, making her believe how fair and good a skin she had; and endeed, she hath a very white thigh and leg, but monstrous fat."

Pepys might fairly be described as a groper and a grabber, who took his pleasures indiscriminately whenever and wherever they presented themselves. None of his household servants was safe from his wandering hands except for the discreet, well-behaved Jane Birch, who intimidated him: "I have . . . a mind to my own wench, but I dare not, for fear she should prove honest and refuse and then tell my wife." He recorded his conquests gloatingly and in detail, usually in a ludicrous patois made up of French and Spanish with the odd Latin or Italian word thrown in:

> Dressed and had my head combed by my little [servant] girle, to whom I confess je sum demasiado kind, nuper ponendo saepe mes mains in sus dos choses de son breast. Mais il faut que je leave it lest it bring me to alguno major inconvenience.
>
> I to Westminster, and to Mrs. Martins and did hazer what yo would con her, and did aussi tocar la thigh de su landlady.

Many have assumed that the foreign words are there for purposes of discretion, but this is an absurd assumption since anyone with even a rudimentary knowledge of Romance languages can understand what he is getting at, and in any case Elizabeth, the person from whom Pepys had the most to fear, was herself French. It is far more likely that the exotic phrases provided Pepys with an additional sexual frisson, and that using them was his way of reliving the experiences with added gusto.

What makes all this particularly amusing is the fact that Pepys could be so extremely censorious about other men's peccadilloes. When the married Lord Sandwich, who appeared to undergo some sort of mid-life crisis in 1663, disgraced himself by going off to live in Chelsea with another woman, Pepys was deeply shocked and even went to the length of writing him a letter to express his concern—an extremely brave gesture from a lifelong dependent and protégé. The example set by the Court was key: when Pepys remarked in 1660 that Sandwich had become "a perfect Courtier" he did not mean it as a compliment, and he frequently expressed his opinion that "there is nothing almost but bawdry at Court from top to bottom"—though disapproval did not keep him from lusting after Lady Castlemaine, the king's glitzy, high-profile mistress: "strange it is, how for her beauty I am willing to conster all this to the best . . . though I know well enough she is a whore."

Pepys's disapproval—again, that of a secular Puritan—seems to have been set in motion principally when adulterous behavior kept a man from doing his work to the best of his ability (something that Pepys never allowed to happen in his own case). It was less the bawdry at Court that Pepys deplored than the lethargy it induced in the royal brothers, who tended to dissipate their not-always-boundless energy in compulsive womanizing. As for Lord Sandwich, his unwise affair turned out to be the first sign of an instability that would eventually damage his career. In 1665 he behaved indiscreetly over a distribution of prize cargoes; there was even talk of impeachment until Charles II saved the day by sending him as ambassador to Spain. He continued to be an important grandee but never regained the high esteem in which he had formerly been held by the Crown, and from that moment the young Pepys was more or less on his own. Pepys's career, which was to be a series of triumphs—he is still revered by historians for his reorganization of the naval administration, and thought by many to have laid the ground for British dominance of the sea during the eighteenth and nineteenth centuries—was, in the end, entirely of his own making.

The most dramatic material in the *Diary* comes toward the end, when Elizabeth at last catches him out. He is with their pretty young paid companion, Deb Willet, and while what he is getting up to with her is, as we know, nothing very unusual for him, it is the first time Elizabeth has been faced with it. She is distraught.

> . . . after supper, to have my head combed by Deb, which occasioned the greatest sorrow to me that ever I knew in this world; for my wife, coming up suddenly, did find me imbracing the girl con my hand sub su coats; and endeed, I was with my main in her cunny. I was at a wonderful loss upon it, and the girl also; and I endeavored to put it off, but my wife was struck mute and grew angry, and as her voice came to her, grew quite out of order. . . .

"At a wonderful loss!" One can just picture them standing there with their mouths open. Elizabeth went ballistic. She ranted, raged, wept; she extracted promises from Pepys not only to send Deb away but to stop seeing all the other attractive women they knew; she attacked him with hot tongs; she even confessed to being a secret Catholic. Pepys admitted the justice of her anger but couldn't help brooding about the departed Deb: "the truth is, I have a great mind for to have the maidenhead of this girl, which I should not doubt to have if yo could get time para be con her—but she will be gone and I know not whither." It was very much a pre-Romantic age, and the concept of being "in love" was foreign to Pepys, but a man in later centuries might well have called himself so. The marital struggle was fought almost to the death, with predictable results: Elizabeth appeared to have won the upper hand, with a contrite Pepys staying home in the evenings reading and even praying with her, but unsurprisingly he had resumed some of his former frolics by the time he brought the diary to its close on May 31, 1669.

In the summer of 1669 Pepys took a holiday to rest his apparently failing eyes, traveling with Elizabeth to France. Upon their return in the autumn, the unthinkable happened: Elizabeth fell ill and, quite quickly, died. Two years later their beloved house burned down; all that Pepys was able to save from the flames were his books, including the *Diary*. The house "that enshrined the memory of his years with Elizabeth" was gone. And Sandwich too was now dead, killed in a sea battle with the Dutch in 1672.

Pepys moved into the Admiralty headquarters at Derby House, and in 1672 was elected to parliament. As secretary to the Admiralty and treasurer for Tangier he exercised considerable power. In 1677 he introduced a new rule that no one should be appointed lieutenant in the navy unless he had served three years, passed an exam in navigation and seamanship, and received a certificate from his captain. "Pepys had made history at a stroke," writes Tomalin, "bringing about a revolution in the way the navy was run, fired by his belief that education and intelligence were more useful to the nation than family background and money; and that however gallant and courageous 'gentlemen' captains might be, the service needed to be professionalized."

Pepys's rise was steady but not without reverses, since his career was linked to and dependent upon the Duke of York, who as a declared Catholic was in a very vulnerable position: Pepys was imprisoned in the Tower on suspicion of treasonable, pro-Catholic correspondence during the Popish Plot, and again in 1690. Still, in 1684 he was appointed King's Secretary for Naval Affairs and was elected president of the Royal Society, and with the accession of James II in 1685 his influence seemed secure.

But the Glorious Revolution and the defeat and exile of James marked the end of Pepys's professional life. Whatever his personal opinion of Charles and James Stuart might have been, he knew he owed his career to them, and he must have felt he was past the age for accommodation. With the accession of William and Mary he joined the group of "nonjurors" who refused to take an oath of allegiance to the new sovereigns, considering themselves still bound by their earlier oaths to James. So Pepys passed, probably with relief, out of the public eye.

He never married again; Tomalin suggests, reasonably enough, that he was so exhausted by his intense, combative union with Elizabeth that he simply couldn't face another round. He did enjoy a thirty-three-year union with a discreet lady, Mary Skynner; they lived together in a suite of rooms in the house of Pepys's former clerk and surrogate son, Will Hewer, and their union was accepted as respectable by all his friends. Pepys died, after a painful illness, in 1703.

"There never was a man," commented Stevenson, "nearer being an artist, who yet was not one." This seems a good judgment on Pepys:

the greatest of diarists, the greatest of observers, but really a commentator rather than an artist. The reason for this lack would seem to be that Pepys was too extrovert to be an artist. He had, at least insofar as the *Diary* tells the truth, no inner life to speak of: everything was on or near the surface. The closest he came to introspection was during the Deb Willet affair, and he did not delve very deeply even then. He possessed, too, a certain emotional naiveté that makes the *Diary* infinitely charming and amusing but deprives it of profound insights.

Pepys's *Diary* was widely read, though in heavily bowdlerized editions, throughout the nineteenth and early twentieth centuries, and up until the Second World War. It is less known to today's readers, possibly because a full enjoyment of it demands at least a rudimentary knowledge of its historical context, which today's general reader does not possess. Tomalin's biography provides that knowledge; perhaps, armed with her work, a new generation will be inspired to tackle this most colorful, absurd, and instinctively witty chronicler.

The Unsentimental Journey of Laurence Sterne

Laurence Sterne's masterpiece, *Tristram Shandy*, is seldom read any more outside of graduate seminars. This is a sad fate for the author whom Nietzsche deemed "the most liberated spirit of all time," and whose style, in its day, was considered "the most rapid, the most happy, the most idiomatic of any that is to be found . . . the pure essence of English conversational style." The novel was wildly popular for years after its appearance. As the enthusiastic James Boswell rhymed, "Who has not *Tristram Shandy* read?/Is any mortal so ill-bred?"

The book's initial success was due in no small part to its heavy flirtation with obscenity. Such smut was considered bad enough, by certain critics, when the book was published anonymously; when it became known that its author was an Anglican minister, it caused an outright scandal. One correspondent in a popular magazine of the day voiced a widespread objection: "[I]t were greatly to be wished he had been more sparing in the use of indecent expressions. Indecent! Nay, even downright gross and obscene expressions are frequently to be met with throughout the book." This revulsion was shared by Samuel Richardson, at that time the torchbearer of high decorum in fiction: "One extenuating circumstance attends [Sterne's] works, that they are too gross to be inflaming. . . . [H]is own character as a clergyman seems much impeached by printing such gross and vulgar tales, as no decent mind can endure without extreme disgust!"

All this notwithstanding, Sterne was always able to evade the charge of outright obscenity by the skillful use of insinuation and *double entendre*: if the reader is dirty-minded enough to draw certain conclusions, the author implies, he has no one but himself to blame. For instance:

> *La Fosseuse*'s voice was naturally soft and low, yet 'twas an articulate voice: and every letter of the word *whiskers* fell distinctly upon the queen of *Navarre*'s ear—Whiskers! cried the queen, laying a greater stress upon the word, and as if she had still distrusted her ears—Whiskers; replied *La Fosseuse*, repeating the word a third time—There is not a cavalier, madam, of his age in Navarre, continued the maid of honour, pressing the page's interest upon the queen, that has so gallant a pair of—Of what? cried *Margaret*, smiling—Of whiskers, said *La Fosseuse*, with infinite modesty.

This is a peculiarly English species of humor that has survived more on stage and television than in fiction: Monty Python and Benny Hill can claim direct descent from *Tristram Shandy*, and so can West End sex farces like *Run for Your Wife* or *When Did You Last See . . . Your Trousers?* The popular and deeply silly *Are You Being Served?*, a long-running sitcom set in the men's and ladies' wear floor of a London department store, is filled with recognizably Shandean humor. For instance, in one episode the salespeople are stuck inside the store due to a transit strike. Mrs. Slocum, a formidable lady of a certain age, telephones her neighbor:

> *Mrs. Slocum:* Mr. Singh, would you be good enough to go over to my flat, look through the letter-slot, and if you see my pussy, drop a sardine on the mat?

In another show, the salespeople shiver while the heat is turned down in the store during the 1973 oil crisis:

> *Captain Peacock* (pompous middle-aged floorwalker): I hope you're not too cold, Miss Brahms?
>
> *Miss Brahms* (buxom twenty-something assistant in the ladies' underwear department): No, I borrowed a pair of earmuffs.

All this is straight Sterne, surprisingly unchanged from his day to ours.

Those who were out of sympathy with this style of humor accused Sterne of inserting it merely to attract the vulgar and the prurient. To give him his due, it seems in fact to have sprung to life perfectly spontaneously. Had not his fellow clerics Rabelais and Swift used obscenity whenever their message required it? "A Very Able Critick & One of My Colour too [i.e., another priest]—who has Read Over tristram—Made Answer Upon My saying I Would consider the colour of my Coat, as I corrected it—That the very Idea in My head would render My Book not worth a groat—still I promise to be Cautious—but I deny I have gone as far as Swift—He keeps a due distance from Rabelais—& I keep a due distance from him—Swift has said a hundred things I durst Not Say," he insisted, adding mischievously, "—Unless I was Dean of St. Patrick's."

Tristram Shandy was published in 1759, when Sterne was forty-six. His sort of dirty joke, or to put it more nicely, Rabelaisian humor, was already going out of style at the time of his death eight years later. Well aware of the changing Zeitgeist, he wrote his travel book, *A Sentimental Journey Through France and Italy* (of which he completed only the first volume), in accordance with the new vogue for pathos and sensibility. Published only three weeks before his death, it was nearly as popular as its predecessor in changing public perceptions of its mercurial author.

Already in 1762 John Langhorne in *The Monthly Review* was opining that Sterne's "excellence lay not so much in the humorous as in the pathetic"—a judgment that seems scarcely credible today. The 1782 publication of a tremendously popular anthology, *The Beauties of Sterne*, completed the author's transformation into a proto-Romantic. The editors of this volume isolated the pathetic and sentimental portions of *Tristram Shandy*, *A Sentimental Journey*, and Sterne's published sermons from their frequently ironic contexts. Thus the Laurence Sterne inherited by the nineteenth century was no longer the famously scandalous parson but was, instead, a gentle, reflective harbinger of Romanticism.

The Victorians rejected Sterne's bawdy side even more emphatically than their Romantic fathers had done. Dickens was highly unusual, for his era, in his enthusiasm for Sterne's humor; Thackeray—hardly the most puritanical man of his age—was more typical in his impatient dismissal: "Some of that dreary *double entendre* may be attributed to freer times and manners than ours, but not all. The foul satyr's eyes leer out of the leaves constantly."

It took the modern age, with its obsession with form and its tolerance for sexual content, to once again appreciate Sterne *in toto*. His influential modern admirers included, along with Nietzsche, James Joyce, Virginia Woolf, and E. M. Forster, who praised the epic's "charmed stagnation." And Sterne has come fully into his own—though perhaps for the wrong reasons—as the darling of the postmodernists, having anticipated by more than two centuries their jokey inversions of fictional conventions and structure. *Tristram Shandy* has a hero who is not even born until well into the third volume; its preface appears in volume three, its dedication in volume nine; it contains chapters that consist of only one or two lines, or of blank pages. Its story line, if it can be said to have one, is no more than a series of increasingly absurd digressions, and at one point the author even inserts a graphic representation of the meandering, self-consuming narrative. "Non enim excursus hic ejus, sed opus ipsum est,"* he quotes in the seventh volume, gently chiding any reader who might still, at that late date, be hoping for the traditional sequence of *protasis*, *epitasis*, *catastasis*, *catastrophe*, and *peripeteia*.

The debts that writers like Beckett, Borges, Nabokov, and Rushdie owe Sterne are only too obvious. Italo Calvino called Sterne "the undoubted progenitor of all the avant-garde novels of our century." Milan Kundera said he was the novelist who taught the world to see the novel as a "great game." Whether or not that is always a good thing is a nice question; so is what Sterne himself, were he to be magically restored to life, might think of his recent disciples. He certainly would have thought playfulness in the novel a good thing, but while postmodern writers are playful as a matter of theoretical doctrine, Sterne was simply having a good time. His humor was both lower and purer than that of his postmodern followers.

Sterne may have been a free spirit, but he was born into constrained circumstances from which he never really escaped: his story, written with sympathy and elegance but without much wit or spark by Ian Campbell Ross (*Laurence Sterne: A Life*), makes for rather sad reading. Sterne was by all accounts an extremely amusing man—Boswell, who was intimately acquainted with some of the most entertaining people of all time, pronounced him "the best companion I ever knew"—but Ross seems incapable of bringing this side of his subject to life. His intelligence, yes; his aberrant and destructive behavior, his dissatisfaction, his lust; but the wild spirits that made him so popular—and with many so unpopular—simply do not come across.

Sterne was born in 1713, the year of the Treaty of Utrecht that ended the War of the Spanish Succession in which his father, Roger Sterne, had served, first as a private and then as an ensign. The Sternes

*"For this is not a digression, but is itself the work." From the letters of Pliny the Younger.

had achieved a position of some prominence in seventeenth-century Yorkshire—the novelist's great-grandfather, a supporter of the Stuarts during the Civil War, had been rewarded with the archbishopric of York by Charles II—but Roger Sterne, the younger son of a younger son, had to make his own way in life, a task for which he was singularly ill-equipped. The novelist would later describe him in a family memoir:

> My Father was a little Smart Man—active to the last Degree in all Exercises—most patient of Fatigue and Disappointments of wch it pleased God to give him in full Measure—He was in his Temper some what Rapid & Hasty—but of a kindly sweet Disposition—void of all Designe; & so innocent in his own Intentions, That he suspected no one, So that you might have cheated him ten times in a Day—if nine had not been sufficient.

Roger's good-heartedness, along with his military experiences—he fought in Flanders, at the sieges of Douai and Béthune—have suggested him as an inspiration for *Tristram Shandy*'s Uncle Toby.

With the Treaty of Utrecht, Roger Sterne, like countless other army officers, was reduced to half-pay. The family was in fairly desperate straits, and the novelist's earliest memories are of moving about from one army barracks to another, in England and abroad. In 1723 or 1724 Roger Sterne took his son from Ireland back to England to leave him at Hipperholme School near Halifax, under the care of his brother, Richard Sterne, who accepted responsibility for this unknown nephew with an ill grace. Roger Sterne never saw his son again; he was to die, in Jamaica, in 1731.

There were very few avenues open to a well-educated but penurious young man at that time, and Laurence Sterne seems never to have questioned the family's decision that he go into the church. It was a career for which, with his intelligence and his sympathetic, imaginative character, he was at least superficially suited, and to the extent that he could rely on any family influence at all it was in that world, for another uncle, Jaques Sterne, was archdeacon of Cleveland and precentor of York Minster. "Jaques Sterne," comments Ross, "might serve as a model of one kind of eighteenth-century clergyman: clever, intensely ambitious, and decidedly worldly"—a sort of precursor to Trollope's Archdeacon Grantly.

Sterne was sent to Jesus College, Cambridge, to prepare for taking orders. He received a scholarship established by his kinsman, the Archbishop of York, for the benefit of poor scholars. He was ordained deacon in 1737 and, benefiting from his uncle's influence, was licensed to a curacy in Huntingdonshire.

Sterne must have been well aware of the precariousness of his position and the uncomfortable degree to which his future depended on his imperious uncle's goodwill. "If, in entering the Church, Sterne was apparently avoiding the frustrations of the military career his father had followed with so little success," Ross points out, "then he was entering an organization whose rigidly hierarchical structure was essentially no different from that of the eighteenth-century army," and he quotes Joseph Addison, who remarked that the clergy, like the military, were divided into "Generals, Field-Officers, and Subalterns." Sterne, while clearly more intelligent than his father, turned out to be not much more provident; he also showed a marked aversion for the hard exercise involved in paying court and currying favor. Despite his superior natural advantages, his ecclesiastical career turned out to be hardly more profitable than his father's military one had been.

Sterne was ordained priest in 1738 and obtained the living of Sutton-on-the-Forest, some eight miles north of York. Soon afterward he met his future wife, Elizabeth Lumley. Elizabeth, of a family as financially straitened as his own, was not much of a catch from a worldly point of view, or from any other point of view for that matter. By the time they married in 1741 she was ill with consumption, as was Sterne himself; she also seems to have been no beauty. A cousin of Elizabeth's summed up the couple's chances rather brutally: "What hopes our relation may have of settling the affections of a light and fickle man I know not, but I imagine she will set about it not by means of beauty but of the arm of flesh."

It is interesting to discover that even at this early age Sterne was considered "light and fickle"; his reputation did not improve with the passing years. The Sternes' marriage, which resulted in several pregnancies but produced only one surviving child, Lydia, was to prove uncomfortable and unhappy almost from the beginning: on the Sunday following the wedding, in fact, Sterne is known to have preached on the text "We have toiled all the night and taken nothing." As the years went on, Sterne affected (when not in the pulpit) to disapprove of marriage in general. Samuel Johnson's confidante Hester Thrale recalled him abusing the institution; when one of his audience dissented, saying that "Jesus Christ once honoured a wedding with his presence," Sterne supposedly replied, "but between You & I Sir . . . that was not the *best* thing he ever did."

In 1741 Sterne became a prebendary in York Minster. To be a prebendary, as one contemporary described it, was "a pretty easy way of dawdling away one's time; praying, walking, visiting;—& as little study as your heart would wish." But Sterne had other responsibilities: Jaques Sterne was cashing in his chips. He was a political power broker dedicated to promoting Whig interests in Yorkshire, and in exchange for his exertions on his nephew's behalf he expected the young man to put his writing talent to work in the Whig cause.

Sterne's career as a political journalist provided him with more stress than pleasure or excitement. While he was a sincere supporter of the Whig political program, sometimes even an ardent one (as he proved by writing some disturbingly anti-Catholic polemics after the Battle of Culloden in 1745), he was in truth not much of a political animal, and eighteenth-century electioneering was violent, corrupt, and unscrupulous—even more so than it is today. He made more enemies than friends during his years of bondage to the Whigs, and eventually abandoned his uncle's cause and, in effect, his own hopes for high office in the church. From then on he was on his own; the solitary battle for preferment was not to be an easy one.

In 1744 Sterne acquired a second living, that of the parish of Stillington which adjoined Sutton-on-the-Forest, and for the next two decades did duty in both parishes, as well as frequent substitute preaching at York Minster for a bit of extra cash. He and Elizabeth also took up farming, which they continued hopefully for years despite their predictable lack of success: "They kept a Dairy Farm at Sutton," remembered one friend, "had seven milch cows, but they always sold their Butter cheaper than their Neighbors, as they had not the least idea of oeconomy, [so] that they were always behindhand and in arrears with Fortune."

Sterne was not entirely unsuited to his priestly calling: he was notably compassionate to his flock and performed numerous acts of private charity in the parish; he was also a gifted preacher. A servant of his claimed that "the audience were quite delighted with him, & he never preached at Sutton but the [congregation] were in tears." Yet he was an odd clergyman: not only was he an indiscreetly unfaithful husband, but he also appears to have been skeptical almost, on occasion, to the point of agnosticism, and he kept company with a famously irreligious social set.

In 1759 Sterne ill-advisedly reentered the political fray when he penned a pamphlet called *A Political Romance*, or *The History of a Good Warm Watch-Coat*, somewhat in the manner of Swift's *Tale of a Tub*, in support of the dean of York Minster in a struggle against the archbishop. Sterne, predictably, had backed the wrong horse, and all five hundred copies of *A Political Romance* were removed from the printers and burned. (A few copies in fact survive, though Sterne himself was not aware of their existence.) It was Sterne's last effort to win favor in the church. Soon he had declared his independence and embarked upon the first volumes of *Tristram Shandy*.

"Now you desire of knowing the reason of my turning author? why truly I am tired of employing my brains for other people's advantage.—'Tis a foolish sacrifice I made for some years to a foolish person." His friends preached caution: "Get Your Preferment first Lory!" said one—"& then Write & Welcome," but Sterne was fed up with patience and diplomacy. "But suppose preferment is long acoming," he objected, "(& for aught I know I may not be preferr'd till the Resurrection of the Just)."

During this time Sterne was as reckless in his personal life as he was in his career. Elizabeth had suffered a severe nervous breakdown, by most accounts the result of her husband's frequent infidelities, and for a time she was so deranged as to imagine herself the queen of Bohemia. Apparently Sterne dallied with a number of ladies but had one particular girlfriend: Catherine Fourmantel, a singer who had created something of a stir at the York Assembly Rooms. "Perhaps because of the unhappy months he had spent during his wife's illness, Sterne threw himself with abandon into this new relationship," Ross writes. "That Sterne did not even scruple to sign his full name to compromising billets-doux suggests that his affection for Catherine Fourmantel was fully reciprocated."

The affair with Fourmantel coincided with his completion of the first two volues of *Tristram Shandy*. Sterne initially offered it to the publisher Robert Dodsley, saying that he thought the book worth fifty pounds; Dodsley disagreed and made a counter offer of twenty. Sterne then decided to stake his own money on it instead, and borrowed enough cash to produce "a lean Edition, in 2 small Vols."

That Sterne had a great deal of confidence in his novel was evident from his willingness to take financial risks he could scarcely afford. His campaign of self-promotion was equally audacious: he wrote out a letter praising the book and induced Catherine Fourmantel to send it to David Garrick as though it were her own. As a special inducement Sterne added, in the person of Fourmantel, that "the Graver People however say, tis not fit for a young Lady to recommend it however the Nobility, & great Folks stand up mightily for it. & say tis a good Book tho' a little tawdry in places."

No such puffery, as it turned out, was needed. Not everyone knew quite what to make of this odd novel; an anonymous reviewer in *The Critical Review*, for one, simply abandoned the attempt to provide a coherent summary. "This is a humorous performance," he wrote, "of which we are unable to convey any distinct ideas to our readers." But sales were brisk, surpassing even Sterne's most sanguine hopes, and he achieved the sort of overnight literary celebrity that comes along only once every two or three decades. Perhaps Boswell described Sterne's rise to fame better than anyone:

> By Fashion's hands completely drest,
> He's everywhere a welcome guest:
> He runs about from place to place,
> Now with my Lord, then with his Grace,
> And, mixing with the brilliant throng,
> He straight commences *Beau Garcon* . . .
> Each Waiter with an eager eye
> Observes him as he passes by;
> "That there is he, do, Thomas, look,
> Who's wrote such a damn'd clever book."

He dined with Lord Chesterfield; he sat for Sir Joshua Reynolds; he was presented to the Duke of York and eventually the young George III himself (though the king, embarrassingly, showed little enthusiasm for either book or author). This period was by any definition the apex of Sterne's life, and, as Ross indicates, he spent the eight years remaining to him in a vain effort to regain the heady excitement of those weeks and months.

Tristram Shandy was on many levels a shocking book, and the fact that it was written by a clergyman made it more shocking still. It was not only its bawdy elements that displeased but also an attitude that could easily be interpreted as freethinking skepticism. The novel cannot be said to have a "message," but it attacks or at the very least calls into question received ideas in almost every field of human inquiry, particularly in ethics, theology, philosophy, sex, and politics. Sterne had described his plan to Dodsley as being "a most extensive one,—taking in, not only, the Weak part of the Sciences, in wch the true point of Ridicule lies—but every Thing else, which I find Laugh-at-able in my way." He employed what he called "the Cervantic humour" for the purpose of "describing silly and trifling Events, with the Circumstantial Pomp of great Ones."

And, of course, though he didn't mention it, the obverse also holds true: great events are all too often exposed as being only silly and trifling. Sterne inserted verbatim, for instance, several pages of transcriptions of the deliberations of French theologians on the viability of intrauterine baptism. As is so often the case, no parody or burlesque could match the unutterable absurdity, madness even, of the proceedings; most readers in fact assumed the insertion was Sterne's satirical invention. Sterne did indeed lavishly parody the excesses of pedantic scholasticism elsewhere in the book, but none of his inventions quite equals the matchless nonsense of the real thing.

Sterne soon decided to capitalize on his success by publishing a collection of his sermons, in two volumes. The contrast between the bawdiness of the novel and the relatively conventional nature of the sermons caused comment, but they sold well—even better, in fact, than *Tristram Shandy* itself. Sterne was beginning, miraculously, to escape his bondage to the time-honored system of ecclesiastical preferment. As Ross demonstrates, he was one of the first "respected and respectable" writers who was able to make a living without the benefit of aristocratic patronage: he was a *commercial* writer, an altogether new species.

In 1760 Sterne acquired a new living, at Coxwold on the edge of the moors north of York. There he lived, performing his parochial duties and working on the next volumes of *Tristram Shandy*. "I shall write as long as I live, 'tis, in fact, my hobbyhorse," he decided. It seems clear that Sterne had no particular plan for his magnum opus; he simply put out two new installments every year or two, and though some critics, notably Wayne Booth, have attempted to demonstrate that *Tristram Shandy* was carefully constructed and that it ends, with volume nine, just as Sterne had always planned it to end, such arguments are exceedingly unconvincing. In fact the novel ends at the moment when Sterne's always-frail health finally gave out, and also at the time when his audience began to tire of the novel's discursive, absurdist style. Even enthusiasts wearied of the fun by the later installments: as Sir Horace Mann remarked, "Nonsense pushed too far becomes insupportable."

Sterne's private life continued as chaotic as ever. By now he and his wife had as little to do with each other as possible. "I don't know what's the matter with me," he wrote, "but I'm more sick and tired of my wife than ever—and possessed by a devil urging me to town . . . a lecherous devil that won't leave me alone, for since I'm no longer sleeping with my wife, I'm more lustful than I can bear." Elizabeth Sterne was not in fact much liked by anyone. As her cousin Elizabeth Montagu put it, "Mrs. Sterne is a woman of great integrity and has many virtues, but they stand like quills upon the fretfull porcupine, ready to go forth in sharp arrows on the least supposed offence."

Sterne dumped Catherine Fourmantel when his success brought him into contact with more sophisticated and interesting women; as time went on he would conduct a number of sentimental liaisons, and in 1767 he fell hopelessly in love with a young woman named Elizabeth Draper and carried on a passionate and foolish flirtation. Three months later she went off to India to join her husband, and Sterne spent the time remaining to him—which turned out to be less than a year—writing to her, and keeping for her eventual perusal a journal whose emotional excesses show what Ross rightly calls "an uneasy mixture of the amorous, paternal, and pastoral." Whether or not he actually had sexual relations with her or any other woman during these years is uncertain: he himself claimed that he did not, and, as Ross points out, there are enough references to impotence in *Tristram Shandy* to give one pause. Sterne died in 1768, a victim to the consumptive attacks that had tormented him for many years.

One of Sterne's many fans was Thomas Jefferson, who once declared surprisingly that "The writings of Sterne . . . form the best course of morality that ever was written." Jefferson was rather an original moralist in his own right, and Sterne, like him, was occasionally accused of paying mere lip service to the tenets of his creed. "Tristram pleads his cause well," the scapegrace John Wilkes remarked upon reading Sterne's collected sermons, "tho' he does not believe one word of it."

Was Jefferson right to represent *Tristram Shandy* as containing in itself a moral system? It is easy for modern readers to appreciate Sterne's spectacular stylistic genius, or his remarkable way with bawdy and innuendo; to appreciate or even to understand the moral underpinnings of his writing one must imaginatively enter the intellectual world of an eighteenth-century freethinker who had little choice but to work within a traditional Christian system not only of values but of beliefs.

Ross somewhat ponderously describes *Tristram Shandy* as dealing in essence with the old unanswerable: "If an all-powerful, ever-present God exists, and is the 'best of beings,' why does He allow accident, mere chance, so often to intervene in human life?" It is hard, though, to find much evidence of such tortured and pointless thought in either *Tristram Shandy* or *A Sentimental Journey*; instead, over and over again, the author hints that both enthusiasm and doctrine are irrelevant if not dangerous (*Tristram Shandy*'s heated debates between the Nosarians and the Antinosarians are a brilliant parody of Reformation polemic), and that true religion lies only in goodness, tolerance, generosity—whether they be of the Protestant variety, as with *Tristram*

Shandy's Uncle Toby, Corporal Trim, and Yorick, or even the Catholic type, as with Father Lorenzo in *A Sentimental Journey*.

Sterne had only contempt for the human race's exalted opinion of its own place in the universe. Man—"with powers which dart him from earth to heaven in a moment—that great, that most excellent, and most noble creature of the world—the *miracle* of nature, as Zoroaster in his book περί φυσεωζ called him—the SHEKINAH of the divine presence, as Chrysostum—the *image* of God, as Moses—the *ray* of divinity, as Plato—the *marvel* of *marvels*, as Aristotle." None of his characters is anything but earthbound. And he significantly makes Tristram's father, who personifies pure intellect detached from judgment and sense, recoil from the new scientific notion that the seat of the soul is in the cerebellum. "The very idea of so noble, so refined, so immaterial, and so exalted a being as the *Anima*, or even the *Animus*, taking up her residence, and sitting dabbling, like a tadpole, all day long, both summer and winter, in a puddle,—or in a liquid of any kind, how thick or thin soever, he would say, shock'd his imagination"—whereas the cannier Tristram knows very well that "the soul and body are joint-sharers in every thing they get."

In fact, if Laurence Sterne had lived two centuries later and had had other means of getting his living, it is extremely unlikely that he would have been any sort of Christian at all—though he would undoubtedly have retained his active, ironical interest in moral questions and human perversity in general. But while a moral system is easier to read into *Tristram Shandy* than any other sort of system, it is finally impossible—and completely undesirable—to impose any interpretation on the book. To do so is instantly to turn oneself into Tristram's pedantic father—though many, God knows, have tried. Here is Sigurd Burckhardt, for instance:

> The omnipresent sexual innuendo in the novel has, as one of its purposes, that of gaining expression for the "unmentionable" in the lit-

eral sense, for what cannot be said except by indirection. In this respect it serves as the metaphor of the unmentionable mystery of the word, of Tristram's paradoxical enterprise of accounting for his "wound" in the very medium of that wound itself. (We might call his quest for health homeopathic, while Uncle Toby's is allopathic.)

This sort of theorizing immediately self-destructs—or deconstructs, if you will—in Sterne's anarchic laughter, and both explicator and reader end up none the wiser. *Tristram Shandy* resists interpretation in the most resolute way, and for that reason its survival more as an academic object than as a popular "fun read" is sad and pointless. Only when it is once again read for its outrageousness, its license, its titillating innuendo, its joy, will it come back into its own.

Boswell: A Quivering Jelly

James Boswell, author of the greatest biography in the English language and one of the most amusing men of his own or any other time, was for many years considered little more than a fool, a toadying sycophant who achieved his literary effects not through any creative effort of his own but from a painstaking fidelity to his great subject: he was, it was held, merely a sort of glorified stenographer.

This image was captured cruelly in 1831 by Thomas Babington Macaulay, who influenced generations of readers. Macaulay began by praising the work: Boswell, he allowed, "is the first of biographers. He has no second. He has outdistanced all his competitors so decidedly that it is not worth while to place them. Eclipse is first, and the rest is nowhere."

But the book, in Macaulay's vision, seems to have generated itself without any particular effort from its author. For Boswell himself, Macaulay continued,

> was one of the smallest men who ever lived . . . a man of the meanest and feeblest intellect . . . servile and impertinent, shallow and pedantic, a bigot and a sot, bloated with family pride, and eternally blustering about the dignity of a born gentleman, yet stooping to be a talebearer, an eaves-dropper, a common butt in the taverns of London.

> . . . He was always laying himself at the feet of some eminent man, and begging to be spat upon and trampled upon. . . . There is not in all his books a single remark of his own on literature, politics, religion, or society, which is not either commonplace or absurd.

There was just enough truth in Macaulay's judgment for it to be taken as the whole truth. It is always risky for an intelligent man to play the buffoon, and this was a role in which Boswell strutted shamelessly throughout his life; even in his own day he was considered a bit of a joke. To Horace Walpole he was "the quintessence of busybodies"; to Edward Gibbon "an ugly, affected, disgusting fellow [who] poisons our literary club to me." Even those who loved him and valued his company—Johnson, Sir Joshua Reynolds, his collaborator Edmund Malone—found it hard to respect him. "You are longer a boy than others," Johnson remarked when Boswell was well into his thirties.

Naiveté, bumptiousness, drunkenness, an almost pathological indiscretion, and a willingness, even an eagerness, to play the stooge: these were Boswell's dominant social qualities, and they were not ones calculated to win the respect he craved, perversely, throughout his undignified life—"Be *retenu*," he often urged himself, in vain. Reflecting upon the ideal of dignity and reserve, he reflected that "in my opinion . . . it is a noble quality. It is sure to beget respect and to keep impertinence at a distance. No doubt . . . one must give up a good bit of social mirth. But this I think should not be too much indulged, except among particular friends."

This was nothing but vain philosophy; social mirth was in fact Boswell's most valuable gift, and it was one he used more wisely than his contemporaries, or in fact he himself, could have known. Had he succeeded in arriving at the high dignity to which he claimed to aspire, the world would have been the poorer, for, as Macaulay pointed out rightly enough, he had little if any talent for abstract thought, and none whatsoever for his chosen profession, the law. "I sometimes," he wrote as a young man, "indulge noble reveries of having a regiment, of getting into Parliament, making a figure, and becoming a man of consequence in the state. But these are checked by dispiriting reflections on my melancholy temper and imbecility of mind."

The real bedrock of Boswell's genius was his infectious ebullience. "Mr. Boswell's frankness and gaity made everybody communicative," as Johnson wrote after the two men toured the Hebrides together. Had he been born in the twentieth century with its flourishing and lucrative celebrity industry, Boswell would never have had to slave away at a profession for which he was manifestly unfit, but would no doubt have commanded a fat salary as a contributing editor to *Talk* or *Vanity Fair*, a sort of superduper Dominick Dunne. We can be grateful that he lived, instead, at a moment when some of the greatest minds and personalities in Western cultural history—Voltaire, Rousseau, Adam Smith, David Hume, Samuel Johnson, and Edmund Burke, among others—were alive, and, thanks to the small-town nature of the eighteenth-century social and intellectual world, readily accessible to a bright provincial like the young Boswell.

Boswell's technique, which he used again and again, was to seek out the great, disarm them with his garrulous good humor, and then direct the conversation so as to encourage them to air their ideas more openly than was their wont. He was genuinely naive, but not so naive as to be unaware of the effect he created:

> I have . . . an admirable talent of leading the conversation; I do not mean leading as in an orchestra, by playing the first fiddle, but leading as one does in examining a witness: starting topics, and making the company pursue them. Mr. Johnson appeared to me like a great mill, into which a subject is thrown to be ground. That is the test of a subject. But indeed it requires fertile minds to furnish materials for this mill.

Boswell insinuated himself into the company of his idols with a puppyish forwardness that seldom failed to disarm, then to charm, those rather jaded older men. On his youthful pilgrimage to Motiers, for example, to worship at the feet of the exiled Rousseau, he was forever pushing the social envelope:

> BOSWELL: "Will you, Sir, assume direction of me?" ROUSSEAU: "I cannot. I can be responsible only for myself." BOSWELL: "But I shall come back." ROUSSEAU: "I don't promise to see you. I am in pain. I need a chamber-pot every minute." BOSWELL: "Yes, you will see me." ROUSSEAU: "Be off; and a good journey to you."

And later:

> ROUSSEAU: " . . . Come back in the afternoon. But put your watch on the table." BOSWELL: "For how long?" ROUSSEAU: "A quarter of an hour, and no longer." BOSWELL: "Twenty minutes." ROUSSEAU: "Be off with you!—Ha! Ha!" Notwithstanding the pain he was in, he was touched with my singular sally and laughed most really. He had a gay look immediately.

So not only did the importunate young man squeeze a few extra minutes out of the eminent philosopher, he also caught, and recorded him, laughing at his guest's foolishness. And in fact the value to posterity of Boswell's account of his visit to Rousseau is not so much in the subjects he got the great man to touch upon—those were all expounded upon better, and at greater length, in Rousseau's published writings—but in the vivid and incongruous glimpses of the sage as a frivolous and amusing host. It was the same technique he would employ on a vastly larger scale in his biography of Johnson.

On his first meeting with Johnson, on May 16, 1763, Boswell had used the same maneuver. "I drank tea at Davies's in Russell Street, and about seven came in the great Mr. Samuel Johnson, whom I have so long wished to see. Mr. Davies introduced me to him. As I knew his mortal antipathy at the Scotch, I cried to Davies, 'Don't tell him where I come from.'" Commentators and biographers have seemed to think that Boswell *really* didn't want Johnson to know where he came from, and that his plea to Davies was sincere; the truth, however, can be found in Boswell's chosen verb, "cried." He wanted Johnson to hear him because, provided he could get a *bon mot* out of the great man, he didn't mind being the butt of his humor, and the ploy paid off handsomely with one of Johnson's most memorable quips: " . . . .'Mr. Johnson,' said I, 'indeed I come from Scotland, but I cannot help it.' 'Sir,' replied he, 'that, I find, is what a great many of your countrymen cannot help.'"

Bingo! Boswell never minded taking a pratfall if it could inspire a laugh, or better yet a scrap of wit, however offensive, for him to snap up for his entertaining, indiscreet journal. "The agreeable scatter-brain, the gay drinking-companion, the quaint Scots chatter-box, the admirable and untiring listener" (as described by the hell-raising politician John Wilkes) was in fact consciously adroit at catching people off guard. As Boswell complacently remarked after his second meeting with Johnson, "He was much pleased with my ingenuous and open way."

In his writings Boswell always seems to be perfectly aware of his own naiveté and to share the reader's laughter. As Adam Sisman observes in his study of Boswell's *chef d'oeuvre* (*Boswell's Presumptuous Task: The Making of the Life of Dr. Johnson*), "much of the pleasure in reading the *Life of Johnson* comes from the presence of Boswell as narrator, just as the presence of Watson (whom Holmes compared to Boswell) supplies much of the pleasure in the Sherlock Holmes stories. There are passages where Johnson appears to be sharing a confidence with the reader, while Boswell struggles to keep up, as if the writer was the last one to be let in on the joke." Boswell's *London Journal*, unknown to the public until the twentieth century and a masterpiece in its own right, contains countless examples of this technique; the long narrative of the twenty-two-year-old Boswell's seduction of "that delicious subject of gallantry, an actress" is perhaps the most memorable.

> A more voluptuous night I never enjoyed. Five times was I fairly lost in supreme rapture. Louisa was madly fond of me; she declared I was a prodigy, and asked me if this was not extraordinary for human nature. . . . She said she was quite fatigued and could neither stir leg nor arm. . . . I have painted this night as well as I could. The description is faint; but surely I may be styled a Man of Pleasure.

> We awaked from sweet repose after the luscious fatigues of the night. . . . I patrolled up and down Fleet Street, thinking on London, the seat of Parliament and the seat of pleasure, and seeming to myself as one of the wits in King Charles the Second's time. . . . I really conducted this affair with a manliness and prudence that pleased me very much. The whole expense was just eighteen shillings.

> I this day began to feel . . . a symptom of that distemper which Venus, when cross, takes it into her head to plague her votaries. But then I had run no risks. I had been with no woman but Louisa; and sure she could not have such a thing.

> Too, too plain was Signor Gonorrhoea. . . . I could scarcely credit my own senses. What! thought I, can this beautiful, this sensible, and this agreeable woman be so sadly defiled? Can corruption lodge beneath so fair a form? Can she who professed delicacy of sentiment and sincere regard for me, use me so very basely and so very cruelly? No, it is impossible.

The ingenuity and openness, though calculated for literary effect, were real enough, and while they provided the extraordinary freshness of the *Life of Johnson* and helped make Boswell's journals among the most readable of all time, they fatally missuited him for serious intellectual endeavor, financial success, or preferment in the influence-mongering political milieu he was always trying to crack. According to the world's lights, and his own—those of a conventional Scottish landowner—he was a sad failure.

Boswell's reputation as an artist in his own right, and not just as the moon circling that more substantial planet, Samuel Johnson, began with the discovery, between the mid-nineteenth and mid-twentieth centuries, of an extraordinary trove of his journals, letters, and other papers. It quickly and surprisingly became apparent just what a careful artist Boswell had actually been, and the publication in 1950 of his hilarious, candid, bawdy, and frequently touching *London Journal* garnered ecstatic reviews and sold almost a million copies. The world became acquainted, as though for the first time, with the major talent that had hitherto been obscured by Johnson's oversized shadow.

As the years go on, Samuel Johnson has receded into the distance while Boswell takes up ever more of the foreground, until now, at the dawn of the twenty-first century, it is Boswell who seems the more considerable, or at least the more interesting, figure—and certainly the more interesting writer. There are a number of reasons for this shift, skillfully examined by Sisman's study and by another new book, *A Life of James Boswell* by Peter Martin. While Sisman's is the more elegantly written and often more readable, both books are excellent portraits of a personality as unexpected and delightful today as it must have been to those of his contemporaries who were tolerant enough to overlook the often crass puerility.

During his adult life, in the second half of the eighteenth century, Boswell was very much a modern, a "new man." Johnson was already old-fashioned, of course, and in this as in other areas it is the contrast of the two that gives Boswell's *Life of Johnson* so much of its humor and force: as John Wain once pointed out, Boswell "is not merely a contrast to the reticent Johnson; he is the all-time, record-breaking contrast." Johnson personified the already dying classical standards of the eighteenth century while Boswell avidly participated in the enthusiasms of nascent Romanticism. As Adam Sisman writes,

> Johnson was a man of reason who believed in God, a philosopher who applied his mind to moral questions, a pious Prometheus. Boswell, by contrast, was imaginative rather than analytical: romantic rather than rational. Johnson was valuable to Boswell *because* they were so unalike; Boswell submissive, Johnson domineering, Boswell a quivering jelly of sensibility, Johnson a solid mass of sense. Boswell was only too pleased to enroll in the Johnsonian school, to abandon any claim to intellectual independence.

Boswell, with his moral and philosophical uncertainty, his guilt and anguish, his easy willingness to laugh at himself, is more appealing to modern notions of relativism than he was to Macaulay's era, while his sexual and alcoholic adventures are not impossible to reconcile with talent for a world that has witnessed the likes of Scott Fitzgerald, Jackson Pollock, William Burroughs, and Dylan Thomas, to name only the first that spring to mind.

Mental illness ran in Boswell's family: his grandfather was "melancholic," in the jargon of the day, an uncle ended his life in a straitjacket, and both his daughter, Euphemia, and his brother, John, spent most of their lives confined in institutions. Boswell was subject all his life to very severe depressions which, combined with a natural disinclination for concentrated effort, made uphill work of any sort of study or professional toil. An important part of his attraction to Johnson was the fact that the older man admitted to sharing his tendency to melancholy and, with his store of solid common sense, offered some techniques for combating it.

> I said I had last summer taken a course of chemistry. "Sir," said he, "take a course of chemistry, or a course of rope-dancing, or a course

> of anything to which you are inclined at the time. Contrive to have as many retreats for your mind as you can, as many things to which it can fly from itself." There was a liberal philosophy in this advice which pleased me much. I *thought* of a course of concubinage, but was afraid to mention it.

The incidence of Boswell's attacks, or "hypochondria," as he termed it, followed a pattern fairly typical of bipolar disorder: in his youth the highs were more frequent than the lows (one of the reasons, of course, he was considered so outrageous and original), but as he aged the lows increasingly dominated. During the last decade of his life, with the natural progression of the illness intensified by the death of his beloved wife, the failure of all his business and political aspirations, and his ever-heavier intake of alcohol, he was in very poor shape indeed, and as Sisman demonstrates, the fact that he was able to undertake and complete the monumental *Life of Johnson*, even with the invaluable help of Edmund Malone, was nothing short of a miracle.

Had Boswell been born into a family where artistic aspirations or even high spirits were valued, the fifty-five years of his life might not have been spent in such a constant state of turmoil. But none of his talents cut any ice with his cold, powerful father, Lord Auchinleck, who set his eldest son upon a life course in which he could not possibly succeed. Lord Auchinleck, a Very Important Person as a member of Edinburgh's Faculty of Advocates and one of the fifteen Lords of Session, was the soul of Scots sobriety and industry, and never saw young Boswell as anything but a rake and a libertine. The plan was that the son would follow his father into a legal practice and prove by his success that he was a worthy heir to the ancient Ayrshire estate of Auchinleck, with its twenty thousand acres. Boswell glowed with romantic feudalism—"I have," he wrote, "the pride of blood in me to the highest pitch"—and wished very much to cut a figure as Laird of Auchinleck, but the fact was that he was bored in the country and depressed by the narrow confines of Edinburgh society. Elysium to him was London, and he spent his life painfully torn between long stretches of dreary, dutiful life in Scotland and heady but all-too-brief descents upon the metropolis.

The first of Boswell's many projects to fail was his plan to obtain a commission in the Guards. There was never much chance that Lord Auchinleck would fund a career that would place his feckless son within easy reach of dissipation, and even Boswell himself admitted that "My great plan in getting into the Guards was not so much to be a soldier as to be in the genteel character of a gentleman." He was forced, instead, into a law career.

> But my mind, once put in ferment, could never apply itself again to solid learning. I had no inclination whatever for the Civil Law. I learned it very superficially. My principles became more and more confused. I ended a complete sceptic. I held all things in contempt, and I had no idea except to get through the passing day agreeably. . . . My fine feelings were absolutely effaced.

He had no confidence in his professional abilities: even in middle age, after years of practice, he would feel "a kind of wonder" at seeing other men defer to his opinion. Boswell's law practice never amounted to much, and after the death of his influential father in 1782 it petered out almost entirely. His efforts to win political preferment were also disastrous: his stint as Recorder of Carlisle, which put him quite literally in bondage to an odious and sadistic power broker, the Earl of Lonsdale, was a humiliation from which he never recovered.

Another scheme to gain fortune and position that came to nothing—fortunately perhaps—was Boswell's hope of making an advantageous marriage. He needed more money than he seemed likely to earn, for Auchinleck was an expensive estate to run. Peter Martin devotes many amusing pages to Boswell's long, adventuresome, and fickle search for a wife: "I must observe of myself," Boswell admitted, "that from my early years I have never seen an agreeable lady but my warm imagination has fancied as how I might marry her and has suggested a crowd of ideas . . . very true but very, very absurd." A number of suitable and not so suitable candidates were considered for the post—including one heiress who frankly admitted that she wished she liked Boswell half as much as she did Auchinleck—before, in a moment of rare sanity, Boswell realized that he really could not do better than to marry his much-loved but penniless cousin, Margaret Montgomerie. Lord Auchinleck was appalled, but Boswell was obdurate for once, and though poor Margaret, what with her husband's compulsive and lecherous womanizing, his depression, drinking, and financial failures, had much to endure, it seems that the two never fell out of love. Boswell never recovered from her death in 1789.

Boswell's only real successes during his lifetime were literary. His *Account of Corsica* was published when he was still in his twenties, and was wildly popular, quickly selling through three editions and earning him the nickname "Corsica Boswell." His *Journal of a Tour to the Hebrides* did not appear until 1785, twelve years after the actual journey and after Johnson's death, for Johnson had published his own account of the trip, and Boswell did not wish to seem to upstage his mentor. ("Between ourselves," he confided to a friend, "he is not apt to encourage one to share reputation with himself.") When it did appear, *The Journal of a Tour to the Hebrides*, like the *Life of Johnson* that would follow several years later, was fresh, original, something entirely new. No one knew quite what to make of it, and not everyone approved of its breezy informality: "it is hard to appreciate," Sisman stresses, "how different and disturbing it seemed two hundred years ago. One aspect of the book that many of Boswell's contemporaries found particularly difficult to accept was its record of private conversations. . . . By publishing so many indiscretions, Boswell jeopardized some of his most valuable friendships and won himself a reputation as an untrustworthy companion."

Samuel Johnson's death in December 1784 set off a feeding frenzy in the publishing world. The very day after hearing the shattering news, Boswell had a letter from the bookseller-publisher Charles Dilly, "in the true spirit of *the trade* wanting to know if I could have an octavo volume of 400 pages of his conversations ready by February." A fortnight after Johnson's death, six biographers were rumored to be at work.

Boswell's two principal rivals were Sir John Hawkins and Mrs. Hester Thrale, with which lady he had suffered through a long and none too friendly competition for Johnson's attention and friendship. Boswell had every intention of writing the biggest and the best biography, but he refused to be rushed, partly because of his worsening depression and alcoholism, and partly because he knew the task was too important not to be done carefully. In the event, it would take him more than six years. "Authenticity is my chief boast," he remarked, and the standards of care and scholarship he established in the *Life* were entirely out of character for himself and entirely new for the literary world: previous generations had set little store by such finicking. Even Johnson, in his influential *Lives of the Poets*, had scorned it.

Boswell proved, too, surprisingly sure of himself in matters of taste and artistic decorum. While deferring in many areas to Edmund Malone (undoubtedly the biography's midwife, to use Martin's phrase, without whom it would never have been completed), Boswell wisely resisted Malone's attempts to elevate the tone of both book and subject. Sometimes he would even sneak back slangy bits that Malone had redpenciled, such as the Earl of Pembroke's wonderful observation that "Dr. Johnson's sayings would not appear so remarkable, were it not for his *bow-wow* way."

The writing and research limped along painfully, with Boswell, toward the end, fearing he might die before the task was done. When his printer begged for a regular supply of text, saying, "You must *feed* the press," Boswell lamented that "Alas, Dinners etc. I *feed myself*." Finally, on May 16, 1791, the completed *Life* appeared.

The book was instantly recognized as one of the most entertaining ever written, which indeed it still is. Sales were brisk. But as with *The Journal of a Tour to the Hebrides*, it was too informal, too gossipy to be taken entirely seriously as literature; in general, as Sisman remarks, people who liked Johnson liked the book, though many were vaguely disturbed by its irreverence. "I profess to write, not his panegyric, but his Life," Boswell stated; "which, great and good as he was, must not be supposed to be entirely perfect." This amounted to a sharp break with biographical tradition, which demanded that a written life be didactic and exemplary. Boswell had revolutionized literary standards, though the fact was not recognized during his own lifetime.

Caught in a downward spiral of depression, dissipation, and alcoholic excess, Boswell died on May 19, 1795. His death was undoubtedly merciful, but he left a sad gap among his dwindling circle of friends. "He was in the constant habit of calling upon me almost daily," wrote the affectionate, long-suffering Malone, "and I used to grumble sometimes at his turbulence, but now miss and regret his noise and his hilarity and his perpetual good humour, which had no bounds."

Thomas Carlyle wrote that Boswell "has given more pleasure than any other man of this time, and perhaps, two or three excepted, has done the world a greater service." The judgment still stands. Boswell, however, also performed a more radical aesthetic function: he effectively killed off the ideal of high decorum in art, and in doing so helped pave the way for new definitions of art and its function—the confessional poetry of Byron and Wordsworth, the later realism of Thackeray and Dickens. In the form of a paean to the great *littérateur* and arbiter Samuel Johnson, whom he genuinely worshipped, Boswell finally slammed the door on Johnson's dying tradition. Looked at retrospectively, the *Life of Johnson* is epochal: Samuel Johnson, representing the fading ideals of the Augustan Age, visibly recedes into the past while James Boswell is very recognizably a man of our own world—for better and for worse.

The Scholar of Scandal

In 1813 Lord Byron, discussing the elderly Richard Brinsley Sheridan with some of his cronies, gave his opinion that

> Whatever Sheridan has done or chooses to do has been, *par exellence*, the *best* of its kind. He has written the best comedy (*School for Scandal*), the best drama (*The Duenna*, to my mind far beyond that St Giles lampoon, *The Beggar's Opera*), the best farce (*The Critic*—it is only too good for a farce), and the best address (Monologue on Garrick); and, to crown all, delivered the very best oration (the famous Begum speech) ever conceived or heard in this country.

It is true that Sheridan was a man of extraordinary gifts. He had two separate and very successful careers: a literary one—upon which his reputation still rests—that lasted, incredibly, only until he was thirty, and a political one, to which he personally attached more importance, that continued until his death at the age of sixty-five.

Sheridan saw himself as a Parliamentarian first, a playwright second, but posterity has never agreed, and when he was buried in Westminster Abbey it was not upon the spot he would have chosen, at the side of his longtime comrade-in-arms, Charles James Fox, but in Poet's

Corner. (With insult added to injury, he was placed next to Richard Cumberland, the writer he had so memorably mocked in *The Critic*.)

A biography of Sheridan by the Irish critic and journalist Fintan O'Toole (*The Traitor's Kiss*) portrays Sheridan as he probably would most like to be remembered: a political radical whose career personified the rapidly developing revolutionary ethos of his time, the growth of liberal thought, and the birth of modern concepts of universal human rights and international law. An Irish nationalist whose political consciousness was formed by the ideals of the American Revolution, Sheridan remained unswervingly on the left throughout an era of dramatically shifting parliamentary alliances. Sheridan held on to his radical principles, as O'Toole demonstrates, at a considerable cost.

Richard Brinsley Sheridan was descended from Donnchadh O Sioradain, a seventeenth-century Gaelic-speaking Irishman who converted to Protestantism, modified his name to Dennis Sheridan, became minister to the Protestant Bishop of Kilmore, William Bedell, and participated in Bedell's project of translating the Old Testament into Irish. This career set a pattern for the Sheridans, who while belonging to the Protestant middle class would continue to identify with the Catholic masses from which they had sprung: Dennis's younger son, William Sheridan, was the sole bishop in the Church of Ireland to refuse to take the Oath of Supremacy and Allegiance to William and Mary in 1688, a stand that cost him his position and his livelihood. The playwright's grandfather, Thomas Sheridan, was a scholar and clergyman, a great friend of Jonathan Swift, whose career in the church was ruined because of a sermon thought by the triumphant Hanoverian dynasty to be seditious.

Sheridan, then, came from a cultivated, politically independent background. His own father, another Thomas Sheridan, had turned away from the church, the traditional family career, and toward that other forum for rhetoric and performance, the theater. At the time of his son Richard's birth in 1751, Thomas was the manager of the

Smock Alley Theater in Dublin and the city's unrivaled "Monarch of the Stage"; his wife Frances, Richard's mother, was a friend of Samuel Richardson and successful in her own right as the author of a popular novel of sensibility, *Memoirs of Miss Sidney Biddulph*. But only too soon Thomas Sheridan experienced a fall from grace as abrupt as that of his father when his production of Voltaire's *Mahomet: The Imposter* incited a six-hour political riot.

The furor was such that Thomas announced that he had "entirely quitted the Stage, and will no more be concerned in the direction of it." Abruptly the Sheridans' prosperous, settled life came to an end, and they left Dublin for London, taking their older and favorite son Charles along but leaving behind three-year-old Richard and his sister Lissy. "The next eight years," O'Toole writes, "were what must have seemed to a little boy a series of expulsions from and re-admittances to the bosom of the family. . . . In all, between the ages of three and eighteen, he spent just four and a half years living with either of his parents."

In August 1759 Richard left Ireland for the last time. Although he would never see his native island again, he staunchly considered himself an Irishman throughout his life, and the country's fate dominated his political agenda and obsessed his imagination. O'Toole points out that Sheridan's younger contemporary the Duke of Wellington, also born in Ireland, opined that "being born in a stable does not make a man a horse." Sheridan would have disagreed.

At the age of eleven he was sent as a boarder to Harrow while the rest of the family decamped to France, pursued by creditors. He was neither academically outstanding nor particularly popular: as one of his teachers put it, "his industry was just sufficient to protect him from disgrace." He seems to have been practically abandoned by his parents, and when his mother died suddenly, in 1766, his father did not even contact him personally.

Modern parents and psychologists attach tremendous importance to the fostering of "self-esteem" in the developing child. Such was not the case during the eighteenth century, but even by the harsh standards of their day Sheridan's parents were both physically and emotionally neglectful. Nevertheless, if the adult Sheridan was to have more than his share of weaknesses, a want of self-esteem was certainly not among them. By the age of seventeen, when he was reunited with his family in London, he was attractive and visibly intelligent, and fully conscious of his own qualities. Lissy describes him as

> handsome, not merely in the eyes of a partial sister, but generally agreed to be so. His cheeks had the glow of health, his eyes, the finest in the world, the brilliancy of genius as soft and tender as an affectionate heart could render them, the same playful fancy, the same innoxious wit that was shown afterwards in his writings, cheered and delighted the family circle. I almost adored him.

Thomas Sheridan was acting at the Haymarket Theatre and giving "Attic Evenings" in which he sang and recited. Richard was studying oratory, mathematics, Latin, fencing, and riding; he was also reading extensively. These were the early days of British radicalism, inspired by the unrest in the American colonies and by general fears of royal despotism. Sheridan was electrified by Montesquieu's *De l'esprit des lois* and by Philip Francis's "Letters of Junius," of which he produced a satirical version.

The family soon removed to Bath, where Thomas Sheridan hoped to establish an academy of elocution and there to make use of his sons as "rhetorical ushers." But this grim prospect happily dissolved, for fashionable Bath was highly amused at the idea of an Irishman teaching correct English speech. As a friend of Sheridan's would relate, "The whole concern was presently laughed off the stage, and then Sheridan described his happiness as beginning. He danced with all the women of Bath, wrote sonnets and verses in praise of some, satires and lampoons upon others and in a very short time became the established wit and fashion of the place."

Bath was an ideal spot for a young man of Sheridan's visible talents and uncertain social status. As O'Toole demonstrates, "Nowhere else in England were the borders of polite society so permeable," and if Sheridan, as the son of an Irish actor, was something less than a gentleman, that fact was not so important in Bath as it would have been elsewhere. Society went there to amuse itself, and although it was a spa, the prevailing spirit of the place was one of festivity: as Horace Walpole quipped, people "went there well and returned home cured."

One of the chief attractions of Bath at the time of the Sheridans' arrival was a young girl named Elizabeth Linley, the daughter of an impoverished musician. A gifted singer and striking beauty, she had been performing on stage from the age of eleven or twelve and had been "transformed into a virtual icon" of the town. Elizabeth seems to have had star quality as well as beauty and talent: she was painted several times by Gainsborough, and her recent broken engagement with a rich and much older man had already become the subject of a London comedy, *The Maid of Bath.*

When the Sheridans met her in 1770, both Charles and Richard inevitably fell in love. Elizabeth (or Eliza, as they soon called her) was being pestered by a persistent suitor, Captain Thomas Mathews, and she confided her irritation to her two best friends, Lissy and Betsy Sheridan, who soon passed the information on to Richard. The idea that he might step forward, save Eliza from Mathews's importunities, and claim her for his own proved irresistible. He would show himself to be a better man than his brother; he would immediately gain fame and glamour by capturing the highly desirable "Maid of Bath"; and he would finally break free from his father. He and Eliza agreed to elope.

Once the decision was made, O'Toole points out, Sheridan "showed the qualities that were to mark his subsequent career—an extraordinary capacity to seize the moment, a genius for improvisation, and powers of persuasion that bordered on the miraculous." The young couple ran off to France, where they were married in a ceremony they must have known was not legally binding, for they did not consummate the marriage.

Mathews challenged Sheridan to a duel; they eventually fought two, of which Sheridan won the first and lost the second. These dramas, which Sheridan played to the house and milked for the maximum of publicity, made the young man a popular hero and even established him as a gentleman—at least up to a point—in a world where an actor was the social equal of a servant. He had begun his career with great éclat, and full in the face of conventional notions of social class, and from that moment on he had no further truck with contemporary pieties on that subject.

> I shall one of these days learnedly confute the idea that God could ever have intended individuals to fill up any particular Stations in which accidents of birth or fortune may have flung them. . . . *The Station* in which it has pleas'd God to place us, (or whatever the words are) is not properly interpreted. And as God very often pleases to let down great folks from the elevated Stations which they might claim as their Birth-right, there can be no reason for us to suppose that he does not mean that others should ascend.

Sheridan had no intention whatever of remaining in his own station, and in the early 1770s he set about to prepare himself for public life. He and Eliza were properly married in 1773, and her career had necessarily to come to an end: a gentleman did not allow his wife to sing on stage.

Yet, uncomfortably enough, the only career in which he was capable of achieving the instant income and fame he desired was a theatrical one. "He was caught between irreconcilable needs—to escape from the stigma of his theatrical connections and to attain public success which only the theater could bring him." And so in the summer of 1774, at the age of twenty-three, he settled down to write what would become *The Rivals*, a piece of work that drew heavily on his own life and recent adventures, with the ingenue couple, Lydia Languish and Jack Absolute, bearing a noticeable resemblance to Richard and Eliza themselves.

The Rivals opened at Covent Garden in January 1775 to mixed reviews. Although there was a general acknowledgment of the author's brilliance, the play was felt to be rather extreme and grotesque where it should have been lighthearted. In a move that was to become the pattern of his theatrical career, Sheridan withdrew the play and rewrote it in ten days, then opened it all over again. This time it was greeted with wild enthusiasm, as audiences recognized timeworn theatrical clichés parodied, twisted, and made altogether fresh and attractive by a young playwright of extraordinary verbal and dramatic inventiveness.

Sheridan's theatrical interests were very soon overshadowed by political ones, as the first shots in the American War of Independence were fired. The Revolution, which bitterly divided conservatives and a new breed of radical, was the most troubled issue in England since the Jacobite uprisings. Sheridan was never in any doubt where he stood. Early in 1776 when George III's government called for a day of fasting and prayer for the success of the war, Sheridan published an openly seditious response in the form of a lyric ode.

Courtiers, forgive the rhyming past,
I'll tell how *I* mean to fast,
And sanctify the day:
So God protect me, as I mean,
With heart all pure, and conscience clean,
To *feast*,—and not to pray.
Or, if I pray, my vows shall be
That every child of Liberty
May hail its parent's name;
And every foe, and every slave,
And ev'ry all-submissive knave,
May glory in his shame.

Sheridan saw himself, as ever, as an Irishman, and to him the principles of Irish and American independence were identical.

David Garrick, who had owned the Drury Lane Theater for nearly thirty years, was at this time talking of selling up and retiring, and so Sheridan saw an opportunity to take over one of the greatest theaters in Europe. He would need more money than he had, though, and to realize his ambitions he set out to write as commercial a comedy as possible. The result was *The Duenna*, a comic opera with music provided by his father-in-law. Written with extraordinary speed, it opened November 21, 1775, and ran for an unprecedented seventy-five performances at Covent Garden. By the beginning of 1776 Sheridan, between his earnings and his borrowings, had become part-owner and effective controller of the Drury Lane.

Fintan O'Toole is an expert on eighteenth-century theatergoing, and he displays his knowledge engagingly: "The underlying expectation of theater in Sheridan's time," he writes, "was not that it might reflect on politics but that it was a form of politics. . . . When Sheridan bought into Drury Lane, he acquired a direct relationship with the King, for Drury Lane and Covent Garden were the 'theatres royal,' operating under license from the King." These two theaters represented opposing political camps: Drury Lane was considered the opposition's theater, while Covent Garden, especially during the long administration of William Pitt the Younger, beginning in 1783, was the government's. "In taking control of Drury Lane," O'Toole says, "[Sheridan] placed himself at a crossroads where culture and politics, money and sex, the real and the imaginary, met and mingled."

Sheridan's next and greatest triumph was *The School for Scandal*. The play is still a crowd-pleaser and one of the standard pieces of the English theatrical repertory. But in its time it was much more than that, a tangible expression of its historical moment "between the American Revolution and the French when a new world seemed to be in the making and that play somehow a part of it." Its principal themes—the deceptive nature of appearances, the fickleness of reputation, the often disreputable guises behind which goodness and honesty can conceal themselves—were all ideas that were being aired in the more intellectual works of the contemporary *philosophes*. Sheridan's feckless Charles Surface and his upright but hypocritical brother Joseph functioned as metaphors for contemporary political and philosophical ideas. Among other things, the play was an attack upon the current cult of sensibility, which Sheridan implied, could too easily become a front for hypocritical prudery. In his early days at the Drury Lane, Sheridan had implicitly attacked the vogue for displays of sensibility by reviving the then-unfashionable Restoration comedies that had been superseded by "ponderous tragedies and sentimental comedies." Now, in his own play, he confronted them far more directly.

The play's impact was phenomenal. "Why can we not always be young, and seeing *The School for Scandal*?" William Hazlitt lamented many years later. "What would we not give to see it once more, as it was then acted, and with the same feelings with which we saw it then?" And in 1822 Charles Lamb wrote that "Amidst the mortifying circumstances attendant upon growing old, it is something to have seen *The School for Scandal* in its glory."

Sheridan quickly followed *The School for Scandal* with *The Critic*, his last comedy, a pure farce exposing the manifold absurdities of the theater business, in which actors were dizzyingly cast as themselves or versions of themselves, the backstage machinations of the scenic illusionists were laid amusingly bare, and the formal excesses of theatrical conventions of the period were mocked. He did not confine himself to backstage; as the title suggests, he also had fun with critics, for whom he had little use. Sheridan would have agreed with Duke Ellington's critical dictum that if it sounds good, it is good; that was about as deep as he liked to get, and he had nothing but scorn for contemporary critical writing, inoffensive as it seems when set against today's equivalent.

As with *The Rivals*, Sheridan didn't actually get around to finishing *The Critic* until opening night was almost upon him. He did not produce the final scene until the other theater owner, a Dr. Ford, locked him in a room with writing materials, food, and drink, and said he would not open the door until the play was finished. Sheridan, according to a contemporary, "took this decided measure in good part; he ate the anchovies, finished the claret, wrote the scene and laughed heartily at the ingenuity of the contrivance."

Sheridan's place in the world was now assured, his way cleared for his long-considered entrance on the political scene. The group to which he naturally gravitated was that of the younger members of the Whig oligarchy, presided over by Georgiana Cavendish, Duchess of Devonshire, and the savvy political manipulator Charles James Fox. George III had toppled the Whigs from their long tenure of power, and they were now in noisy opposition. In the persons of Fox and Edmund Burke, the left wing of the Whig party combined radical chic with aristocratic glamour, and Sheridan fit right in. He became a regular at Brooks's, the group's preferred watering hole, and began a steamy affair with an available beauty.

In 1780 Sheridan was elected to Parliament as the member for Stafford, running on a popular platform of a shorter work day and the taxation of the rich rather than the poor. Except for very brief administrations in 1782 and 1783, the Whigs, and Sheridan, were in opposition for nearly a generation, during which period the Tory William Pitt, Sheridan's nemesis, was prime minister.

Parliament was still to a large degree controlled by the monarchy, and the fact that Sheridan was inevitably disliked by the conservative George III induced him to look elsewhere for royal favor. He found it all too easily in the spoiled, unprincipled person of the Prince of Wales (the future Prince Regent, later George IV), who showered his favor on the Whigs purely as a gesture of defiance toward the oppressive father whose power he so resented. In 1785 the prince had contracted a secret marriage with a widow, Mrs. Maria Fitzherbert. Public knowledge of his union with this fervent Catholic would have spelled disaster for the prince, for the Act of Settlement and the Royal Marriage Act forbade the monarch's marriage to a Papist; exposure would have cost the prince his throne and might even have jeopardized the monarchy itself.

Fox's disapproval of Mrs. Fitzherbert alienated him from the prince, who now turned to Sheridan, making him his confidential adviser. Sheridan urged discretion upon the couple, and when the question of whether or not the prince was married was brought up in Parliament, Sheridan rushed into the breach, managing to distract public fears with a speech that was a masterpiece of equivocation.

The marriage was successfully hushed up and eventually annulled, making way for the prince's spectacularly disastrous alliance with Princess Caroline of Brunswick. But Sheridan's discretion at this crucial point earned him the prince's difficult and demanding allegiance for the next twenty years. It was a friendship that eventually proved illusory and was to harm Sheridan's career, "conjuring up," in O'Toole's words, "a tantalizing vision of great power always within sight and always out of reach."

Sheridan was as celebrated a speaker as he was a writer, possibly the greatest of the great eighteenth-century orators. His most resounding triumph, *The School for Scandal* of his political career, was his role in the impeachment and subsequent trial of Warren Hastings, governor-general of India, for corruption and cruelty. Burke and Sheridan were the driving forces behind the trial, and Sheridan the star turn. In the impeachment hearing Sheridan, with a flair for melodrama worthy of Agatha Christie, called Hastings himself as the chief witness, then proceeded to deliver a five-and-a-half-hour speech that left the House, for the first time in its history, in an eruption of cheering and applause.

But he had saved even bigger guns for the trial that followed. Public interest was at fever pitch; tickets were being sold for as much as fifty guineas, and "Many fashionable ladies lost their shoes in the mêlée, some going into the hall barefoot." One of the contemporary MPs described "a rush as there is at the pit of the playhouse when Garrick plays *King Lear*." Sheridan spoke four and a half hours the first day, then, after a hiatus of several days, finished his address with a peroration on true justice that left his audience in ecstasies.

> . . . the *real image—Justice!* I have now before me, august and pure, that abstract idea of all that would be perfect in the spirits and the aspirings of men; where the mind rises; where the heart expands; where the countenance is ever placid and benign; where her favorite attitude is—to stoop to the unfortunate; to hear their cry; and to help them; to rescue and relieve; to succour and to save!

At last, with a cry of "My Lords, I have done!" he fainted histrionically into the arms of the waiting Burke. Edward Gibbon took the performance with a grain of salt: "Sheridan at the close of his speech sank into Burke's arms;—a good actor; but I called this morning he is perfectly well." Still, Sheridan's tour-de-force was one of the great public events of the era, remembered for the rest of their lives by those who were there.

The ideas about the rights and responsibilities of man that Sheridan enunciated in these speeches held a special significance in the context of the impending revolution in France, an event that would create an irreparable fissure within the Whig party as Burke moved to the right, Sheridan to the left. Sheridan passionately attacked Burke in Parliament when the latter charged the French with having pulled down their laws, revenues, and industry. "What were their laws?" Sheridan demanded. "The arbitrary mandates of capricious despotism. What their justice? The partial adjudications of venal magistrates. What their revenues? National bankruptcy."

Although Sheridan was disgusted by the excesses of the Jacobins, he kept Girondin contacts and remained sympathetic to the basic tenets of the revolution throughout the reactionary period that set in after England and France went to war in 1792. As O'Toole persuasively demonstrates, he even committed acts that would have been thought treasonous in that fearful time. He was sympathetic with the popular radical societies, agreed in principle with the use of force to uphold Irish rights, and joined with Lord Edward Fitzgerald in the Society of Friends of the People, a challenge to the anti-revolutionary wing of the Whig party led by Burke. He did not countenance the overthrow of the British government, but he saw fit to remind Parliament, apropos of the constitution, that "We have, at this day, nothing in it that is beautiful, that had not been forced from tyrants, and taken from the usurpations of despotism."

Sheridan stuck to his political principles throughout his life: no small feat at that time for a self-made man without inherited wealth or surefire aristocratic influence who was patronized by the Whig oligarchs only so long as they continued to find him useful. In the conduct of his personal life he was less fastidious. He and Eliza, like many another glamour couple, soon fell prey to sexual temptation. Sheridan enjoyed a long liaison with Lady Harriet Duncannon, the Duchess of Devonshire's sister, while Eliza was tempted by many suitors, among them the Duke of Clarence, later King William IV. By 1790 Eliza was writing to Mrs. Canning that "S and I shall most probably come to an amicable separation when I return to town. We have been sometime separated *in fact* as man and wife. The world, my dear Hetty, is a bad one and we are both victims of its Seductions."

A year later Eliza was in love with the romantic revolutionary Lord Edward Fitzgerald and pregnant with his child. She died, however, shortly after the little girl's birth, and Lord Edward and Sheridan, who seemed never to waver in their unusual friendship, decided that the child should be baptized as Sheridan's daughter. When little Mary died in infancy, the two men were equally heartbroken.

In 1795 Sheridan married Esther Jane Ogle, called Hecca, a flighty girl twenty-five years his junior. The aging and increasingly dissolute man was invigorated by Hecca's presence, even imagining that he might once again succeed as a dramatist. And in fact he did write one more play, *Pizarro* (1799), a romantic fantasy in which the Indians defeat the conquistadors and resume their peaceful lives. It was a tremendous box-office hit and remained a reliable item in the Drury Lane repertoire until the late nineteenth century, but it has not aged well.

With Pitt's fall in 1801, Sheridan was finally in a position to seize power; the new prime minister, Addington, urged him to accept a place in his government and so, surprisingly, did his old enemy, the king. Had he done so he could have had almost anything he wanted: a hereditary peerage, a government sinecure. Instead he refused, claiming, according to a friend, that "his receiving anything like emolument . . . from Ministers would *contaminate the purity* of his support and dishonour him forever."

Although Sheridan remained in Parliament almost until his death, his influence now began to decline. He became increasingly subject to depression and paranoia fueled by alcohol. The grotesque caricatures of the elderly Sheridan from the pens of Gillray and Cruikshank testify to the Tory press's extreme dislike for "Old Sherry," but to revolutionary young men like Byron he was a consummately glamorous relic. The turning point was 1806, which brought the death of all the most notable of his friends and enemies: Pitt, Fox, the Duchess of Devonshire, and his own brother Charles, with whom he had had a troubled relationship since childhood. With the disappearance of Fox and Pitt (Burke had died in 1797), Sheridan became an anachronism, the last of the great eighteenth-century orators.

Sheridan's private life continued to deteriorate. His marriage was stormy; he drank far too much; he continued to pursue his onetime love, Harriet Duncannon, sending her pornographic pictures, threatening her, and even crushing her hand. ("Confess," she wrote to a friend, "that the rarity of this makes it worth telling—people don't usually maim grandmothers for the sake of their *beaux yeux*. One may boast a little when it happens to one.") He continued to be active in Parliament, especially in the cause of Catholic emancipation and enfranchisement in Ireland, but he would never hold power. When the leadership of the Opposition finally became vacant in 1807, he was visibly unequal to the task. "It has always been his ambition to lead the Op[position]," Harriet Duncannon observed, "and with talents and Eloquence to entitle him to any thing he had chose it, he has so degraded a mind and character that there is scarce anyone who has sunk so low as to look up to Sheridan as his chief."

In 1809 the Drury Lane burned to the ground, hideously underinsured. It was a financial disaster for Sheridan, who was pushed out of the business by his partner and investors. With foolhardy courage, he chose this moment to sever, on a matter of political principle, his dependent relationship with the Prince of Wales. "His decision to do so, in the battered and vulnerable state in which he found himself, was the bravest of his life," O'Toole ventures, "far more courageous than any elopement, duel, or gamble. He knew that if he left the prince's protection and then failed to win a seat for himself, he would be at the mercy of his creditors." Fail he did, and as a result was imprisoned twice for his debts. He was compelled to sell nearly all his possessions, even his treasured portrait of Eliza by Sir Joshua Reynolds.

Sheridan died destitute in 1816. He was given a splendiferous funeral at Westminster Abbey: the coffin of the man who had disdained to "hide his head in a coronet" was carried by six noblemen and followed by a gorgeous procession of princes, dukes, earls, and viscounts. "Such a catalogue of Mourners!" wrote Samuel Rogers to Walter Scott. "And yet he was suffered to die in the hands of the Sheriff."

It is always tempting to draw a sententious lesson from the spectacle of golden youth sunk to aged debauchery, and such a moralizing strain was to become a regular feature in Sheridan's biographies. O'Toole, thankfully, does not go in for such easy conclusions. His sympathetic portrait makes it clear that the personal excesses that cost

Sheridan so much in old age were the very same excesses that had prompted him to aim so high in youth, and that made his life the stunning success it was. Sheridan wrote the best plays of his time; he had a long and eventful political career; he enjoyed the favors of some of England's most beautiful and fascinating women. A quiet, philosophical old age would have been too much to hope for.

The Self-renewing Jane Austen

"Jane Austen: A Woman for the '90's," says the Everyman's Library ad in *Publishers Weekly*. "She's sensible, she's persuasive, she's proud. And she's the hottest film property since E. M. Forster."

Austenites will soon have a film of *Sense and Sensibility*, starring Emma Thompson. The BBC is putting out a new version of *Pride and Prejudice* and has collaborated with Sony in an ungraceful adaptation of *Persuasion*. (In their attempts to purify the movie of Hollywood sheen and give it an air of naturalism, the producers of *Persuasion* have too zealously ripped away the romantic gauze: the distressing results are an unappealing Anne Elliot, a pockmarked Captain Wentworth, a greasy-locked Benwick, and a slovenly Lady Russell.) And in an offbeat film adaptation, Austen's meddling heroine Emma Woodhouse has been charmingly resurrected as a dizzy Bel Air babe in *Clueless*.

It is heartening to see that the works of Jane Austen live on in the mainstream of our culture. She is indeed a woman for the nineties and for every decade. Though her books are almost two hundred years old, they gleam with an immediate freshness that no previous or subsequent novelist has quite achieved. They are entirely free, for example, of the lumbering contrivances and verbosity of her major predecessors in the novel, Fielding and Richardson; as for her own era, the works of Fanny Burney, Maria Edgeworth, and even Sir Walter Scott have badly withered in the intervening centuries; her immediate heirs the Brontës, for all their qualities, lack her universal and timeless appeal. The great Dickens should finally be reckoned inferior to Austen, because while she addressed her readers as intellectual equals, he too often did so in the spirit of a conjurer manipulating an audience. And the heavy-hitting moderns like James, Woolf, and Joyce were disproportionately concerned with aesthetic problems over moral ones. Shortly before his death Anthony Burgess stated his opinion, arrived at after a lifetime of studying Joyce, that "probably the novel is a middlebrow form and both Joyce and Woolf were on the wrong track." If he is right, then this middlebrow form has produced its most perfect practitioner in Jane Austen, and, in *Pride and Prejudice*, the greatest expression of sheer joyfulness in our language.

It is easy to love Austen, too easy. E. M Forster ridiculed the Austen idolator in a 1925 essay:

> I am a Jane Austenite, and therefore slightly imbecile about Jane Austen. My fatuous expression and airs of personal immunity—how ill they set on the face, say, of a Stevensonian! But Jane Austen is so different. She is my favorite author! I read and re-read, the mouth open and the mind closed. Shut up in measureless content, I greet her by the name of most kind hostess, while criticism slumbers. The Jane Austenite possesses little of the brightness he ascribes so freely to his idol. Like all regular churchgoers, he scarcely notices what is being said.

Austen fans perusing their idol's masterpieces, Forster wrote, have a tendency to fall into a "primal stupor." There is a great deal of truth in this little squib. Austen's accessibility, her wit and her jokes, the reader's confidence that there will be happy endings for all his or her favorite characters, has led to a widespread perception of Austen as a cozy novelist whose role is to provide a comforting illusion that all's right with the world. This incomplete assessment has become so widely accepted that in an article in the *Times Literary Supplement* earlier this year Joyce Carol Oates made the bizarre statement that

> there is no war, no harm, no sin, scarcely any blame, nor any blemish on a heroine's complexion. . . . If there are complications, they will be resolved; if there are misunderstandings, they will be cleared up. People make mistakes, but never fatally. Irony is not a principle of discourse. Forgiveness, compassion, generosity, warmth; lovingly detailed interiors, clothes, social mannerisms, the habits of "eccentric" characters; plots that might be disastrous, but are not.

Can Ms. Oates and I be reading the same novels? No sin? What about Maria Rushworth, Henry Crawford, Willoughby, Wickham, Mrs. Norris? On a finer, more ambiguous level, what about Mr. Bennet, Sir Thomas Bertram, Frank Churchill, Mrs. Dashwood, Mr. Price? Even some of Austen's ostensible heroes are not without sin: what reader not caught up in the Austenite's "primal stupor" can hold Edmund Bertram or Edward Ferrars to be spotless or even particularly deserving young men?

As for blemishes on the complexion, who can fail to be moved by Anne Elliot's faded bloom? And Jane Austen is of all her contemporaries the very least inclined to give us lovingly detailed interiors or descriptions of dress. With the possible exception of Northanger Abbey and Mr. Darcy's Pemberley, very few particulars of interior decoration are offered; and how many readers can say with certainty whether their favorite heroine is dark or fair, or even what color Elizabeth Bennet's fine eyes might be? Gardens and exteriors are described in rather more detail than are interiors, but this is always for the purpose of indicating subtle points of character in the house's owner or its visitor (as with Darcy and Elizabeth at Pemberley, or the various members of the Bertram family at Sotherton Court) and not for description's own sake. Far from lavishing her books with minutiae, Austen streamlined them in a manner that was almost revolutionary for her day, and she was proud of her ruthless cutting: "I have lopt & cropt so successfully," she said of *Pride and Prejudice*, "that I imagine it must be rather shorter than [*Sense and Sensibility*] altogether," and it is surely the verbal constraint, the tight focus upon character and motivation, that keep her novels living and breathing in a world whose exterior aspect is changed almost beyond recognition.

Oates's thoughtless assertion that Austen's characters make no fatal mistakes fails to take into account the fact that Austen was a highly religious woman with a stoic cast of mind. Maria Rushworth, Henry and Mary Crawford, John Willoughby are the possessors of souls, souls which are eventually lost through the characters' own actions. Willoughby's own eloquent words to Elinor Dashwood in *Sense and Sensibility* show him to be fully aware of the evil in his decision to marry a rich woman rather than the portionless Marianne, for whom he had come to feel something approaching love: "To avoid a comparative poverty, which her affection and her society would have deprived of all its horrors, I have, by raising myself to affluence, lost everything that could make it a blessing." Even a paragon of good intentions like *Pride and Prejudice*'s Mr. Bingley is capable through sheer passivity of doing irreparable damage: as Elizabeth points out, "without scheming to do wrong, or make others unhappy, there may be error, and there may be misery. Thoughtlessness, want of attention to other people's feelings, and want of resolution, will do the business." In Austen's novels mistakes, fatal mistakes, are frequently made. It is the real possibility of disaster that gives *Emma* and *Persuasion*, for example, their power; things could so easily have turned out differently, tragically. Austen's biographer Park Honan wrote that she viewed life "as a struggle never won." Even her Cinderella endings imply a lifetime of sustained moral effort beyond the longed-for marriages.

The fate of Charlotte Lucas in *Pride and Prejudice* is an example of just how ambiguous Austen could make her characters' choices, how carefully she asked her readers to consider and judge. Charlotte, hitherto a sensible young woman, decides to accept the ridiculous Mr. Collins's offer of marriage and defends herself with a reasoned, though chilling, display of what her contemporaries called Sense. We are invited to consider Charlotte's decision in the light of her possibilities and even, perhaps, to condone it; Charlotte is not made an object of judgment by the author. Yet to what extent does Austen actually sympathize with Charlotte? Is Charlotte in fact guilty of an unforgivable sin against nature and truth? In 1814 Austen herself was urging her own niece, Fanny Knight, not to think of accepting her suitor "unless you really do like him. Anything is to be preferred or endured rather than marrying without Affection."

Thus Anne Elliot's final speech to Captain Wentworth, which has startled so many readers, should by no means be taken as Austen's final judgment on the issue of persuasion. "I must believe that I was right," Anne says, "much as I suffered for it, that I was perfectly right in being guided. . . . I was right in submitting to [Lady Russell], and that if I had done otherwise, I should have suffered more in continuing the engagement than I did even in giving it up"—quite a contrast with Austen's own advice to Fanny: "Your affection gives me the greatest pleasure, but indeed you must not let anything depend on my opinion. Your own feelings & none but your own, should determine such an important point." How reliable in fact is Anne as a mouthpiece for the moralizing author? It is such tantalizing ambiguities that keep Austen's novels alive for every generation.

Oates's weirdest opinion on Austen is her assertion that "irony is not a principle of discourse." On the contrary, irony is probably the most consistent and pervasive principle of discourse in Austen's work. For the most part it is an irony that delicately adheres to the story and the characters, so much a part of the structure that it melts into its background, requiring a certain quickness of response from the reader. (To her sister she joked: "I do not write for such dull Elves / As have not a great deal of Ingenuity themselves.") It is not the heavily constructed irony of situation of the Conrad or Hardy type; Austen's meanings, her moral dichotomies, tend to be more challenging and elusive. By the end of *Sense and Sensibility* we realize that the two sisters are not opposites but complements—at times Marianne displays more sense than Elinor, Elinor more sensibility than Marianne. Elizabeth Bennet may be prejudiced, but she is also far more perceptive than most of the society around her. Darcy is proud, yet at the same time curiously humble.

It is when Austen lets her irony become too obvious—when she demands the reader's concurrence without earning it, explicitly instructing her readers as to how they ought to think—that she occasionally fails. In the very first chapter of *Mansfield Park* the omniscient narrator reveals as much about the characters of Sir Thomas, Lady Bertram, and Mrs. Norris as we learn in the entire novel: they are described, summed up, and dismissed, and from that moment they can offer no further surprises. Maria and Julia Bertram, too, on whose behavior so much of the psychological drama of the novel is to depend, are served up on a platter very early in the story. "Their vanity was in such good order," the narrator states, "that they seemed to be quite free from it, and gave themselves no airs."

How different, and how much less effective than the slow unfolding, the almost imperceptible growth of a character like Darcy's, or Elizabeth's, or Emma's. The reader loves them because his susceptibilities are beguiled and his good judgment is appealed to—but Austen *tells* us to love Fanny, and in spite of the author's obvious partiality, many readers are not convinced. In the same manner Henry Crawford is said by the narrator, again and again, to be charming. *Northanger Abbey*'s Henry Tilney, on the other hand, has no need for his author's recommendations: his own conversation demonstrates his real charm without a doubt.

Films are not the only item on the Austenite's agenda. We have also a new edition of Austen's letters, edited by Deirdre Le Faye. This is the third edition of the complete letters, following up the work of the great Austen editor R. W. Chapman, who originally published the letters in 1932 and twenty years later revised them in a second edition containing five new letters. Several new fragments have turned up since then, and additional family manuscripts have also been made available. Accordingly a number of the letters have changed places in the sequence, and Le Faye has effected some textual alterations.

The new edition, with its extensive notes on matters like provenance, watermarks, and postmarks, is of interest to scholars and is the most comprehensive edition we have—yet the general reader would probably do better to get his hands on a copy of Penelope Hughes-Hallett's 1990 selection, which is lavishly illustrated and introduces each letter with a generous measure of background material. The format favored by both Chapman and Le Faye is extremely difficult for any reader who does not know quite a lot about Jane Austen and her large extended family and circle of friends: there are endnotes rather than footnotes, so that the reader must turn to the back of the book several times per page in order to find out whom the often cryptic comments refer to, and while these notes are heavy on recondite editorial information, they contain very little about the personalities Austen is referring to, which will naturally be the principal point of interest for most readers. These are gossipy letters, and need gossipy footnotes, which Le Faye, a serious scholar, is not in the business of supplying.

Even by an Austenite it must be admitted that Jane Austen was not one of the world's great letter writers. One cannot criticize her for failing to address posterity—indeed, her modest assessment of her own claim to literary immortality is one of her more attractive qualities; it simply did not occur to her that anyone other than her correspondents might read this inconsequential tittle-tattle and household chat. Nevertheless the mundanity of her usual subject matter is not encouraging, and though, as she said, she herself found the purchase of a sponge cake interesting and might well be able to make it interesting in a novel, she seldom troubles to do so in her correspondence. Here is a typical excerpt:

> I wonder whether the Ink bottle has been filled.
>
> —Does Butcher's meat keep up at the same price? & is not Bread lower than 2/6—Mary's blue gown! —My mother must be in agonies. —I have a great mind to have *my* blue gown dyed some time or other—I proposed it once to you & you made some objection, I forget what. —It is the fashion of flounces that gives it particular Expediency. —Mrs & Miss Wildman have just been here. Miss is very plain.

And so on, and so on. There is a great deal of talk about clothes and food, clothes predominating in the author's early years, food in the later ones.

The fact is that Jane Austen led an uneventful life. She was the seventh child in her family, which consisted of six sons (James, a clergyman; Francis and Charles, both naval officers; Edward Austen Knight, adopted by a rich couple who made him their heir; Henry, the most colorful of the siblings, who pursued a variety of careers; George, a deaf-mute who lived apart from the family) and two daughters, Cassandra and Jane. The Austens were a harmonious family and remained close to one another throughout their lives. Neither of the two girls married; they lived with their parents in the village of Steventon, where their father was rector, until 1801 when Jane was twenty-five years old, then moved to Bath when Mr. Austen retired. Upon his death in 1805 the mother and two daughters settled in the Hampshire village of Chawton, on the estate of Jane's brother Edward Knight. Jane died at the age of forty-one of Addison's disease, which was at that time incurable.

Jane Austen was shy about her writing and tried to keep the fact of her authorship a secret. Her books were published with "By a Lady" in place of the author's name on the title page. Eventually the well-meaning boasts of her proud brothers and friends blew her cover; by

1813 she was writing that "the Secret has spread so far as to be scarcely the Shadow of a secret now. . . . I beleive [sic] whenever the 3rd appears, I shall not even attempt to tell Lies about it.—I shall rather try to make all the Money than all the Mystery I can of it."

In the last three or four years of her life she achieved a modest degree of celebrity, even receiving an invitation to the Prince Regent's Carlton House and a request from the Regent that she dedicate *Emma* to him. (She felt it was an offer she could not refuse, though she had always held him in contempt as a rake.) Though Austen's works never sold on the scale of Maria Edgeworth's or Fanny Burney's, both *Mansfield Park* and *Emma* did well (*Northanger Abbey* and *Persuasion* were not published until after Austen's death), and *Pride and Prejudice*, the most popular of her books during her lifetime, went into a third edition. She earned a grand total of £685 during her writing life—not a fortune, even by the standards of the time—and she complained that "People are more ready to borrow & praise, than to buy—which I cannot wonder at;—but tho' I like praise as well as anybody, I like what Edward calls *Pewter* too."

Austen took pride in her abilities and knew when she had done well (of Elizabeth Bennet she wrote, "I must confess that *I* think her as delightful a creature as ever appeared in print, & how I shall be able to tolerate those who do not like *her* at least, I do not know"); she enjoyed reading her works in progress to her family; but writing was strictly a private activity for her, and the face she presented to the world was not that of an authoress but of a rural gentlewoman. To everyone, including her family, she played down her writing as secondary in importance to her role within the household and the community. Her letters, accordingly, are much richer in domestic detail than in insights into her creative life. A reader of the correspondence who happened to be unacquainted with her novels would think her to have been a sharp, acidly amusing woman but hardly one of the immortals.

Not that the letters that survive would present her much scope for aesthetic or philosophical speculation; a few were written to her young nieces Anna and Fanny, but the vast majority were short, newsy bulletins to Cassandra during one or the other sister's absences from home, missives that Le Faye likens to telephone calls. It should be said that it is high time readers stopped maligning Cassandra Austen for destroying some of her sister's letters (mostly, it turns out, ones that contained references to ill-health or unnecessarily hurtful comments about family members still living). Cassandra in fact deserves posterity's gratitude for preserving the great majority of the letters her sister sent her; none of Austen's other correspondents did. The six Austen brothers and their parents kept none of Jane's letters, her nieces only a few.

Cassandra merits praise not only for retaining her sister's correspondence but, even more important, for taking on the lion's share of the household work, leaving Jane enough free time to write—a boon of which Jane must have been very sensible. In the last year of her life she wrote of a fellow authoress, "how good Mrs West cd have written such Books & collected so many hard words, with all her family cares, is . . . a matter of astonishment! Composition seems to me Impossible, with a head full of joints of Mutton & doses of rhubarb."

Much has been made of the fact that in neither her novels nor her letters did Jane Austen discuss the really momentous events that were being played out upon the world stage during her lifetime. In actuality Austen was alert to political events and also to the intellectual currents of her age, one in which ideas, as the historian J. Christopher Herold has written, "were in marvelous disorder, in a veritable orgy of cross-fertilization. . . . [T]hings of the mind mixed freely for a brief moment, heedless of former labels and classifications, dressed up in a riot of fantastic new fashions." Austen was the contemporary of Napoleon, Beethoven, Constable, Wordsworth, Schiller, Turner, Blake, and Byron; she was an avid reader of poetry, particularly her favorite Crabbe and Cowper; she followed with interest the wild roller coaster of contemporary politics.

But her genius stood peculiarly apart from the genius of her age. A member of the first generation of Romanticism, she remained wedded to a Johnsonian ideal of common sense; while her contemporaries courted the spark of divine madness, she was and is perhaps the sanest writer in the language. She was a faithful communicant of the Church of England and an unswerving Tory during the ascendancy of liberals and reformers. The few political reflections to which she makes her correspondents privy seem remarkably commonplace for a woman capable of such subtle reasoning in the area of human relations: in 1814, during the war with America, she wrote to a friend, "If we *are* to be ruined, it cannot be helped—but I place my hope of better things on a claim to the protection of Heaven, as a Religious Nation, a Nation in spite of much evil improving in Religion, which I cannot believe the Americans to possess"—sentiments, and prose, which point ahead to those of Queen Victoria.

Austen's recoil from serious matters was a marked characteristic. Even her own personal crises—the defection of Tom Lefroy, a young man she was growing to love, the death of Cassandra's fiancé, the death of another young man whom the family believed Jane would marry, Jane's acceptance and then almost immediate rejection of a friend's proposal—are not touched on in these letters. Austen makes light of the great dangers that threatened her two sailor brothers in the English navy's struggle against Napoleonic France; she much preferred cracking jokes to discussing painful feelings.

It is interesting to observe the way in which the distrust of emotional display shown in her letters became a major theme in her novels, for not just *Northanger Abbey* and *Sense and Sensibility* but all of Austen's fiction, from the farcical *Love and Freindship* [sic] which she wrote at the age of fourteen for the amusement of her family, right through *Persuasion*, can be seen as a rebuttal of the contemporary convention of sensibility whereby society measures intensity of emotion, and moral worth itself, by visible demonstrations of feeling.

Many of Austen's finest characters—Darcy, Elinor Dashwood, Anne Elliot, Jane Fairfax, Mr. Knightley, Jane Bennet—struggle not to express but to hide their emotions, and Austen often indicates, by contrast, that emotional transparency springs from an essential vulgarity and light-mindedness, as the easy confidences of Harriet Smith, Lydia Bennet, Wickham, Lucy Steele, Mary Crawford, and even Edmund Bertram show.

In her letters Austen's dislike of sentiment could reveal a hardness that has repelled many readers. As a clever young woman of twenty-two she wrote to Cassandra, "Mrs Hall of Sherbourn was brought to bed yesterday of a dead child, some weeks before she expected, oweing to a fright. I suppose she happened unawares to look at her husband"—a crack that can seem either funny or appalling, depending on the reader and his mood. Recounting a ball two years later, Austen ran through her fellow revelers:

> There were very few Beauties, & such as there were, were not very handsome. Miss Iremonger did not look well & Mrs Blount was the only one much admired. She appeared exactly as she did in September, with the same broad face, diamond bandeau, white shoes, pink husband, & fat neck. . . . Miss Debary, Susan & Sally all in black, but without any Statues, made their appearance, & I was as civil to them as their bad breath would allow me.

Such brittle, bitchy humor amuses for a while but fades quickly without the complementary virtues (always present in the novels) of balance, fairness, and even—yes—sentiment, or at any rate respect for the genuine feelings that underlie sentimental demonstrations. As a fictional character even fat Mrs. Musgrove is allowed her measure of real grief for her worthless son, but all too often Austen, at least in confidence to her sister, denied that right to the actual humans around her.

Yet as Austen matured and aged she gained compassion, and in any case the cruel jokes between the sisters were very much a private affair; by her family and friends Jane Austen was remembered as an exceptionally kind woman. Her elder brother Francis described her as "cheerful and not easily irritated, and tho' rather reserved with strangers so as to have been accused by some of haughtiness of manner, yet in the company of those she loved the native benevolence of her heart and kindliness of her disposition were forcibly displayed." After Jane's death Cassandra mourned her as "the sun of my life, the gilder of every pleasure, the soother of every sorrow."

It is this essential kindness, allied with the famous wit, that made Jane Austen the artist she was. "Nobody ever feels or acts, suffers or enjoys, as one expects!" she exclaims in 1813, a few months later writing, "After having much praised or much blamed anybody, one is generally sensible of something just the reverse soon afterwards"—the very foundation of her gift for irony and surprise. A trip to two London museums inspires "some amusement at each, tho' my preference for Men & Women, always inclines me to attend more to the company than the sight."

This says everything about Austen's particular outlook: well-read and cultured though she may have been, hers was a mind to which every pleasure of the intellect and spirit—art, literature, even nature—was subordinated to her real interest, the vagaries of the human animal. Like Barbara Pym, a novelist often compared with Austen, she uses cultural references purely for the purpose of illuminating her characters. The fatuity of Sir Edward, in Austen's fragment *The Watsons*, is fatally exposed by his passion for Robert Burns: "His soul was the altar in which lovely woman sat enshrined," gushes the foolish baronet, "his spirit truly breathed the immortal incense which is her due." And just as Pym has her characters either rhapsodize or yawn over a visit to Keats's Hampstead house in *The Sweet Dove Died*, Austen has Captain Benwick and Anne Elliot speak of Scott and Byron not in order to weave the work of the poets into her own thematic pattern but to enrich her characterization of Anne and poke gentle fun at Benwick:

> . . . having talked of poetry, the richness of the present age, and gone through a brief comparison of opinion as to the first-rate poets, trying to ascertain whether *Marmion* or *The Lady of the Lake* were to be preferred, and how ranked the *Giaour* and *The Bridge of Abydos*; and, moreover, how the *Giaour* was to be pronounced, he shewed himself so intimately acquainted with all the tenderest songs of the one poet, and all the impassioned descriptions of hopeless agony of the other . . . that she ventured to hope he did not always read only poetry; and to say, that she thought it was the misfortune of poetry, to be seldom safely enjoyed by those who enjoyed it completely; and that the strong feelings which alone could estimate it truly, were the very feelings which ought to taste it but sparingly.

In spite of the tedium of much of the correspondence, it does give us some marvelous insights into the mind of a woman who was a great artist without being a great thinker. Her advice to her young niece Anna, an aspiring authoress, is valuable in that it contains all we possess of Austen's ideas on fiction writing; in other letters we catch glimpses of the distinctive humor that marks her own work (one can detect the author of *Northanger Abbey* in Austen's laughter at Fanny Knight's love life: "Your trying to excite your own feelings by a visit to his room amused me excessively.—The dirty Shaving Rag was exquisite!—Such a circumstance ought to be in print"). And there are gems, such as the little correspondence between Austen and the Rev. James Stanier-Clarke, the Regent's librarian and an ardent Austen fan. Clarke, a delicious mixture of obsequiousness and innocence, showers Austen with his ideas on potential subjects for her genius: perhaps a novel about an English clergyman "Fond of, & entirely engaged in Literature—no man's Enemy but his own," or "a Historical Romance illustrative of the History of the august house of Cobourg." Austen's graceful refusals are models of tact. "I could no more write a Romance than an Epic Poem. . . . No—I must keep to my own style & go on in my own Way; And though I may never succeed in that, I am convinced that I should totally fail in any other."

And occasionally there are moments of pure delight—as when Austen accompanied her brother Henry to a picture gallery in London and caught a glimpse there of one of her own characters:

> It is not thought a very good collection, but I was very well pleased—particularly . . . with a small portrait of Mrs Bingley, excessively like her. I went in hopes of seeing one of her Sister, but there was no Mrs Darcy. . . . Mrs Bingley's is exactly herself, size, shaped face, features & sweetness; there never was a greater likeness. She is dressed in a white gown, with green ornaments, which convinces me of what I had always supposed, that green was a favourite colour with her. I dare say Mrs D. will be in Yellow.

But Elizabeth Darcy was to remain elusive even after Jane and Henry visited two more exhibitions. "There was nothing like Mrs D. at either," she wrote. "I can only imagine that Mr D. prizes any Picture of her too much to like that it should be exposed to the public eye.—I can imagine he wd have that sort of feeling—that mixture of Love, Pride, & Delicacy."

Hans Christian Andersen: A Fight for Love and Glory

*I*n "The Little Mermaid," Hans Christian Andersen suggests that immortality can serve as a substitute, however unsatisfactory, for human love. This story is clearly an allegory for his own life, for the unloved Andersen, more than 125 years after his death, can lay as good a claim as anyone to artistic immortality. At a time when children's stories were exclusively moral and didactic, he revolutionized the genre by infusing it with the humor, anarchy, and sorrow of great literature. He expressed the most painful and rawest emotions with extraordinary aesthetic control; the results rivaled anything produced by the great Romantic writers who were his contemporaries. In his simple, unpretentious way he told us as much about the human condition (think of "The Emperor's New Clothes," "The Snow Queen," "The Fir Tree") as any of the world's writers and philosophers.

"The history of my life will be the best commentary on my work," Andersen wrote. Most Americans, unfortunately, derive what little knowledge they have of it from the saccharine 1952 Danny Kaye musical bio-pic. Apart from Andersen's provincial background and his early emigration to the metropolis of Copenhagen, there was no truth in the film: Kaye's Andersen, handsome, self-confident, and heterosexual, bore no resemblance whatever to the original. The real story is infinitely stranger, sadder, and more interesting.

"The Ugly Duckling" is Andersen's most obviously autobiographical piece of work. Andersen was ugly, to be sure, almost grotesquely so; like the duckling, he was ridiculed in youth but lived to have the last laugh. In Andersen's case, however, the psychic scars were so severe that it would be hard to view his later life of international acclaim as a true happy ending.

He was born in the Danish town of Odense in 1805. His father was a shoemaker, intelligent and self-educated, depressed by the poverty and limitations of his life; he died when his son was eleven years old. Andersen's mother was a superstitious, barely literate peasant who gave him two inestimable gifts: a connection with the immemorial folklore of their native region and an unswerving belief, against all early evidence to the contrary, in her son's genius.

Even in childhood Andersen stood out as a bit of a freak. Unnaturally tall, gawky, and homely, he was also startlingly effeminate. While other boys played out of doors, he preferred to stay home, sewing dolls' clothes and rehearsing plays and ballets with his puppet theater. His tolerant mother encouraged his obsession with the arts and did what she could to provide him with the rudiments of an education. When, as a small child, he was beaten by his teacher, she enrolled him in Odense's Jewish school, a very enlightened step for someone of her time and class.

Andersen used what developed into a beautiful soprano voice to insinuate himself into the homes of the local bourgeoisie, who allowed him to sing and recite for them. Sent to work in a cloth mill at an early age, he was called upon to perform for the other workers. There was some speculation among Andersen's young colleagues as to whether he was not in fact a girl, and they pinned him down and pulled off his clothes to find out. A subsequent stint in a tobacco factory ended in more humiliation.

No amount of ridicule shook Andersen's belief that he possessed a unique destiny. At fourteen, having saved up the tiny sum of thirteen Danish rix-dollars, he persuaded his mother to let him seek his fortune in the great city of Copenhagen, where he knew no one. "Like generations of histrionic, effeminate, artistically talented boys," Jackie Wullschlager, the author of a fascinating Andersen biography, has commented, "he wanted to enter the theater in any capacity whatsoever." His first, absurd idea was to become a dancer, and in pursuit of this pipe dream he presented himself at the home of Mme. Schall, Copenhagen's leading ballerina. Andersen later recalled: "I improvised both text and music, and to be able to execute better the dance scene with the tambourine . . . I placed my shoes in a corner and danced wearing only socks on my feet." Mme. Schall not unnaturally assumed he was a lunatic and had him removed from the house.

Andersen's one and only strong suit at that time was his voice, and he eventually finagled an informal scholarship at the Royal Choir School. That ended when his voice broke; again, he managed to persuade some generous backers to help finance his ambitions. "The desperation to perform, the burning ambition, the implacable self-belief—all this stood out from the comedy of Andersen's incongruous exhibitionism and made other people believe in him," Wullschlager noted. One day a much-admired patroness casually referred to the boy as a poet. It was a seminal moment: "It was the first time anybody had connected my name with that of a poet," Andersen later wrote. "It went through me, body and soul, and tears filled my eyes. I knew that, from this very moment, my mind was awake to writing and poetry."

That was all very well, but he was almost completely uneducated. It was decided by a group of supporters, led by a powerful businessman, Jonas Collin, that Andersen should finally stop floundering and get a grammar school education, and he was sent, at their expense, to the town of Slagelse for his belated schooling. Andersen was by this time seventeen, gangling and overgrown; he had to join a class of eleven-year-olds. He spent the next five years in the school, a dogs-body-cum-baby-sitter for his rather sadistic teacher, and a definite oddball. He was too dreamy and distractible to make a scholar, but he stuck out the standard course of studies and in 1827 embarked upon his literary career, producing in short order poetry, a Romantic novel, a comic fantasy, and a successful play.

He spent the next several years experimenting, trying to find his own voice. In 1834 he began to turn his attention to fairy tales, drawing on the folklore he had heard as a child. His qualification for this work turned out to be exceptional, possibly unique. The ancient folk culture of the Scandinavian countryside was still very much alive during Andersen's youth, and he, scarcely out of the peasantry, was exposed to it all. In later life, thanks to the new social mobility of the nineteenth century, the educated, upwardly mobile Andersen was able to spread this culture to the larger world as storytellers of earlier generations would not have been.

Jacob and Wilhelm Grimm's *Kinder- und Hausmärchen* had appeared between 1812 and 1815; exciting and colorful as the tales were, they were not original creations but faithful transcriptions of oral tradition rendered by scholars rather than artists. Fairy tales of a more personal sort, consciously artistic creations known as *Kunstmärchen*, had been written by E. T. A. Hoffmann and Ludwig Tieck. What Andersen was conceiving was something different, and in 1835 his first volume of fairy tales, *Eventyr, Fortale for Børn, Forste Hefte* (*Fairy Tales, Told for Children, First Volume*) was published, introducing Danish readers to "The Tinderbox," "Little Claus and Big Claus," and "The Princess and the Pea." All these stories were based on folk originals, but Andersen was well aware that he was pioneering a new genre. "I . . . have written them exactly the way I would tell them to a *child*," he confided to a friend, and the opening words of "The Tinderbox" confirm the description:

> A soldier was marching along the high road: Left, right! Left, right! He had his knapsack on his back and a sword at his side, for he had been to the wars and was going home. And on the way he met an old witch. Oh, she was horrid: her bottom lip came right down to her chest.

Chatty, conversational, unpolished—altogether shocking to contemporary standards, and a world away from the high-flown language and didactic content of the usual children's fare. Andersen's prose exuded humor, and the tales were constructed with an unadorned purity of form that was radically new to their readers. A second volume soon appeared, which included "Thumbelina," "The Naughty Boy," and "The Traveling Companion."

Andersen quickly saw possibilities in the fairy-tale form that no previous author had divined. Its formality and fantastic subject matter provided a perfect metaphoric structure in which he could express his own pain as a social and romantic outsider. The outsider's role, so often assumed for dramatic effect by other artists, was in Andersen's case literally true: despite his great celebrity abroad, he never much impressed the audience he really yearned after, the insular, conformist Copenhagen intelligentsia personified by the Collin family, in particular Edvard, Jonas Collin's son, with whom he remained obsessed all his life. Andersen had a number of crushes on both men and women (including the other Scandinavian superstar of his day, Jenny Lind) and at least one happy love affair with a man, but he went through life essentially alone. No one, perhaps least of all the buttoned-up, withholding, and definitely heterosexual Edvard, was equipped to return Andersen's devouring love. Andersen's emotional incapacities must certainly have been exacerbated by his unsettled early life, in which he was pathetically dependent on the generosity and good opinion of his social betters. The obsequiousness, the eagerness to please, and the incessant craving for praise and attention were adolescent qualities that Andersen never outgrew, and they became ever more ridiculous as he aged.

By now, though, he was reaching the height of his powers as an artist. In 1837 he published the third *Eventyr* volume, which contained "The Little Mermaid" and "The Emperor's New Clothes"—a masterpiece whose very title has become a byword for human vanity. The next year there appeared "The Steadfast Tin Soldier," a metaphor for fidelity to love and vocation that has deeply affected artists as different as George Balanchine and Thomas Mann; it was the first of Andersen's stories to be entirely original, with no folk sources. And in 1844 he published "The Ugly Duckling," "The Nightingale," "The Snow Queen," and "The Fir Tree."

If Andersen was never able to win the admiration of Edvard Collin and his ilk, he found friendship of a sort among the rich and powerful, and soon began dancing endlessly through the courts of Europe—in Wullschlager's apt comparison, like his own character Karen in her red shoes. With royalty he played the fawning lapdog, and Heinrich Heine remarked on Andersen's "servile lack of self-confidence which is appreciated by dukes and princes. He fulfills exactly a prince's idea of a poet. . . . Otherwise Andersen is a man of some spirit."

As with so many artists, there was a bizarre contrast between Andersen's stunted personality and his work, which became ever more sophisticated and allusive. His later fiction, directed now toward an adult audience, anticipated surrealism and Freudian ideas of the unconscious; it was experimental, self-referential, protomodernist. In his personal life he displayed no such maturity. It was in the role of the unworldly naif that he had first won recognition, and he played it to the hilt for the rest of his life, often to ludicrous effect. One observer described Andersen in late middle age as "a child, according to the ideal of childhood; keenly sensitive, entirely egoistical, innocently vain, the center of life, interest, concern and meaning to himself."

Andersen died in 1875. His influence had been remarkable, and it continues to be so despite the best efforts of cartoon animators, bowdlerizing children's authors, the Walt Disney Company, and other barbarians to distort the meaning of his tales. As is not always the case, Andersen's contemporaries were aware that his death marked the passing of a very great artist. There were crowned heads at his funeral, though there were no blood relations. At Andersen's suggestion, Edvard Collin and his wife had agreed to be buried with him, and on their deaths in 1866 and 1894 his dying wish was granted. A few years later, though, family members dug up the Collins' bodies and had them moved to the Collin family plot in another cemetery. In death as in life, Andersen was left alone.

The Byronic Melodrama

The main task for any biographer intrepid enough to take on the subject of George Gordon, the sixth Lord Byron, is to give equal time to both versions of the man: Byron as he really was, and Byron as a symbol—what he meant to the world, what he stood for and to some extent still stands for today. These two Byrons are so very different that it is sometimes hard to make them coalesce into a single figure.

To Napoleonic and post-Napoleonic Europe, Byron meant, quite simply, Liberty. His life, his poetry, and especially his death in Missolonghi, where he had gone to assist in the Greek war for independence, inspired political and artistic revolutionaries for generations. The Risorgimento leader Giuseppe Mazzini claimed to know "no more beautiful symbol of the future destiny and mission of art than the death of Byron in Greece. The holy alliance of poetry with the cause of the peoples; the union—still so rare—of thought and action which alone completes the human Word." Victor Hugo and Alfred de Vigny openly identified themselves with Byron and what they perceived to be his ethos. One of the plotters executed in Russia's Decembrist rising went to the scaffold clutching a volume of Byron's poetry. Heine, Pushkin, Liszt, and any number of later Romantics constructed their own ideas of love and liberty around Byron's. Delacroix and Verdi based some of their most passionate works on his poems and dramas. Hector Berlioz, only half-jokingly, summed it all up as he recalled his youthful worship and emulation of the great Romantic: "He was loved! He was a poet! . . . He was free! . . . He was rich! . . . He had it all!"

Benita Eisler, one of Byron's recent biographers, claimed that since neither music nor painting lend themselves to irony, Byronists like Verdi and Delacroix took only the unironic surface that Byron presented to the world and disseminated it for posterity. This is not strictly true: Mozart was an ironic composer, and in painting Byron's contemporary, Goya, put irony to work superbly in an *oeuvre* that was every bit as political as Byron's own. I think it is probably more accurate to say that Byron's continental worshippers never understood his extremely English style of irony. The bitchy, insinuating English dandy who watched his weight, fussed over his clothes, and enjoyed gossiping with malicious old ladies is a side of Byron that the mythologizers rejected—or, rather, never really absorbed in the first place. Shelley, who knew him almost as well as anyone, believed that Byron was never a revolutionary so much as a libertine.

One thing we can be sure of: Byron took great pains to construct and groom his public image, and his relationship with his own renown is strikingly modern; like many a twenty-first-century celebrity, Byron courted fame and then backed away when its embrace became too rough. He sought fame, needed it, feared it, scorned it, craved it. His ambition was, perhaps, not so much to *do* great things as to project a great image. Already, at the age of sixteen, he knew what he wanted: "I will cut a path through the world or perish in the attempt. Others have begun life with nothing and ended Greatly. And shall I who have a competent if not a large fortune, remain idle, No, I will carve myself the path to Grandeur, but never with Dishonour." At the end of his life this ambition had not abated in the slightest. His friend Lady Blessington observed in 1823 that "Byron had so unquenchable a thirst for celebrity, that no means were left untried that might attain it: this frequently led to his expressing opinions totally at variance with his notions and real sentiments. . . . There was no sort of celebrity he did not, at some period or other, condescend to seek, and he was not over nice in the means, provided he obtained it in the end."

In *Don Juan* Byron presented the public with his ruminations on celebrity:

What is the end of fame? 'tis but to fill
  A certain portion of uncertain paper:
Some liken it to climbing up a hill,
  Whose summit, like all hills, is lost in vapour;
For this men write, speak, preach, and heroes kill,
  And bards burn what they call their 'midnight taper,'
To have, when the original is dust,
A name, a wretched picture, and worse bust.

What are the hopes of man? Old Egypt's King
  Cheops erected the first pyramid
And largest, thinking it was just the thing
  To keep his memory whole, and mummy hid:
But somebody or other rummaging,
  Burglariously broke his coffin's lid.
Let not a moment give you or me hopes,
Since not a pinch of dust remains of Cheops.

Byron certainly got his share of wretched pictures, and worse busts: T. S. Eliot memorably described the Thorwaldsen bust as having immortalized "that weakly sensual mouth, that restless triviality of expression, and most of all that kind of look of self-conscious beauty." Leigh Hunt's wife Marianne cruelly and quite accurately commented that the famous Harlow portrait of the young Byron "resembled a great schoolboy, who had a plain bun given him, instead of a plum one": once one has read this remark, one can never take the painting seriously again.

The lines of poetry quoted above, though written in Byron's characteristically facetious vernacular, express a conventional view on fame, that of Shelley's *Ozymandias*. They were not in any way what Byron actually believed, and he refuted them in practice, manipulating his own image so brilliantly that he may well have achieved an immortality denied poor Cheops, definitely less gifted in the all-important art of public relations.

The fascination that Byron exerts from far beyond the grave is such that new, "definitive" biographies get churned out at extremely short intervals even though there is very little left to be said. Fiona MacCarthy has recently added a hefty tome to their number: *Byron: Life and Legend*, published here and simultaneously in Britain by the firm of John Murray, the same house that originally published the bulk of Byron's poetry: while Byron dealt with John Murray II, Fiona MacCarthy has worked with the seventh of that name.

MacCarthy's book follows hard on the heels of two full-length biographies, Phyllis Grosskurth's *Byron: The Flawed Angel* and Benita Eisler's *Byron: Child of Passion, Fool of Fame*. Even Eisler was accused by critics of having produced an essentially unnecessary book; MacCarthy's is the more unnecessary, then, except for the two issues that she uses to justify it: her connection with Murray which afforded her access to the complete correspondence between Byron and John Murray II, and her contention that Byron was not a heterosexual who slept with boys but a homosexual who slept with women. Neither of these reasons is really enough to warrant another big biography; but why complain since the material is, as ever, fascinating? MacCarthy's book is a fun read, lavishly illustrated, and quite convincing in the presentation of its homosexual thesis.

Like many another Englishman, Byron was initiated into the Greek ideal of romantic friendships between men at his public school, and later, as with many of his countrymen, his relations with young boys assumed a pattern of *de haut en bas*. Byron's principal romance at Harrow was with the young Earl of Clare, four years his junior, and he clearly retained a *tendresse* for this old flame throughout his life, shedding tears when they met by chance in 1821 after an interval of many years. At Cambridge he fell passionately in love with the choir-boy John Edleston. Byron's love for Edleston was as intense as any in his life; the famous 1811 "Thyrza" cycle of elegiac poems was written not, as contemporaries assumed, about a woman but about Edleston, who had recently died, and Byron wore the cornelian ring the young boy had given him until his own death thirteen years later.

Installed at Newstead Abbey after his departure from Cambridge, Byron bestowed his sexual favors on both his pages and his housemaids; significantly, he often dressed his boyish, nubile female conquests in male garb. This was to become a major feature in his overheated affair with the equally androgynous and unstable Lady Caroline Lamb, who liked to disguise herself as a page and procured page boys for Byron's enjoyment and apparently for her own as well.

Sodomy was a hanging offense in England during Byron's lifetime, and though he talked and wrote freely of his "Horatian" (a private code word for homosexual) adventures with a select group of old friends including John Cam Hobhouse, Scrope Davies, and Charles Skinner Matthews, he was as discreet as it was ever in his nature to be when it came to guarding his public image. Caroline Lamb's indiscretions terrified him, and when she blackmailed him by threatening to make public some letters he had foolishly written her about his homosexual exploits, he contemplated leaving the country, a step he would in fact soon take, permanently. He was notoriously indiscreet, however, about his relations with women, which quickly became the stuff of legend: Caroline Lamb, Byron's half-sister Augusta Leigh, Annabella Millbanke, whom in a fit of insanity he married, and the relatively stable Teresa Guiccioli—each of these ladies has a starring role in the Byron melodrama.

Fiona MacCarthy believes that "Byron liked the chase, the reassurance of heterosexual conquest. But in general, Byron's female attachments dwindled quickly in intensity. Byron himself, half-jokingly, gave them a limit of three months—an estimate that proved fairly accurate in practice. . . ." Only Augusta and Teresa exceeded this limit, and the signs seem clear that Byron had had enough of Teresa by the time he left for Greece. Augusta, perhaps because of rather than in spite of the illicitness of their passion, was thus the only woman who inspired lasting love in him. ("[T]he kind of feeling which has lately absorbed me," he wrote early in his *liaison* with Augusta, "has a mixture of the *terrible* which renders all other—even passion (pour les autres) insipid to a degree.") "What fools we are!" he exclaimed, thinking of his relations with women. "We cry for a plaything, which like children we are never satisfied till we break it open, though unlike them, we cannot get rid of it, by putting it in the fire."

On some occasions he came perilously close to this extremity, shunning his female groupies in truly humiliating ways. Women threw themselves at him, of course, but they would not have done so had he not exuded some perverse invitation to emotional excess in which they were fawningly complicit. His future wife Annabella saw, during the great *Childe Harold* season of "Byromania," "how all the women were absurdly courting him and trying to *deserve* the lash of his Satire." And when the women became too hysterical the lash could be brutal indeed: "I shall ever continue to be your friend," he wrote to Caroline Lamb, "if your Ladyship will permit me so to style myself; and, as a first proof of my regard, I offer you this advice, correct your vanity, which is ridiculous; exert your absurd caprices upon others; and leave me in peace."

With women he mixed hatred with lust and behaved in a sadistic fashion, especially during his grisly marriage, to which the term "mental cruelty" can never have been more literally applicable. But this was not the case for his friendships with boys, to whom he was both affectionate and generous. With boys he was the Lover, with women the impatient Beloved.

The last passion of his life was for a Greek teenager he took into his service, Lukas Chalandritsanos, and his two final poems, "Love and Death" and "Last Words on Greece," reveal his erotic obsession with this boy.

> Thus much and more—and yet thou lov'st me not,
> And never wilt—Love dwells not in our will—
> Nor can I blame thee—though it be my lot
> To strongly—wrongly—vainly—love thee still.—
>
> (the last stanza of "Love and Death")

John Cam Hobhouse, Byron's oldest friend and his executor, explained that "A note attached to these verses by Lord Byron states they were addressed to nobody and were a mere poetical scherzo," but details of the poems, particularly a description of a high fever their subject suffered, make it clear that they were written for Lukas, as does the fact that the discreet Hobhouse was seen to destroy a third poem, probably the last that Byron wrote.

MacCarthy describes the conspiracy of silence, begun by Hobhouse and Byron's other cronies, that was carried on for the next century and a half. Sir Harold Nicolson, himself a closeted homosexual, wrote a book about Byron in 1924, the centenary of the poet's death; he claimed to have been horror-struck as he unearthed the truth about Byron's sexual propensities, and dithered to John Murray IV over just how honest he ought to be. "Amidst all the aspersions which have been flung upon B's reputation by his own descendants," replied Murray smoothly, "my constant policy (& my Father's) has been to keep away as much as possible from his personal characteristics and to concentrate on his powers as a poet and letter writer"—advice which the nervous Sir Harold followed. Byron's other major biographer of the period,

Peter Quennell, was in MacCarthy's fine phrase "rampantly heterosexual" and responded primarily to the Errol Flynn side of his subject. The image he propagated in his two popular books was of Byron as a serial lady-killer, a cliché that has largely remained fixed in the public mind.

Byron was a paradoxical character: on the one hand he was one of the great shits of history, while on the other he was, obviously, deeply loved by countless friends. Reading about him, one is overcome by waves of revulsion for his cruelty, his pride, his posturing. MacCarthy does not exonerate him, but she shows us that much of this behavior was the result of what was in effect a pathological condition. Byron was descended, on both sides, from deeply unstable families. "The Byrons," wrote the poet's 1957 biographer Leslie Marchand, "seem to have grown more irresponsible with each generation, until the summit of social irregularity is reached in the character and conduct of the great-uncle [known as the Wicked Lord] and the father ["Mad Jack"] of the poet, if not indeed in the poet himself." And, he continued, the Gordons of Gight, Byron's maternal family, presented "a startling record of violence rare even in the annals of Scottish lairds," "a spectacle of unrestrained barbarity." Byron's maternal grandfather and great-grandfather both drowned, apparent suicides, and his mother was unstable, to say the least, with violent mood swings and tempers the poet described as "phrenzy."

"It is ridiculous," Byron told Lady Blessington, "to say that we do not inherit our passions, as well as . . . any other disorder"; he assured Teresa that "My melancholy is something temperamental, inherited." His personality was explosive from the very beginning—"I like a row—and always did from a boy," he told Sir Walter Scott—and periods of depression began to manifest themselves during his late adolescence. During his early travels in Greece and Albania, the fits of "caprice and feline temper" noticed by his traveling companions made some of them wonder whether he was mad. His mood swings were cyclical, and he was familiar with the impulse to suicide, as this verse attests:

> The Mind, that broods o'er guilty woes,
> Is like the Scorpion girt by fire,
> In circle narrowing as it glows
> The flames around their captive close,
> Till inly search'd by thousand throes,
> And maddening in her ire,
> One sad and sole relief she knows,
> The sting she nourish'd for her foes,
> Whose venom never yet was vain,
> Gives but one pang, and cures all pain,
> And darts into her desperate brain.—
> So do the dark in soul expire,
> Or live like Scorpion girt by fire.

And at times, as during his myriad erotic entanglements of 1814 (hypersexuality, by the way, is one of the more common symptoms of manic-depression, as is the alternation between parsimony and lavishness, to which Byron also fell prey), he sank into "intense unhappiness and instability so great that Byron's condition came close to schizophrenia," as MacCarthy writes. The condition worsened with the advancing years, as is usually the case. During the last year of his life the symptoms became particularly pronounced; as a result, the idea of an early death held no horrors for him. "I am not sure that long life is desirable for one of my temper & constitutional depression of Spirits," he told John Murray in 1821.

What contemporaries found fascinating in Byron was the flip side of this dangerous moodiness: his gift, which amounted to genius, for empathy. He was preeminent during his time in his ability not only to attract adulation but to inspire profound affection and understanding in his friends—usually men but sometimes, as with Lady Melbourne or Lady Blessington, women. After his death John Cam Hobhouse, responding privately to Byron's obituary in the *Times*, tried to formulate his companion's extraordinary appeal:

> . . . no man lived who had such devoted friends his power of attaching those about him was such as no one I ever knew possessed—no human being could approach him without being sensible of this magical influence—there was something commanding but not overawing in his manner—He was neither grave nor gay nor out of place and he seemed always made for that company in which he found himself—there was a mildness and yet a decision in his mode of conversing which are seldom united in the same person—He appeared exceedingly free open and unreserved with every body—yet he continued at all times to retain just as much self restraint as to preserve the respect of even his most intimate friends.

Aha. Hobhouse knew all of Byron's faults, probably better than anyone: yet this, finally, was his summing up of the man. It is good to hold it in mind when perusing the terrifying marital experiences of Lady Byron, or the caustic memoirs of Leigh Hunt. When he could hold his demon at bay, Byron was not only one of the most gifted men of his time but one of the most delightful as well.

So much for the man and the myth. What of the artist? During his lifetime and for quite a few years afterward, Byron was widely considered the greatest poet in the world. Today he is read by few. Anthologies still include his simpler pieces, "She Walks in Beauty Like the Night" or "So We'll No More Go a Roving," but the works that ravished his contemporaries, *The Pilgrimage of Childe Harold* and *Don Juan*, have become highly inaccessible to the general reader.

These long poems were intensely political, allusive, and up to the minute; they spoke to contemporary readers, resoundingly, but the world has moved on in ways that even Byron's feverish imagination could not have encompassed, and the society he wrote about has faded away; his lines, once so racy and topical, are now dense and obscure. The work of his contemporaries, Shelley, Keats, Coleridge, and to a certain degree Wordsworth, has retained its universality. To read Shelley one needs only sensibility and imagination, but to read Byron demands intellect and a detailed sense of history, and people who turn to his work nowadays are struck not so much by its poetic force as by its sheer brainpower. Children of Byron's generation did not have their intelligence quotients measured, but it is safe to say that Byron's must have been extremely high. His friendship with Shelley seems to have grown less from their mutual interest in poetry, revolution, or free love than from the simple fact that in Shelley he found, possibly for the only time in his life, an intellectual peer.

Poetry was the most prestigious and vital art form of Byron's day, and he therefore made it his natural mode of expression. Would he have been a poet had he lived today? One wonders, and doubts. Other forms have usurped poetry's role and drained its power. What might Byron have become in our time? A major novelist? A pornography king? A gonzo journalist? Whatever the answer, he certainly wouldn't have settled for suburban obscurity.

Hawthorne's Twilit Soul

A perpetual twilight reigned over Nathaniel Hawthorne's spirit, according to Henry James. James put it well: Hawthorne's was essentially a negative, elusive character. This negativity—not pessimism, for which it was often mistaken—distinguished him from his New England peers, an extroverted crowd that included Ralph Waldo Emerson, Margaret Fuller, Bronson Alcott, and the heroic transcendentalist George Ripley. Hawthorne was "morbidly shy and reserved," according to one friend; another admitted, "I love Hawthorne, I admire him; but I do not know him. He lives in a mysterious world of thought and imagination which he never permits me to enter."

Hawthorne's biographers, then, have not had an easy task. Yet early chroniclers like Henry James (1879) and Newton Arvin (1929) had a certain advantage: they wrote at a moment when Hawthorne was not only canonical but popular too. James could even remember the aura of scandal that had wafted about the great man's name during his own childhood, "the sensation [*The Scarlet Letter*] produced, and the little shudder with which people alluded to it, as if a peculiar horror were mixed with its attractions."

The Scarlet Letter still inspires horror, but only in the hapless high school students who have it shoved down their throats like castor oil. It is still a great novel, in some expert opinions *the* Great American Novel, but it is singularly inappropriate for modern teenagers—no longer because of its shocking subject but because of the high artificiality of its style and construction, the prominence given to an abstract and alien construct of Sin, and the novel's ruthless subordination of character to allegory. "One thing is clear," Edgar Allan Poe commented, apropos Hawthorne, "that if allegory ever establishes a fact, it is by dint of overturning a fiction"—and teenagers tend to be more interested in a good story than an apt allegory. If secondary educators insist on administering tonic doses of Hawthorne, they ought to consider substituting *The Scarlet Letter* with *The Blithedale Romance*, an entertaining and far more accessible piece of work.

Brenda Wineapple, the author of biographies of Janet Flanner and of Gertrude and Leo Stein, is the latest writer to tackle Hawthorne's life and try to distill his shadowy essence. If the attempt is in any way unsatisfactory, it is probably because of something unsatisfactory in the subject's own character; Hawthorne withdraws from the biographer as successfully as he did from his family and friends. But Wineapple is a good storyteller and has created a vivid account of a highly interesting life; she has also managed to communicate, if not to resolve, the man's puzzling contradictions.

The self-defined recluse was simultaneously, according to his friend Longfellow, "much of a lion [in Salem], sought after, fed, and expected to roar." The artist who created strong, passionate, brilliant heroines turns out to have disapproved of bluestockings, and refused to educate his own intelligent daughters. The moralist who was so deeply preoccupied with the sins of the past was content to condone the preeminent sin of his own day, slavery, and to reject the activism that obsessed his social circle (his two sisters-in-law, Elizabeth Peabody and Mary—Mrs. Horace—Mann, were famous abolitionists) in favor of the doomed states' rights policies of his crony, Franklin Pierce. How do all these pieces add up? "He was a man," Mary Mann believed, "of natural tenderness & imaginative nature, rather than a man of lofty principle"—but as an artist he was uncompromising, and while his total output, for so major a figure, might seem slight, "some of his projects," as Malcolm Cowley once pointed out, "were finished with perfect workmanship at a time when circumstances were hostile to Hawthorne's type of richly meditated fiction. His talent had to be robust in order to survive and had to be exceptionally fertile in order to produce, against obstacles, the few books he succeeded in writing."

Wineapple covers a great deal of well-trodden ground: Hawthorne's childhood in Puritan-haunted Salem; his family's morally ambiguous history in the town (one ancestor was a hanging judge at the witchcraft trials, another a brutal prosecutor of the nonconforming Quakers); his father's early death, and his upbringing in a household of women. At Bowdoin College in Maine he was a member of the famous class of 1825—which, out of a total of thirty-eight students, also included Longfellow and Pierce.

Hawthorne was a late bloomer, and though he began writing soon after his graduation, he was reluctant to declare himself a professional man of letters. Such diffidence was unsurprising: scarcely a dozen Americans had attempted to do so until that time. He lived at home with his mother and sisters, and spent two stints in Boston, as the editor of a minor magazine and, later, working as a weigher and gauger in the Boston Custom House. Here he began a lifelong pattern; whenever he was in government office, he hankered after his desk and his pen, but once in his room and faced with the hard chore of composition, he found himself longing for the steady income and undemanding work of a civil service post.

Unsatisfied with his early fiction, he destroyed his first short story collection, *Seven Stories*, after a single rejection letter; no trace of it remains. His first novel, *Fanshawe*, was published anonymously and forgotten. It was not until the publication of *Twice-Told Tales* in 1837 that Hawthorne caught the attention of intellectual circles. It was a striking collection in which he included "The Minister's Black Veil," "Wakefield," and "The Wedding-Knell" but omitted, for reasons known only to himself, future classics like "My Kinsman, Major Molineux" and "Young Goodman Brown."

Even after this *succès d'estime* Hawthorne felt himself to be obscure and unappreciated, but in provincial Salem he cut a wide swath. Not only gifted but remarkably handsome, he was an irresistible prize to women. The energetic, earnest Elizabeth Peabody, famous many years later as the original for the elderly Miss Birdseye in Henry James's *The Bostonians*, cast a proprietary eye: Hawthorne was, she insisted, "one of nature's ordained priests, an Ariel breathing moral ambrosia, a second Homer." But as is so often the sad case, Hawthorne preferred her pretty, conventional sister Sophia. Neither intellectually nor artistically aspiring, Sophia presented no threat to her insecure suitor and was more than content to play the role of helpmeet. "To be the means in any way of calling forth one of his divine creations, is no small happiness, is it?" she asked Elizabeth smugly.

Wineapple dislikes Sophia, who was undoubtedly vain and narcissistic. But she was also amusing, and many readers will develop a sneaking affection for her. Clearly, too, she was the right wife for Hawthorne, and the two were happy together for the rest of his life.

Hawthorne loved Sophia, but he was incapable of shedding his habitual ambivalence even in her case: their engagement lasted three years. It was during this period that Hawthorne took up residence at the transcendentalist commune, Brook Farm. Margaret Fuller, among others, was skeptical of the endeavor: "I doubt they will get free from all they deprecate in society," she predicted, and of course she was right. But Hawthorne's stint there eventually bore fruit in *The Blithedale Romance*, a delightful send-up of the commune and its pretensions.

Brook Farm was only the first of Hawthorne's many failed attempts to find the Great Good Place, every writer's holy grail. The Concord of Emerson and Thoreau, where the Hawthornes moved upon their marriage in 1842, seemed idyllic at first, but the Hawthornes were poor and became poorer, eventually having to resort to selling apples, potatoes, and even grass to make ends meet. "The treasure of intellectual gold, which I hoped to find in our secluded dwelling, had never come to life," he later wrote, and the stories he wrote there, collected as *Mosses from an Old Manse*, were, in Wineapple's words, "hermetic, rarefied." Contemporary literary powerhouses like Fuller and Poe agreed.

In 1846 he was back in Salem as surveyor of the Custom House, a job he held until he was fired three years later. This rejection further embittered him: "I detest this town so much that I hate to go out into the streets, or to have people see me." In a state of rage over his ousting and grief at his mother's recent death, he composed *The Scarlet Letter* at high speed: it was written, he later said, "all in one tone. I had to get my pitch, and then could go on interminably." He did not, of course: *The Scarlet Letter* is remarkably taut for a nineteenth-century novel, and its unified tone, or pitch, is one of the qualities which makes it so unusual. He knew, as Wineapple says, that "his strengths as a writer did not lie in consistently sustained narrative": "In all my stories, I think," he reflected, "there is one idea running through them like an iron rod, and to which all other ideas are referred and subordinate." The one time he did attempt what was then considered a full-length novel, *The Marble Faun*, the result seems wavering and artificially drawn out: it is the least successful of the author's novels.

Hawthorne's days of obscurity ended forever upon *The Scarlet Letter*'s publication in 1850. It was a critical and popular hit from the beginning, selling out its first edition in two weeks. He followed it, a year later, with *The House of the Seven Gables*, another brilliant portrait of his New England, blighted by class, heredity, intolerance, family pride, and baneful tradition.

Money worries did not abate: "I have never yet seen the year, since I was married, when I could have spared even a hundred dollars from the necessary expense of living," he complained. In 1849, with few prospects, he had accepted an offer to live in a handyman's cottage on the Tanglewood estate in the Berkshires. His disenchantment was swift and predictable: "I hate Berkshire with my whole soul, and would joyfully see its mountains laid flat." Two years later he was back in Concord, aptly christening his new house there "The Wayside."

Salem, Concord, Tanglewood, Brook Farm, the Custom House: Hawthorne was an outsider everywhere. He was coming to feel particularly out of place as the 1850s progressed and New England became increasingly caught up in abolitionist fever. Hawthorne was not proslavery, but he was constitutionally opposed to enthusiasm, even the reforming variety, and doubted the world could ever be much improved. "He was a fatalist," Wineapple writes, "apprehensive of action—associated with aggression—skeptical of result."

Feeling few ties to home, then, Hawthorne lobbied enthusiastically for the consulship to Liverpool when his old friend Franklin Pierce was elected president in 1852, and a few months later he and his family sailed, for the first time, to Europe. Liverpool was a cultural backwater, but Hawthorne's ambitions were narrow: "perform well, avoid attention, count his money." Traveling around the Continent, the great writer exposed himself as a shocking provincial, but the sights he saw, especially in Rome, haunted his imagination almost in spite of himself; the result was *The Marble Faun* (1860).

The Civil War, which broke out soon after Hawthorne's return to America, inspired from him an extraordinary article in *The Atlantic*, "Chiefly About War Matters by a Peaceable Man," characterized by Charles Eliot Norton as "pure intellect, without emotion, without sympathy, without principle." This, combined with his not wholly flattering sketches about his travels in England, collected as *Our Old Home*, bolstered his already considerable reputation as a contrarian. Upon the author's death in 1864, the nation's future was still unresolved. Hawthorne held no high hopes for it; but then, he never had. His subject had always been, Wineapple writes, "national hypocrisy."

That is true, but it was not his only subject, any more than Sin, or the Puritan legacy, was. He was the first great pathologist of American Protestantism, and his observations and analyses appalled him, and still appall us, his readers. As Herman Melville pointed out, "There is a grand truth about Nathaniel Hawthorne. He says NO! in thunder; but the Devil himself cannot make him say *yes*."

Hawthorne cannot be called a literary biography; Wineapple gives very little space to analysis of her subject's novels and stories. Perhaps that is not really necessary, for Hawthorne's fiction, after all, has been as much discussed as that of any writer of his time. And while she has written a compelling narrative, there is something basically discordant about the work. Wineapple's slangy style, combined with frequent solecisms and awkward sentences, sometimes seems untrue to Hawthorne's fastidious artistry and smooth Latinate diction. Were he, from beyond the grave, to get his hands on a copy of this volume he would be disappointed, as indeed he was with everything in life. As his fictional alter ego Miles Coverdale remarked, "We may be very sure . . . that the good we aim at will not be attained. People never do get just the good they seek. If it come at all, it is something else, which they never dreamed of, and did not particularly want."

The Tragic Life and Comic Art of William Makepeace Thackeray

Throughout William Makepeace Thackeray's professional life, he was plagued by explicit and implied comparisons with his great contemporary, Charles Dickens. Thackeray was born in 1811, Dickens a year later. By the mid-1830s, when the callow young Thackeray was knocking at the doors of literary London, Dickens had already claimed the spotlight: he was the established star of the coming generation and very much the man to be measured against. As the two men aged, their relationship, cordial on the surface, would remain uneasy, and they found real friendship impossible. Thackeray, despite occasional spasms of confidence in himself and his style of writing, too often felt himself the inferior artist while Dickens, though he never lost his position at the head of the pack, was uneasily aware of the challenge. As Thackeray was to claim late in their careers, "He [Dickens] knows that my books are a protest against his—that if one set are true, the other must be false."

In this he was wrong, of course, for felt truth can be as powerful, or more so, than the intellectual variety. In any case the comparison is unfair and pointless, for the two authors were as different as chalk and cheese. But the final score must be decisive: Thackeray produced only one entirely successful novel, *Vanity Fair*, while Dickens never wrote a bad book; his was an extraordinary, almost superhuman achievement. There is a case to be made for *Vanity Fair* as the best English novel of the nineteenth century, but it does not outweigh, on its own, the riches of Dickens's output—*David Copperfield*, *Bleak House*, *Dombey and Son*, *Our Mutual Friend*, *A Christmas Carol*, and all the others.

But Dickens was one of those great artists whose flaws were on as extravagant a scale as his gifts, and a significant number of readers have always been repelled by him. As D. J. Taylor writes in his new biography of Thackeray, "A certain kind of late-Victorian middle-class home . . . found Dickens vulgar; a certain kind of late-Victorian intellectual found him incorrigibly sentimental. In both cases Thackeray was a highly acceptable substitute." This is true, and Taylor need not have limited his statement to the Victorian period. Thackeray was the anti-sentimentalist *par exellence*, to the point where he was constitutionally unable to provide happy endings even for his most deserving characters in his most conventional novels; life itself provided no such happy endings, as he knew only too well. This tough emotional realism unfortunately earned him the label of cynic, a charge against which he fought throughout his life.

The issue of Dickens's vulgarity, and of Thackeray's cultivation of a deliberately gentlemanly style, is not really of any importance at all. Gentlemanliness is as irrelevant—and possibly even detrimental—to art as is the dubious advantage of good taste. Dickens, uninhibited by mere taste, was consistently able to achieve a high emotional power that was far beyond Thackeray's reach. Yet Thackeray, to whose nature artistic excess was anathema, had compensatory qualities that eluded all other English novelists of the era, Dickens included. His very diffidence now appears, in our own age of increased moral relativism, an artistic strength. His muted, perpetually qualified style indicates an admirable suspicion of rhetoric and absolutes. And his stance of gentlemanliness—understated, unobtrusive—is the outward sign of a refreshing unwillingness to assert himself too rudely, or to advance his own theories or observations as facts.

George Henry Lewes's brilliant review of *Vanity Fair* in *The Athenaeum* still stands, after more than a century and a half, as the shrewdest assessment of Thackeray at the height of his powers.

> The style of *Vanity Fair* is winning, easy, masculine, felicitous, and humorous. Its pleasant pages are nowhere distorted by rant. The author indulges in no sentimentalities—inflicts no fine writing on his readers. Trusting to the force of truth and humour, he is the *quietest* of contemporary writers,—a merit worth noting in a literary age which has a tendency to mistake spasm for force. The book has abundant faults of its own . . . but they are not the faults most current in our literature. The writer is quite free from theatricality. No glare from the foot-lights is thrown upon human nature, exaggerating and distorting it. He is guiltless too—let us be thankful for such a boon in the sense here intended—of a "purpose." Unfettered by political or social theories, his views of men and classes are not cramped.

All true, and Lewes also grasped the fatal flaw of both novel and author. Thackeray is deficient, he goes on to say, "in passion:—a deficiency that sits lightly upon a satirist, but is serious in a writer of fiction. He has no command over this quality—apparently but little knowledge of it."

It is a hard and surely a wrong judgment of any man to surmise that he knows little of passion. But it is true to say that Thackeray's works are oddly deficient in the quality, and perhaps this lack can be blamed on the cultivation of gentlemanly detachment as opposed to uninhibited engagement. Thackeray, as Geoffrey Tillotson wrote, "saw the world represented in his novels as spectacle rather than as an arena in which the author and his personages interlock. He felt that

Charlotte Brontë was too much embroiled in the moments as they came. He himself is not embroiled."

But if Thackeray was inhibited and emotionally constipated, he had good reason to be so, and if his works suffer from a want of passion it is probably because his own circumstances—for which "tragic" is not too strong a word—and the conventions of his era necessarily pushed passion onto the sidelines.

It was a sad life, one of enforced and undeserved emotional deprivation, and Taylor's sympathetic biography, while not providing much new material or even superseding previous works (Catherine Peters's excellent *Thackeray: A Writer's Life* was published in 1987, with a revised edition in 1999) provides a fine portrait of its contradictory subject: a high-spirited voluptuary forced into a life of unremitting labor; an uxorious family man forever denied marriage or acknowledged love.

Thackeray was born in Calcutta on July 18, 1811. His father, Richmond Thackeray, was a rising young official from a family prominent in the Indian Civil Service, his mother a beauty from another important Bengal family. Richmond Thackeray had not been Anne Becher's original choice; she had fallen in love back in England with Lieutenant Henry Carmichael-Smyth, an officer in the Bengal Engineers. But Anne's grandmother, who disapproved of the match, disposed of the suitor by telling Carmichael-Smyth that Anne no longer cared for him and informing Anne that her lover was dead of a fever. Anne departed for India, where she met and married Richmond Thackeray. And then one evening in 1812, not long after her son's birth, she was stunned to see Henry Carmichael-Smyth enter her drawing room as a guest of her husband. Three years later Richmond Thackeray died, and Anne married Carmichael-Smyth with almost unseemly haste.

The effect these events had on the novelist's life is hard to assess. Thackeray was only four when his father, of whom he was to retain almost no memory, died; Carmichael-Smyth was to prove a father and more than a father to his stepson until his death only two years before Thackeray's own. Still, it is a disturbing story, and it is hard not to agree with Taylor's opinion that it influenced the novels, which are "full of unheralded revenants—Amory, for instance, in *Pendennis*, whose wife has grown rich and married a baronet—and well-kept premarital secrets."

At the age of five, young Thackeray, like other Anglo-Indian children, was sent back to England to school. The little boy was predictably unhappy, first with relatives and later at Walpole House in Chiswick, which stood more or less as the model for Miss Pinkerton's Academy in *Vanity Fair*. The Carmichael-Smyths returned to England in 1820, and in 1822 the ten-and-a-half-year-old Thackeray enrolled at Charterhouse.

Like his literary alter ego Arthur Pendennis, Thackeray was not a happy or successful scholar; as one contemporary remembered, "no one could in those early days have believed that there was much work in him, or that he would ever get to the top of any tree by hard activity." He deeply disliked the school with its narrow, outdated curriculum and its headmaster, Dr. Russell, whom he was to lampoon years later in *Dr. Birch and His Young Friends*. "There are but 370 in the school," he wrote wistfully during his last year there. "I wish there were only 369."

At Charterhouse and later at Cambridge he quickly established "a routine that involved the minimum of work and the cultivation of his own interests." These consisted of the theater, with which he was obsessed, and of the production of hundreds of comical drawings burlesquing fellow pupils, masters, literary characters, and theatrical personalities. He also applied himself to written parodies which, along with the drawings, were essentially rehearsals for his early journalism, his later triumphs like *The Yellowplush Papers*, and, eventually, the sort of episodic novel of which *Vanity Fair* is the great example.

Readers familiar with Arthur Pendennis's misadventures at "St. Boniface College, Oxbridge" will already have a clear picture of Thackeray's university career. Taylor points out, though, that Pendennis, "who cuts a considerable public dash, has his verses for the chancellor's poetry medal printed up in morocco bindings and enjoys cosy dinners with titled friends, is a much more conspicuous figure than Thackeray ever was. At the same time his debts are nothing like as great." Richmond Thackeray left his son a modest fortune of some £18,000, to be kept in trust until his twenty-first birthday. With the assurance of this legacy casting a rosy hue over his future, Thackeray, thrilled to exchange the Spartan Charterhouse for Cambridge, threw himself into wine parties, dinners, the theater, rackety visits to Paris, cards (he was what we would now call a compulsive gambler), sartorial excess, and (unlike Arthur Pendennis, denied such joys by the prudery of the Victorian reading public) casual sex. Although he read avidly, he more or less ignored the syllabus, took a fourth in the Tripos exam and a poor second in the Previous. An academic failure, he left Trinity College in June 1830—with no degree, heavy debts (he could not touch his legacy until his twenty-first birthday), and a gonorrheal infection that was to plague him for the rest of his life.

Thackeray needed a profession, and now accepted the fact that it would probably have to be the law. "I have thought a great deal on the profession I *must* take; & the more I think of it the less I like it—However I believe it is the best among the positive professions & as such I must take it, for better or worse." He accordingly enrolled with a Mr. Taprell in the Middle Temple, commenced a course of study even more desultory than the one he had pursued at Cambridge, and took rooms very like those in which Pendennis and his friend George Warrington read for the law.

Thackeray never scratched the surface of his chosen subject. After some months of study he was writing in his diary, "I find I cannot read I have tried it at all hours & it fails—I don't know so much now as when I came to town & that God knows was little enough." Despairing of the entire project, he turned once again to his old enjoyments: "In a London made up of taverns and gaming-houses, theatres and print-shops, pleasure boats to Richmond and Greenwich, study assumed a low priority."

Late in 1833 Thackeray's fortunes, already uncertain, took a disastrous turn. The Indian banking houses in which most of his father's legacy was invested collapsed, and what remained of his capital vanished forever. "He was twenty-one-and-a-half, and had squandered or had removed the best part of £20,000. How was he to live?"

Law was clearly not an option, but by this time Thackeray had begun to realize that his talents for caricature and burlesque might provide a living. He was still not clear as to whether his forte was to be art or literature, but he covered both fronts. He and his stepfather embarked on a short-lived career as newspaper publishers—no one has ever figured out how they raised the cash—and Thackeray began to study art in earnest, spending several months in a Paris atelier. He made his first real entry on the London literary scene in 1834 with a contribution to the lively magazine *Fraser's*.

It was at this turning point that Thackeray fell in love and his life took a heartbreaking turn, sharply contrasting with the rather low comedy that had so far marked it. His choice fell upon an immature seventeen-year-old named Isabella Gethin Shawe, who lived with her mother and sisters in a Paris boardinghouse. She was a passive, childish girl, in thrall to a domineering mother and afraid of claiming independence: "Reading the letters exchanged prior to the marriage," Taylor writes, "it becomes clear that a less tenacious man would not have got what he wanted." Thackeray's letters, admonitory, cajoling, gently bullying, outnumber Isabella's three to one.

> So, dearest, make the little shirts ready, and the pretty night caps, and we will in a few months, go & hear Bishop Luscombe read, and be

> married, and have children, & be happy ever after, as they are in the story books. Does this please you as it does me?

The tone, as patronizing as though addressed to a small child and with a distinctly saccharine view of domesticity, is typical of Thackeray's attitude to his chosen mate. When he wrote of Isabella to others, the adjective "little" popped up often, and "The sense that in choosing Isabella he had deliberately selected an immature intelligence he could form to his own design is sometimes rather too strong for comfort." But if Thackeray's ideas about marriage seem like pure fantasy at best, and at worst what many nowadays like to call patriarchal oppression, let it only be said that he was to be punished out of all proportion for his folly.

For the moment, though, he was happy: he had won his Isabella, after an epic struggle with Mrs. Shawe and, indeed, with the girl herself—for she seems to have been fully aware of her own intellectual and emotional shortcomings—and the couple embarked on married life in 1836 with a precarious income. But Thackeray was gaining confidence in his earning abilities. As the 1830s progressed he was established as a fertile and reliable source of comic and political writing. Thackeray had accepted the fact that he did not have the talent to become a first-rate painter, but he knew his caricatures and illustrations were more than adequate: his first published "book" in fact was an 1836 pamphlet of eighty lithographed cartoons of ballet dancers called *Flore et Zephyre*.

The crucial moment came with *The Yellowplush Papers*, a series that ran in *Fraser's* throughout much of 1838. Its narrator, James de la Pluche, is "a gentleman's gentleman who trains his worm's eye view on the society in which his various employers operate"; the text, full of cockney malapropisms, sharp detail, and sly observations about social pretensions, is both an effective spoof of the etiquette books that were popular at the time and a forerunner of the way "society" would be depicted in *Vanity Fair*. *The Yellowplush Papers*, serialized in 1837, and *The Paris Sketch-Book*, published in 1840, established his reputation; he also published his first novel, *Catherine*, a takeoff on the lurid Newgate crime novels then current, which was received without much enthusiasm. For this Thackeray could hardly blame his readers: he had chosen, he admitted, "A disgusting subject & no mistake."

Thackeray's family was growing. Anne, called Anny, was born in 1837; Jane, a year younger, lived only a few months. Thackeray responded to the death with a stoicism that would become fixed during the many hard years to follow. It seemed wrong, to him, to pray or to hold God responsible: "For specific requests to God are impertinencies I think, and all we should ask from him is to learn to acquiesce."

Money was tight, and Isabella was proving to be a singularly bad housekeeper. She had always been passive and sluggish, and now spent more and more of her time in an ominous haze. The house was noisy and disorganized, and Thackeray began a lifelong habit of writing in clubs, inns, and public houses. Harriet Marian, whom her parents called Minny, was born in 1840, after which Isabella lapsed into what seemed to be a typical postpartum depression. But she did not get better, and soon she was suffering what Thackeray called an "extraordinary state of languour and depression." The doctor ordered sea air, and he took the family to Margate for a holiday they could ill afford. It was there that Isabella's state suddenly degenerated from depression to outright insanity. Walking on the beach with three-year-old Anny, she suddenly threw the child into the sea. Although Isabella soon came to her senses and fished her out again, it was a trauma Anny Thackeray never forgot.

Distraught over his wife's condition and the state of their finances, Thackeray accepted an advance from Chapman and Hall for a travel book about Ireland. He could leave Isabella and the girls with her family in Cork, he decided, while he traveled around the country in search of material. On the steamer from London, however, Isabella locked herself in the lavatory and jumped out of the window, and it was only by chance that, several minutes later, another passenger noticed her in the water: the air in her crinoline had kept her afloat.

She was determined to end her life, and it was with the greatest difficulty that her husband managed to get her and the children to Mrs. Shawe's. There he stayed for weeks, watching his wife deteriorate and chafing in the hands of his intolerable mother-in-law. The situation was desperate; he was down to his last twenty pounds, and Chapman and Hall had even required that he leave the family plate in their office as security for their advance. The only place he could turn for help was to the Carmichael-Smyths, now installed in Paris. They were warmly welcoming, but their funds were limited and the space was cramped; the presence of the Thackeray family, including the now fully demented Isabella, pushed everyone's financial and emotional resources to the limit. In her memoirs Anny Thackeray recalled one particularly awful day when a servant asked her father for money, causing him to change his last five-pound note—"and we children were in one room crying and mamma was raving in the other."

Isabella could not be cared for at home. Thackeray placed her initially in a "Maison de Santé" outside of Paris; eventually she would lodge with a private caregiver in England. Over the rest of her long life—Isabella was to outlive her husband by more than thirty years—she never recovered her reason. What was really wrong with her, and how might she be diagnosed today? Taylor suggests a form of autism, but autism appears in early childhood, not in a grown woman who has all her life been more or less normal. A more plausible explanation is schizophrenia. Yet Isabella's granddaughter, Minny's daughter Laura Stephen (half-sister to Virginia Woolf), seems to have been autistic, and autism probably is an inherited condition.

At first Thackeray visited Isabella regularly, but as she was indifferent to him and sometimes even disturbed by his presence, he eventually learned to keep away. He could never remarry, of course, and since this was the Victorian age and Thackeray was not, socially at any rate, a nonconformist, he was never allowed to enjoy any sort of acknowledged love affair with another woman, either. He did fall in love: but his relationship with Jane Brookfield was in all probability unconsummated. It was a tragic impasse for a man who had so desperately longed for married bliss, and when Charlotte Brontë, who admired *Vanity Fair* extravagantly, dedicated *Jane Eyre* to her favorite novelist, Thackeray was bitterly aware of the irony: Brontë might not have known the facts, but his situation was horribly similar to that of her Mr. Rochester.

Thackeray was depressed but not self-pitying, for now as at all the crises of his life he was painfully convinced that the fault lay not in his stars but in himself. He prayed for help "to work out the vices of character wh. have borne such bitter fruit already." It is true that Thackeray had often behaved badly, and in pressuring the unwilling Isabella into marriage he had been both thoughtless and cruel—but how more than adequately he had been punished for actions that were not vicious so much as simply thoughtless! It is at this period that shame and remorse begin to seep into the fabric of his novels, giving them their characteristic disabused tone alongside their equally distinctive gentleness and tolerance. The critic Alexander Welsh noted with acuity that "Thackeray's Christianity differs from that of most Victorian writers, including Dickens and George Eliot: he believes more strongly in the possibility of repentance. . . . Thackeray . . . is a veritable student of botching and repenting." His extremely dubious "happy endings" are those where what little satisfaction the heroes find comes not through married happiness but instead from the exceedingly cold comfort of self-knowledge.

The next five years saw Thackeray struggling to support his family and keep his wife well cared for. Freelance work being what it always is, he found it a challenge, and during that period Anny and Minny had to remain in Paris with their grandparents while the novelist lived alone in cheap, bleak rooms back in England. He began two novels at this time, one of which, *The Great Hoggarty Diamond*, would eventually be completed and published. According to his friends, he was consumed with an "awareness of what his marriage was costing him" and "the conviction that he was wasting his talents and that the great novel he believed he had within him—references to which start to crop up regularly in his letters—might remain permanently unwritten."

But his work was getting steadily more assured. *The Luck of Barry Lyndon* was published, with modest success, in 1844, and his association with a new magazine—"a very low paper," he called it in a letter to his mother, "only it's good pay and a great opportunity for unrestrained laughing sneering kicking and gambadoing"—now made his name famous at last with a wide reading public. *Punch* burst upon the scene with a tonic freshness, and Thackeray's particular style of satire suited it exactly. His work for *Punch* in the 1840s comprised the best of his journalism and sketch-writing: *The Snobs of England*, serialized in 1847 and brilliantly illustrated by the author, is still a source of great pleasure in its own right as well as being, as Taylor notices, "a series of rehearsals" for *Vanity Fair*.

With commercial success Thackeray was finally able to buy a house large enough for his family to join him: Anny and Minnie, Major and Mrs. Carmichael-Smyth, Thackeray's ancient grandmother Mrs. Butler, a governess, and servants could all be accommodated at the new establishment in Kensington. Here in 1846 the newly solvent Thackeray worked on *The Snobs of England* and on a new novel, not yet named *Vanity Fair*. He was "working every day, and yet not advancing somehow, and poor too—although everybody gives me credit for making a fortune." But poverty is a relative term. Thackeray never got so rich that he could stop worrying about the next contract and the next book: even in 1855, when he was an international celebrity, he commented dryly that "when I have written 2 more novels, for which I shall get £5000 a piece—why then, at 50, I shall be as I was at 21."

But from this point his immediate, driving needs, and those of his family, were seen to.

Vanity Fair began serialization in January 1847; it had been postponed so that it would not have to compete with Dickens's inevitably better-selling *Dombey and Son*. The early numbers aroused interest without selling particularly well: there were suggestions of canceling it altogether, and Thackeray went out of his way to inject more suspense, most obviously by making a mystery of Becky Sharp's secret marriage. Taylor is of the school of thought that "the development of *Vanity Fair* was almost startlingly *ad hoc*." Many critics disagree—perhaps out of wishful thinking, an unwillingness to believe that such a masterpiece could have been planned in a haphazard fashion or that such crystalline characters might have been changed quite drastically during the course of composition. But Thackeray was no modernist and would never have denied creating what Henry James denigrated as a "loose baggy monster." In any case, the looseness is almost the point of the whole thing: one of the joys of reading *Vanity Fair* is the sense that the author is discovering his characters alongside the reader, and that his opinion of them alters and develops as he writes.

It must be said, of course, that when his opinions alter it is for the worse and that the novel darkens as it progresses. George Osborne begins as a selfish and thoughtless but not bad-spirited young man; by the time he is dead ("with a ball in his odious bowels," as Thackeray remarked privately, with grim satisfaction), he is purely bad. At the outset of the novel Amelia is charming if lightweight; as life delivers its lessons and she learns nothing from them, her value sinks until by the end she is all but worthless. Even Dobbin, the novel's only fully admirable character, is hopelessly cheapened by the poor object on which he bestows the invaluable gift of his love.

Becky Sharp, one of the great characters of English literature, is a special case. Taylor speaks for a large proportion of readers when he claims that "*Vanity Fair* is not merely a 'novel without a hero'; it is also, at any rate covertly, a novel without a heroine." Others, without going so far as to call Becky the book's heroine, have noted the author's liking for her or at any rate a rare ambiguity in his treatment of a character who by all conventional standards is thoroughly rotten. It is true that not only Becky's craftiness but also her cheerful pragmatism and lack of malice—so long at least as her own interests are not threatened—are oddly attractive, and when she says, famously, that she thinks she could be a good woman on five thousand a year, one feels almost ready to believe her. But the Becky who angles after Jos Sedley and charms Sir Pitt Crawley is a very different proposition from the Becky who neglects and mistreats her son, and it is with the birth of little Rawdon Crawley that Thackeray's affection for Becky noticeably withers. By the end of the narrative, with the broad hints that Becky has murdered Jos (and Thackeray's line drawing of her in the role of Clytemnestra), she has ceased to be an engaging anti-heroine and has become an entirely evil woman.

Thackeray is hard on his characters, then, but he is not cruel; there is no last judgment in the novel. George dies a hero's death; Amelia finds satisfaction if not passion in her second marriage; Becky finally attains bourgeois respectability. Only Dobbin has the reflective powers to understand the irony of his own "happy ending": that the prize he had spent the better part of his life in fighting for had never been worth the taking.

In a wonderful essay on Thackeray called "The Method of Allusive Irrelevancy," G. K. Chesterton outlined the novelist's way of treating his characters and their manifold faults.

> No novelist ever carried to such perfection as Thackeray the art of saying a thing without saying it. Human life is (so to speak) so dense with delicacies, so thickly sown with things that are true and yet may be understood, that this is a very valuable faculty in a man telling tales about men. . . . When Thackeray wished to hint a truth which was just

> not true enough to bear his whole weight, his way was to wander off into similes and allegories which repeated and yet mocked the main story like derisive and dying echoes. . . . In this connection it is specially unjust to call Thackeray a cynic. He falls away into philosophizing not because his satire is merciless but because it is merciful; he wishes to soften the fall of his characters with a sense and suggestion of the weakness of all flesh. He often employs a universal cynicism because it is kinder than a personal sarcasm. He says that all men are liars, rather than say directly that Pendennis was lying. He says easily that all is vanity, so as not to say that Ethel Newcome was vain.

That is exactly what made Thackeray so very attractive a figure: his acceptance of human frailty sets him apart from many writers, most particularly those of his own era. As Lord David Cecil observed, his particular gift "needs for its full expression moral tolerance." This he did not receive in Victorian England, which is probably why he set his books in a more tolerant past—during the Regency period, as in *Vanity Fair*, or back to the eighteenth century and even beyond. "His genius, in fact," Cecil continued, "and his age, were always pulling him different ways. And he yielded to the age."

Yielded slowly, that is, and only after *Vanity Fair*. John Carey has characterized Thackeray's post–*Vanity Fair* career as "the history of a capitulation," and this is true. But a capitulation to what? To the spirit of the age, in part: as Thackeray grew older, more established, and more bourgeois, he became more conventional, or at any rate more accepting of other people's conventions. Starting in 1847 he was taken up by grand society, and as the years went by he spent more and more time hobnobbing with the rich and powerful, and far less in the bohemian company that had always stimulated his imagination. His critics accuse him of pandering to upper-class and bourgeois taste in his later novels, and there is some truth in the charge.

More serious, though, was the physical and emotional toll that his long push for fame and solvency, culminating in the huge effort of *Vanity Fair*, had cost him. Although large and powerfully built, Thackeray had never been a strong man. He was troubled by recurrent digestive ailments that his contemporaries blamed on his compulsive dining out but actually seem to have been caused by some chronic illness, possibly Crohn's disease. He was also plagued by an urethral stricture left over from the early bout with gonorrhea and was badly debilitated by a serious case of cholera. His long romantic friendship with Jane Brookfield, the wife of his friend William Brookfield, provided more frustration than relief, and it was broken off in 1851.

Pendennis had been published the previous year. It is an autobiographical *Bildungsroman*, Thackeray's answer to *David Copperfield*. While not a masterpiece like *Vanity Fair*, it is still on a very high level, one of the most rewarding of Victorian novels and now unjustly forgotten. One character in particular, the worldly old Major Pendennis, is sublime, on a par with almost any of Dickens's creations. Nevertheless *Pendennis* marks the beginning of Thackeray's decline: it bears the marks, Taylor rightly notes, of "his efforts to adjust his temperament to the sensibilities of the people for whom he wrote, and its ultimate aesthetic effect is compromised by a reliance on what its audience expected from the fiction they read." The central romance between Pendennis and the insipid Laura Bell, in particular, is intolerable to anyone who knows the levels of ambiguity of which Thackeray was capable.

Thackeray had enjoyed writing *Pendennis*, but he was tired and began to cast about for some money-making scheme that would not involve writing. Lecturing was an acceptable alternative—Dickens had made enormous sums in this way—and though he hated and feared the limelight, Thackeray thought it might behoove him to try his own hand at public speaking. He prepared a series of talks on English humorists of the eighteenth century, and despite his initial panic attacks, they proved a hit. They were not taken seriously by historians and intellectuals, however, and the irritable Carlyle remarked, "I wish I could persuade Thackeray that the test of a great man is not whether he would like to meet him at a tea-party."

The publisher George Smith had offered Thackeray generous terms for a new novel and now, with the eighteenth-century background fresh in his mind, he turned to the composition of *The History of Henry Esmond*, a narrative spanning the period from the Glorious Revolution through the reign of Queen Anne. *Esmond* has some interesting points: the central love triangle, involving Henry, his adoptive mother Rachel Castlewood, and her beautiful, imperious daughter Beatrix, is odd and incestuous enough to have disturbed a number of readers. On the debit side, though, the novel is stuffy and even ponderous. Catherine Peters criticizes "the suffocating blanket of Victorian respectability which weighs down the eighteenth-century action," and even Thackeray, as he later admitted to Trollope, found Esmond "a prig." His privately expressed opinion of the novel was that "it is clever but it is also stupid and no mistake."

In 1852, seeking a wider audience for his lectures, he headed for the United States. He enjoyed himself immensely, but the six months took their toll, and his exhaustion persisted. "Life was full of obligations: to write a book, to think about his next series of lectures, to eat a dinner or make his bow in somebody's drawing-room. To write or dictate the letters by which his social and professional life was transacted." The girls, quickly growing up now, required guidance that he did not always feel qualified to give them, and he went through a seemingly endless string of governesses. ("Unless I liked a Governess I couldn't live with her and if I did—O fie. The flesh is very weak, le Coeur sent toujours le besoin d'aimer," he confided to a friend.)

He was nearly worn out when he embarked on *The Newcomes*, his last major effort, which Elizabeth Bowen later described only too accurately as "the shell of a great novel." But he needed the money. He was afraid that the novel would mark a "retreat"—"however if I can get £3000 for my darters I mean 3000 *to put away* . . . I will go backwards or forwards or anyway." While *The Newcomes* displays the same high intelligence as *Vanity Fair* and *Pendennis*, it is ruined by what Taylor calls "a creeping emollience" of which Thackeray, as ever, was gloomily conscious. By the time he began his next book, *The Virginians*—"a horribly stupid story," as he later called it—he had almost completely worn out his imaginative powers and his energy.

Thackeray's last important work was the founding, with the publisher George Smith, of the *Cornhill*, one of the great Victorian literary magazines. While his own powers were on the ebb, he was an effective figurehead and, his susceptibility to pretty female contributors notwithstanding, a good editor as well: his choice for the magazine's first full-length serial fell on the young Anthony Trollope, who provided *Framley Parsonage*, the novel that made his name.

"I have outlived my health, popularity and inventive faculties," Thackeray wrote in 1860, at the age of not quite fifty: he was being brutally honest, as he always was about himself. He still wrote—*Philip* was serialized in *Cornhill* in 1861–1862, and *Denis Duval*, unfinished at the time of his death, was in the future—but he readily admitted that "the novel writing vein is used up through and through" (to which his lifelong friend Edward FitzGerald commented, "it is a pity he was not convinced of this before") and told friends that if he were not obliged to do so for financial reasons, he would never take up his pen again. His letters became increasingly valedictory, and he seemed disinclined to take a stand against the premature death that was obviously stalking him. "I wouldn't care to travel over the ground again," he wrote, "though I have had some pleasant days and dear companions." On Christmas Eve, 1863, he was found dead of a stroke, aged only fifty-two.

Although Thackeray had been in manifest decline, his death shocked literary London, and there was a huge turnout of writers and artists at his funeral, including Browning, Trollope, Millais, John Tenniel, Henry Mayhew, G. H. Lewes, and Dickens, who was visibly distressed. The obituaries were deeply affectionate, as were the diaries and letters of his friends as they reflected upon his life. "He had many fine qualities," wrote the prickly Thomas Carlyle, whose friendship with the novelist had not always been smooth: "no guile or malice against any mortal: a big mass of soul, but not strong in proportion: a beautiful vein of genius lay struggling about him—Poor Thackeray, adieu, adieu!"

The daughters over whose future Thackeray had long fretted both had happy lives, although Minnie's was to be a short one. She married Leslie Stephen; their daughter Laura was born in 1870, and Minnie became pregnant again, but both she and the new baby died shortly before its birth. Anny Thackeray, her father's greatest friend, became the keeper of his flame and wrote introductions to his books. At the age of forty she married a cousin, Richmond Ritchie. She produced two children, enjoyed her own distinguished career as a novelist, was the friend of many eminent writers and artists, and as an old lady was the model for Mrs. Hilbery in her stepniece Virginia Woolf's novel *Night and Day*.

D. J. Taylor's biography makes a good read, but it is not really a *necessary* book. Although slightly longer and more detailed than Catherine Peters's life of the novelist, it is noticeably less acute. It offers no new interpretations of Thackeray's work, for Taylor does not aspire to write a critical biography: "critics criticize, biographers write biographies," he insists. And it ultimately fails in its stated purpose, "to demonstrate that [Thackeray] was the greatest English writer (writer, you note, not novelist) of the nineteenth century. And perhaps the greatest of all time." I did not believe this before reading the biography, and I found nothing in its pages to change my opinion.

But—as is not always the case with writers—to know about Thackeray's life is to enrich one's feeling for his work. On a first reading of *Vanity Fair* its sparkle and wit simply overwhelm the reader; it is one of the funniest books ever written. Coming back to the novel in later life, and with a knowledge of Thackeray's personal struggles, the book's sadness overwhelms or at least balances the wit: the sense of lost chances and love squandered, of moral slackening, personal disgust, and the hopelessness of poor, dissatisfied, and disappointed humankind is realized in a manner that has seldom been equaled. Let Thackeray himself have the last word:

> I want to leave everybody dissatisfied and unhappy at the end of the story [he wrote to a sympathetic critic]—we ought all to be with our own and all other stories. Good God don't I see (in that may-be cracked and warped looking-glass in which I am always looking) my own weaknesses wickednesses lusts follies shortcomings? . . . You have all of you taken my misanthropy to task—I wish I could myself: but take the world by a certain standard (you know what I mean) and who dares talk of having any virtue at all? . . . In fact, I've a strong impression that we are most of us not fit for—never mind.

Wilkie Collins: An Enlightened Libertine

Wilkie Collins, the author of Victorian masterpieces of suspense including *The Woman in White* and *The Moonstone*, seems to have found the secret to a happy life: do as you please and be damned. He had not one ounce of Anglo-Saxon puritanism. He loved pleasure of all kinds: food, drink, women, the theater. Visits to France and Italy early in life had confirmed him in the belief that his fellow Englishmen were hypocrites regarding sex and barbarians when it came to the arts of the table, that "a man who eats a plain joint is only one remove from a cannibal—or a butcher." His self-indulgent habits caught up with him, and in middle age, according to Julian Hawthorne, the son of the novelist, "he was soft, plump, and pale, suffered from various ailments, his liver was wrong, his heart weak, his lungs faint, his stomach incompetent, he ate too much and the wrong things." Still, he continued to take his pleasures however and whenever he could, determined to make the most of life.

He despised social convention. A radical and a bohemian with a bourgeois fondness for comfort, Collins did exactly as he liked, shocking many people in the process. From 1858 until the end of his life he lived with a semi-respectable widow, Caroline Graves, and her daughter Elizabeth (called Carrie); from about 1865 he had also a second mistress, Martha Rudd, by whom he fathered two children. This he called his "morganatic family." Public disapproval bothered Collins not at all: he had always hated "Society" and was only too pleased to be rejected by it. His friends remained his friends.

In any case, many of his circle enjoyed or suffered from marital irregularities. There was Charles Dickens's separation from his wife, Catherine; Holman Hunt's long and stormy liaison with his illiterate model, Annie Miller; John Everett Millais's union with Mrs. John Ruskin, whose first union had never been consummated; William Frith's seven children by his mistress and twelve by his wife. Marianne Evans (George Eliot) and George Henry Lewes, unmarried, lived together openly, as did Charles Reade and the actress Laura Seymour.

What set Collins apart was his specific dislike for the institution of marriage, and he was not afraid to express his objection in print. "The real fact seems to be, that the general idea of the scope and purpose of the Institution of Marriage is a miserably narrow one. . . . The social advantages which it is fitted to produce ought to extend beyond one man and one woman, to the circle of society amid which they move," he wrote in "Bold Words by a Bachelor" (1856). Collins did not shy from the responsibilities that marriage involved—he willingly supported both his households—or even from a more settled way of life; his relationship with Caroline was a long-standing one, and time with his "morganatic family" was spent in a conventional, domestic fashion. His stated objections to the institution appear to have been quite sincere, and when in 1868 Caroline tried to pressure him into wedlock by threatening to marry another man, he called her bluff. (She lived with her new husband, Joseph Clow, for two years, then returned to Collins upon exactly the same basis as before.)

Alert though he was to the selfishness of marriage, Collins was remarkably obtuse when it came to the selfishness of his own bachelor existence. As the author of *No Name*, he had passionately criticized the law that deprived illegitimate children of their legal rights and place in society; as a father, he blandly condemned his own children to suffer these indignities. As a result, his daughters, who lived until 1955, never married and never acknowledged their connection with the novelist. It seems that Collins, generous friend though he was, had a strong streak of egotism, or at least of stubbornness. But he was a kind man, and most of his acquaintances were very fond of him. His charm stemmed partly from his lack of interest in social advancement. "Wilkie was entirely without ambition to take a place in the competition of society," wrote Holman Hunt, "and avoided plans of life that necessitated the making up of his mind enough to forecast the future. In this respect he left all to circumstance." Yet Collins was anything but careless; he worked industriously, with a conscientious professionalism, and met his deadlines even when incapacitated by illness, as he was throughout his last years.

To today's readers he is known simply as the author of *The Moonstone* and *The Woman in White.* A few others have read *Armadale* and *No Name*, and though Collins was the author of thirty-three books as well as many plays and magazine articles, his modern reputation rests exclusively on these four novels, all published in the 1860s.

They are extremely good, especially since they belong, at least in part, to the literary genre with the shortest shelf life: melodrama. T. S. Eliot, one of Collins's most influential admirers, wrote of *Armadale* that "it has no merit beyond melodrama, and it has every merit that melodrama can have." I think it is time that Eliot's judgment, taken as gospel by so many twentieth-century readers, be challenged, or at least broadened. Collins's best fiction comprises melodrama, suspense, and mystery; but it is made complete, made literature rather than simply genre fiction, by a strange and passionate moral vision. This perhaps is one of the reasons the books are as startlingly vivid and readable today as they were upon their appearance. Comparing *The Woman in White* or *No Name* with other popular melodramas of the nineteenth century—*The Mysteries of Udolpho*, say, or *Uncle Tom's Cabin*—Collins's novels have the ring of absolute modernity while the others have dwindled into fusty, faintly ridiculous dullness. Suspense novels with great longevity are rare, and for this reason alone Wilkie Collins might be accounted an extraordinary writer. But there are many other reasons.

First among these is Collins's gift for invention, so great that he was able to be profligate with his ideas. With *The Moonstone* he practically invented the modern detective novel. (Poe had already written his tales of C. Auguste Dupin, but the book-length, fleshed-out plot with a crime at its center was Collins's creation, and many of the book's details have now become conventions of the genre.) But while *The Moonstone*'s innovations have been refined, elaborated, and imitated by thousands of writers over more than a century, Collins himself never again exploited the genre he had created.

Another characteristic that gives Collins's work its life was the assurance, which he shared with many of his contemporaries—Thackeray, Trollope, Charlotte Brontë, Dickens—that writing for the masses did not necessitate writing down to them. In Collins's day, highbrow and lowbrow had not yet parted company; the best literature was popular literature, and Collins considered his readers (measured in volume of sales) to be the final judges of his work rather than the convention-bound critics. Had he lived long enough to witness the Joycean ideal of godlike aesthetic detachment, he would have been disgusted. As it was, he sought an audience even broader than the voracious general readership of his own period, trying again and again to entrap even the lowest echelon of readers, the "Unknown Public" that read cheap and sensational newspapers rather than books. Though he never succeeded in this final goal, Collins was throughout his career a democratic artist who boldly made his bid for popularity and won it in almost unhoped-for measure. Swinburne was correct when he offered that "though Dickens was not a Shakespeare, and though Collins was not a Dickens, it is permissible to anticipate that their names and their works will be familiar to generations unacquainted with the existence and unaware of the eclipse of their most shining, most scornful, and most superior critics."

Collins was exceptional, too, in the way he adorned his sensational plots with a finely drawn psychological truth. Unlike the typical characters of melodrama, his are no mere types but living people, sometimes etched with a delicacy more reminiscent of George Eliot than of his fellow melodramatists, even the greatest melodramatist of all, Dickens. In spite of Collins's friendship with Dickens—and it was certainly the formative friendship of his career, if not of his life—it was to Balzac that Collins looked for inspiration, and to Balzac's breadth of vision that never excluded the petty, the sordid, the contradictory. Balzac he saw as the greatest portrayer of women while Dickens was limited in this area: Collins believed Nancy in *Oliver Twist* to be the "the finest thing [Dickens] ever did. He never afterwards saw all sides of a woman's character—saw all round her." He himself tried always, with varying levels of success, to see "all round" his women characters, an attempt that did not commend him to certain of his critics. When *No Name* was published in 1862, the reviewer Margaret Oliphant wrote in horror of Magdalen Vanstone, the book's heroine, revolted by her "career of vulgar and aimless trickery and wickedness . . . from all the pollutions of which he intends us to believe that she emerges, at the cost of a fever, as pure, as high-minded, and as spotless as the most dazzling white of heroines." Of course Collins never intended even the reformed Magdalen to seem high-minded or spotless; she remains the flawed but attractive character she has been from the beginning. Her sister Norah, who bears the sisters' discovery of their illegitimacy and their subsequent fall into penury with modest resignation, ultimately wins back the family fortune by virtue alone, but it seems almost as though Collins simply threw her in as a sop for those who require virtue in their heroines. It is always the ruthless Magdalen with whom the reader identifies, though she goes so far as to prostitute herself by tricking into marriage a man who disgusts her. Collins deftly manipulates the reader's sympathies so that they turn against Norah and the girls' governess, who have Magdalen's best interests at heart, perversely presenting them as mere encumbrances to Magdalen's quest for revenge against the cousin who has robbed her of her fortune and her name.

He again employs a "double heroine" in *The Woman in White*. Here is the most memorable character in all his fiction, the magnificent Marian Halcombe, a vigorous, passionate, strong-minded young woman who is the most active force for good in the book. Yet, as though to comment upon society's ideal of feminine dependency, Collins condemns Marian to permanent spinsterhood, making the helpless Laura Fairlie the book's nominal heroine. When Laura agrees to marry the sinister Sir Percival Glyde, her father's choice, rather than the young drawing instructor Walter Hartright, whom she loves, her passive betrayal not only of her lover but of herself means that she more or less colludes in the plot to steal her identity and lock her up in an insane asylum. Yet the colorless Laura is rewarded with a loving husband and son; Marian, the fighter, who risks her life for Laura, must content herself with the role of aunt. Again Collins manipulates the reader's sympathies so that they are at odds with the accepted moral code and the role it assigned to women.

He simply felt that life was more complicated, circumstances more extenuating than middle-class English society was willing to admit. Sex, and sex among the unmarried, was a fact of life. Why could others not acknowledge it? He was outraged by the concurrence of Dickens's friend and biographer, John Forster, in the platitude that all of Dickens's work could be put into the hands of children. "It is impossible to read such stuff as this without a word of protest," he wrote.

> If it is true, which it is not, it would imply the condemnation of Dickens's books as works of art, it would declare him to be guilty of deliberately presenting to his readers a false reflection of human life. If this wretched English claptrap means anything it means that the nov-

> elist is forbidden to touch on the sexual relations which literally swarm about him, and influence the lives of millions of his fellow-creatures, [except when] those relations are licensed by the ceremony called marriage. One expects this essentially immoral view of the functions of the novelist from a professor of claptrap like the late Bishop of Manchester. But that Forster should quote it with approval is a sad discovery indeed.

The modernity of Collins's books, then, is largely due to his moral vision, which harmonizes far more readily with the attitudes of our own time than it did with the popular standards of the 1860s. Many have called Collins an atheist. He was not a churchgoer, but he was emphatically not an atheist; he simply believed God's tolerance and forgiveness to be extended far beyond some narrow elect—a belief to be found throughout *No Name*, an essentially Christian book. Cruelty was hard to forgive, sexual weakness easy.

How was this easygoing iconoclast formed? In her new and entertaining biography of Wilkie Collins, *The King of Inventors*, Catherine Peters proposes that he determined to escape "the mental inhibitions of the obsession with class that his father had allowed to throttle his freedom." For though Collins's childhood was a happy one, his parents prosperous and affectionate, there can be no doubt that the father's character—represented by Peters as a "mixture of groveling humility, anxiety and family affection"—forced an uncongenial code of behavior upon the son.

William Collins was a well-known painter, a member of the Royal Academy, and very much a pillar of England's artistic establishment. His work would not appeal much to modern tastes, for he ran to heavy-handed conversation pieces with titles like *The Burial-Place of a Favourite Bird* and *The Sale of the Pet Lamb*. Nor was he greatly admired by his more brilliant contemporaries. Constable, who despised his work, described one of William's contributions to the Academy Exhibition as "a coast scene with fish, as usual, and a landscape like a large cow-turd." Nevertheless William gave his sons William Wilkie (born 1824) and Charles Allston (born 1828) a wonderful education in the art of seeing and an appreciation for the privileges of an artist's life. He often expressed his belief that "the study of the Art was in itself so delightful, that it balanced almost all the evils of life . . . that an artist with tolerable success had no right to complain of anything." Wilkie (who dropped the "William" from his name in adolescence) later wrote of his father that "an excursion with him in the country was a privilege. . . . He possessed the peculiar facility of divesting his profession of all its mysteries and technicalities, and of enabling the most uneducated in his Art to look at Nature with *his* eyes, and enjoy Nature with *his* zest."

Wilkie Collins was always a visual writer, constructing his scenes in a vivid, painterly fashion. In this his father's training was instrumental, as was the fact that he spent his entire life around painters. As a child he was surrounded by his father's friends in the profession, who included Turner; his aunt, Margaret Carpenter, was one of the best portraitists of her time; his younger brother, Charley, was a fairly considerable Pre-Raphaelite painter; Wilkie himself studied painting and even had a work exhibited at the Academy Exhibition of 1849. Wilkie included among his own intimate friends the Pre-Raphaelites Rossetti, Millais, and Holman Hunt as well as the Academy painters (whose work he preferred) W. P. Frith, Augustus Egg, and Edward Ward.

A careful (some said niggling) artist, William Collins was anything but a bohemian. His modest gifts had afforded him an escape from the obscurity and near poverty of his youth to the privilege and social position he craved, and he passionately embraced the values of the upper middle class. Among the perks of his trade were professional visits to the country houses of the great, from where, Peters tells us, "his loving letters to his wife often contain, as well as chat about the titled and famous people he is mixing with, reference to a good sermon, or a pious exhortation not to forget the blessings of the Almighty." When he sent Wilkie to school, he chose Mr. Cole's establishment at Highbury, telling the boy that there "you will make aristocratic connections which will be of the greatest use to you in life."

But Wilkie never made use of any such connections. He had already rejected his father's upwardly mobile striving, turning with gusto toward the raffish and the sybaritic. He became a conscientious nonconformist: "He had only to identify a conventional attitude," writes Peters, "to want instantly to outrage it; to hear a platitude and contradict it; to have an expectation held of him and disappoint it." The boy cheerfully failed at each new start in life his father arranged for him, including a five-year stint with a tea merchant in the Strand, an establishment Wilkie baldly called "a prison."

William Collins took his family on a long visit to Italy and France from 1836 to 1838, when Wilkie was an adolescent, and from that moment the boy adopted continental attitudes to religion, sex, and food, in blatant contrast to his father's xenophobia and piety. Also in contrast to his father, Wilkie was bumptious and sexually self-confident, in spite of his strange appearance: he stood under five feet six inches, his hands and feet were smaller than a woman's, and there was a bulging protuberance on his forehead.

Though Wilkie began studying law in 1846, his ambitions were by that time wholly literary, and he had started a novel. Its composition was interrupted, however, by the death of William Collins, and Wilkie set about the task of writing his father's official "Life." The finished biography was Collins's first published book, and it was received with enthusiasm: ". . . no better work upon art and artists has been given to the world in the last half-century," raved the *Observer* critic.

Though she had been devoted to her husband, Harriet Collins felt unexpectedly liberated by his death. After years as the sober helpmeet of a serious and ambitious man, she became ebullient and witty, the dominant force in her sons' lives. She moved to a new house and began running what was in effect a salon for the artists who were her sons' friends: Millais, Frith, and Egg, among others. Wilkie and Charley were content for many years to live with Harriet, using her as landlady, banker, and hostess. She had a firmer hold on her sons than did any of the women in their lives, and Collins was repeatedly to speak of her death (in 1868) as the greatest sorrow of his life.

The new atmosphere at home proved a fruitful one for Collins. He at last completed his novel, *Antonina: or the Fall of Rome*, published in 1850. It was a historical romance modeled upon the works of Bulwer-Lytton and Scott, and dealt with the destructive nature of religious fanaticism and extremism of all sorts; it was a great success with reviewers. He followed this with a light travel book about Cornwall, *Rambles Beyond Railways* (1851). His publisher was Richard Bentley, a useful connection in that he also put out a magazine, *Bentley's Miscellany*, which became an outlet for Collins's growing stream of articles and stories. The first editor of this periodical had been Charles Dickens, and it was at this point in his life that Collins first became acquainted with the older novelist.

Dickens was producing a new play, *Not So Bad as We Seem*, in aid of the Guild of Literature and Art. Himself the star, he recruited Collins to play a small part. Dickens's rehearsal pace—long, grueling hours followed by riotous parties—suited Collins's temperament, and the two men quickly became friends. John Forster's jealousy of Collins's friendship with Dickens caused him practically to omit Collins from what was for years the definitive biography of the great man, but we now know that during the mid-fifties Collins became Dickens's bosom friend, taking the place of earlier companions like Forster and Daniel Maclise. Collins's professionalism matched Dickens's own, and his liking for fun and dissipation made him especially attractive. For Dickens had become something of a prisoner in the role of household deity he had created for himself, and family life was growing less congenial to him as he became estranged from his wife and disappointed in his children. Collins's taste for brothels, music halls, and actresses was shared by Dickens; his openness about sexual matters was exciting, if a little threatening to Dickens's chosen image. They traveled together in Europe, Collins flaunting his knowledge of painting and his adolescent sexual experiences in Italy before the more insular Dickens, but generally making himself agreeable: "Collins eats and drinks everything," Dickens wrote home to his wife. "Gets on very well everywhere, and is always in good spirits."

Dickens gave Collins valuable business advice about the publication of *Basil* (1852), his first novel with a modern setting; he gave him work writing stories for his magazine *Household Words*, one of which, "A Terribly Strange Bed," would become a classic; and, in 1853, he made Collins one of the "young men" on the magazine's staff. Collins attacked social convention here and in *The Leader*, a radical newspaper founded by George Lewes and Thornton Leigh Hunt: "A Plea for Sunday Reform," for instance, or an editorial on the dreadful legal status accorded married women. When his outbursts became too radical for *Household Words'* more middle-of-the-road politics, Dickens would discreetly edit them.

Peters demonstrates that it required an effort for Collins to retain his independence from the Dickens juggernaut. "All Wilkie's good-humored stubbornness was needed to keep his own style and literary integrity, to remain something more than one of Dickens's 'young men.'" And though Collins continued to publish his own novels (*Hide and Seek*, 1854; *The Dead Secret*, 1857), his output was markedly slower during these years than at other times in his life. Dickens could be high-handed: when Collins showed him a play he had written, *The Lighthouse*, Dickens appropriated it, did some rewriting, and gave it an amateur production with himself in the lead, rather than the professional one through which Collins sought to break into the theatrical world. Nevertheless Collins's long apprenticeship with Dickens strengthened his work. The older man's energy and rich imagination were infectious, and it is worth noting that after Dickens's death in 1870 Collins never again wrote anything of great imaginative force.

In 1858 the lives of both men changed direction. Dickens's love for the young actress Ellen Ternan forced him to a final break with his wife, and Collins began living openly with Caroline Graves, leaving his mother's house for the first time at the age of thirty-four. (In his biography of his father, John Guille Millais tells a melodramatic story of Collins's first meeting with Caroline: alone and dressed entirely in white, fleeing a mesmerist at dead of night, she appeared like a ghost to Collins and his companions. Peters ridicules the unsubstantiated story.) The way in which Dickens and Collins dealt with their personal crises marks the profound differences between them. Collins was perfectly open about his relationship with Caroline, and if he did not invite her everywhere he went, it was not out of shame but because he often preferred traveling as a bachelor. Dickens took the opposite tack. But while he tried to keep his link with Ellen Ternan a secret, his separation from his wife was inevitably made public, and he responded with defensive bluster, even destroying *Household Words* because its publishers refused to print his own version of the separation in *Punch*.

The dissolution of the magazine gave birth to a larger one, however, when Dickens replaced it with *All the Year Round*. He decided that each number would begin with a serialized piece of fiction by a well-known author. He himself launched the periodical with *A Tale of Two Cities*, and he asked Collins to follow it up with a new novel of his own. The result was *The Woman in White*.

The kernel of the story, based on a true case, Collins described as "a conspiracy in private life, in which circumstances are so handled as to rob a woman of her identity by confounding her with another woman, sufficiently like her in personal appearance to answer the wicked purpose." Challenged by Dickens's example, Collins set out to write, above all, a page-turner. "I *must* stagger the public into attention, if possible, at the outset. They shan't drop a number, when I begin, if *I* can help it." But he overstepped the mark in his zeal. "I have yielded to the worst temptation that besets a novelist—the temptation to begin with a striking incident, without counting the cost in the shape of the explanations that must and will follow." He had to begin again—but the new beginning, of course, was more striking yet: Walter Hartright's famous meeting with Anne Catherick, the Woman in White, late in the evening on a Hampstead road.

Unlike so many of his contemporaries, Collins chose to ignore the stringencies of serial publication. He felt that the most important thing was to keep "the story always advancing, without paying the smallest attention to the serial division in parts, or to the book publication in volumes." The fortunate result is a free-flowing, suspenseful narrative, unmarred (at least for modern tastes) by subplots or comic supporting characters. Unquestionably thrilling, the book has many other virtues. Its narration by a series of characters in turn (inspired by Collins's visit to a criminal trial) ensures a continual freshness of outlook, gives differing interpretations of the events, and shows, in Collins's best style, the relativism of any received moral notions. The feminist heroine, Marian Halcombe, is something quite new in English literature; the arch-villain, Count Fosco, is an equally fine creation, with his brilliantly persuasive attacks on the English moral code. Most striking of all is Collins's use of humor, which is always intrinsic to the central situation and never, as in so many popular novels of the period, appended as mere filler. Take, for example, Walter's first meeting with Marian.

> I looked from the table to the window farthest from me, and saw a lady standing at it, with her back turned towards me. The instant my eyes rested on her, I was struck by the rare beauty of her form, and by the unaffected grace of her attitude. Her figure was tall, yet not too tall; comely and well-developed, yet not fat; her head set on her shoulders with an easy, pliant firmness; her waist, perfection in the eyes of a

man, for it occupied its natural place, it filled out its natural circle, it was visibly and delightfully undeformed by stays. . . . She turned towards me immediately. The easy elegance of every movement of her limbs and body as soon as she began to advance from the far end of the room, set me in a flutter of expectation to see her face clearly. She left the window—and I said to myself, The lady is dark. She moved forward a few steps—and I said to myself, The lady is young. She approached nearer—and I said to myself (with a sense of surprise which words fail me to express), The lady is ugly!

The Woman in White was nothing less than a blockbuster. Lines formed to buy each new number of *All the Year Round*, and the periodical achieved staggering circulation figures, three times that of *Household Words*. There were "Woman in White" perfumes and toiletries, cloaks and bonnets; there was a Fosco Galop and a Woman in White Waltz. Collins's commercial success now allowed him to dictate his own price to publishers, and though the highbrow *Cornhill* was too late to snag his next book, already promised to *All the Year Round*, its editor offered him an enormous sum for the following one. Collins was gleeful. "Five Thousand Pounds!!!!!! Ha! ha! ha! Five thousand pounds for nine months or at most a year's work—nobody but Dickens has made as much."

He was already at work on *No Name*. Dickens was excited by what he read but gave his protégé a suggestion:

> It seems to me that great care is needed not to tell the story too severely. In exact proportion as you play around it here and there, and mitigate the severity of your own sticking to it, you will enhance and intensify the power with which Magdalen holds on to her purpose. For this reason I should have given Mr. Pendril some touches of comicality, and should have generally lighted up the house with some such capital touches of whimsicality and humour as those with which you have irradiated the private theatricals.

Fortunately Collins ignored this advice. Only a writer of Dickens's own genius could have carried off such "whimsicality" and "comicality" without destroying the straightforward narrative rush that was Collins's particular strength. *No Name* sold well, though critics were repelled by its heroine. *Armadale*, Collins's next novel, was serialized in *Cornhill* from 1865 to 1866. Again he chose a heroine who would shock: Lydia Gwilt was even more cynical and tough than Magdalen Vanstone. *Armadale* did not justify the magazine's financial outlay, selling relatively slowly. But it is one of Collins's best books, in fact the very acme of the "sensation novel" of the sixties that he did so much to define and popularize. The sensation novel dealt with crime, adultery, bigamy, illegitimacy, sex, murder, or any combination thereof. *Armadale* and *No Name* are the best the genre has to offer; Collins now set out to challenge his audience's expectation by changing the rules of the game.

In doing so he created a new and much more durable genre. "*The Moonstone* is the first and greatest of English detective novels," wrote T. S. Eliot, and many have shared his opinion. In this novel the detective story as we know it bursts fully matured onto the scene. Its predecessors were few. There was the Inspector Bucket subplot of Dickens's *Bleak House*. There were the Dupin stories. But as Eliot pointed out, "the detective story, as created by Poe is something as specialized and intellectual as a chess problem; whereas the best English detective fiction has relied less on the beauty of the mathematical problem and much more on the intangible human element." Sergeant Cuff, with his inductive reasoning and his passion for roses, is the direct ancestor of Sherlock Holmes and Hercule Poirot.

Like *The Woman in White*, *The Moonstone* has many virtues other than those of its genre. The first is the respect accorded the Hindu religion. The jewel has been stolen from a Hindu temple by the wicked John Herncastle and left in his will to his niece Rachel Verinder. Though the book's series of narrators all treat the diamond as Rachel's rightful property—and indeed, Rachel is innocent of any taint of theft—Collins gently enlists our sympathies with the mysterious, even murderous Brahmin priests who seek the stone, and we rejoice at the moonstone's ultimate return to its temple. This may seem straightforward enough today, but the novel was written hardly a decade after the Indian Mutiny, and the vengeful jingoism that event had caused in England was still the overwhelmingly dominant attitude there.

The novel was also remarkable in its bold sympathy for poor working women. With *The Moonstone*'s Rosanna Spearman, the ugly housemaid who dares to fall in love with the young gentleman Franklin Blake and commits suicide for her unrequited love, Collins cast a very uncomfortable shadow over the reader's feelings for the charming Franklin. His inability to recognize the girl's love and her pain is a real fault: as Rosanna's friend Lucy says, "He bewitched her. Don't tell me he didn't mean it, and didn't know it. . . . Cruel, cruel, cruel."

The Moonstone was another best-seller, spawning imitations of all kinds: Trollope's *The Eustace Diamonds*, Dickens's *The Mystery of Edwin Drood*, and Conan Doyle's *The Sign of Four* are three of the more famous books that drew inspiration from the story. But *The Moonstone* was the last of Collins's major novels. After this his talent seemed to fade, for several reasons.

His health, never good, began to handicap him intolerably. He suffered from a debilitating condition which he described as "rheumatic gout," and as it grew more severe he became increasingly dependent on laudanum (an opium-based drug) to ease his discomfort. Eventually he was taking massive doses, and the disease and the drug combined to make long periods of concentrated work a painful process. The death of Dickens, two years after the publication of *The Moonstone*, ended Collins's most fruitful working relationship. Also, his success as a playwright began to play havoc with his fiction: he took to writing his books with one eye on their immediate transformation into plays, and his fictional constructions suffered for it. Some feel, too, that his consuming political interests—the rights of women, anti-vivisection, divorce law reform—began during this period to take precedence over his attention to art, and that in Dickens's absence he became a disciple of Charles Reade, the leading proponent of "Fiction with a Purpose." Swinburne's parody of Pope—

> What brought good Wilkie's genius nigh perdition?
> Some demon whispered—'Wilkie! have a mission'

—is, perhaps, partly true.

Meanwhile, in the eyes of the great public, Collins was becoming old hat. The most intelligent readers no longer turned to melodrama, and the style of the time, naturalism, was a closed book to him. He was too highbrow for the new mass-readership newspapers, yet out of touch with the tastes of educated readers. He was in fact one of the first victims of the new rift between literature for the elite and literature for the masses, and Peters points out that "Collins, who had always believed passionately that the two could and should be combined, found himself caught in the middle." A younger writer such as Robert Louis Stevenson was able to take Collins's material and turn it once more to magic—for surely Collins, with his recurrent motif of the double, is one inspiration behind both *Dr. Jekyll and Mr. Hyde* and *The Master of Ballantrae*. But for Collins himself the magic no longer worked. He wrote several more novels, notably *Heart and Science* (1883), *The Evil Genius* (1886), and *Blind Love*, which he was still working on when he died, in agonizing pain, in 1889. Walter Besant finished the novel on Collins's request and following his fantastically thorough notes.

Meredith, Hardy, and Harry Quilter raised a subscription for a memorial to Collins in St. Paul's, but the dean and chapter refused to consider memorializing so notorious a fornicator. The money was used in a way that Collins would in any case have preferred, to create the "Wilkie Collins Memorial Library of Fiction" at the People's Palace in the East End, later Queen Mary's College.

Catherine Peters's biography is timely, for Wilkie Collins is a strangely modern character, his eccentricities likely to appeal to readers of our own time, his books worthy of a new surge of interest. His disdain for cant and social niceties is as merciless as any opinions of the last two hundred years. "Shall I tell you what a lady is?" Magdalen Vanstone asks her maid. "A lady is a woman who wears a silk gown, and has a sense of her own importance. I shall put the gown on your back, and the sense in your head." Collins knew that gentility and respectability are constructed of surfaces, with no more solidity than air. But any disdain he felt for the human race was always far overshadowed by his principal quality—kindness. Collins was above all a kind man, and he knew that kindness is not an easy quality but a difficult one, closely allied with intelligence, sensibility, and the rarest of all virtues, tolerance. "Examples may be found every day of a fool who is no coward," he wrote; "examples may occasionally be found of a fool who is not cunning; but it may be reasonably doubted whether there is a producible instance anywhere of a fool who is not cruel."

Henty's Christian Gentlemen

Some children's books seem to be timeless: *Peter Rabbit*, for instance, or *Charlotte's Web*. Others are unmistakably a product of their Zeitgeist and become less accessible with each passing generation: it will be surprising if today's best-selling author Judy Blume appeals to children in the year 2050 or so. In the case of G. A Henty (1832–1902), even the titles, with their potent whiff of Victorian imperial verve and muscular Christianity, are enough to elicit a condescending smile from modern readers: *By Sheer Pluck: A Tale of the Ashanti War*; or *With Buller in Natal*; or *A Dash for Khartoum: A Tale of the Nile Expedition*; or *The Tiger of Mysore: A Story of the War With Tippoo Sahib*.

Henty's eighty historical adventure novels for boys (yes, for boys—it goes without saying that no writer today would get away with this sort of gender stereotyping) were wildly popular in their day and continued to find a healthy readership right up to the Second World War. Thereafter the breakup of the British Empire and the degradation of its once-proud ethos put them almost instantly out of date. And nowadays, with "multiculturalism" and political correctness dominating children's publishing, the kind of broad cultural assumptions Henty held are downright taboo. How many schoolteachers, for instance, would dare recommend a book with the title *A Tale of the Western*

Plains: or, Redskin and Cowboy? And how seriously will anyone take dialogue like the following (from *A Knight of the White Cross*):

> "Well, young sir, how like you the prospect of your pageship?"
> "I like it greatly, sir, but shall like still more the time when I can buckle on armor and take a share of fighting with the infidels."

Today all children's literature is furiously vetted by publishers, educators, and librarians fearful of causing offense to some ethnic or social group. I recently read my children a book that had given me great pleasure as a child: Lois Lenski's *Indian Captive*, the true story of a young girl, an eighteenth-century colonist, who was captured by Seneca Indians and eventually became a full-fledged member of the tribe. *Indian Captive* is extraordinarily sensitive to the Seneca way of life as it describes Mary Jemison's slow and sometimes painful acculturation; in the end, when she is given the choice of staying with the Senecas or returning to the white world, she realizes that the Senecas have become her true family. Yet when I mentioned this book to a librarian at a prominent New York school, I was told in no uncertain terms that it was "racist."

How much more racist, classist, sexist, and every other type of -ist then is Henty, whose young heroes have internalized an ideal of their own *mission civilisatrice* and would certainly concur with the author's younger contemporary Winston Churchill when he rhetorically inquired, upon joining Kitchener's mission to the Sudan in 1898, "What enterprise that an enlightened community may attempt is more noble and profitable than the reclamation from barbarism of fertile regions and large populations? To give peace to warring tribes where all was violence, to strike the chains off the slave, to draw the richness from the soil . . . what more beautiful ideal or more valuable reward can inspire human effort?"

Quaintly written on the one hand, culturally passé on the other, Henty's books were all but forgotten during the second half of the twentieth century, despite the fact that he had inspired not only generations of future soldiers and administrators but also an array of future intellectuals from Henry Miller to Roy Jenkins, for his research and attention to detail was stunning, his historical and local flavor flawless, his battle accounts impeccable. Henty's descriptions of eighteenth-century Madras in *With Clive in India*, for instance, and of Hannibal's heterogeneous, exotic army in *The Young Carthaginian*, are really masterful. A. J. P. Taylor recalls of Henty's books that "the best feature was the battle diagrams with the oblongs for the opposing forces of cavalry and infantry. I reproduced them on the attic floor with my toy soldiers. . . . As a matter of fact . . . vague recollections from Henty carried me through when I had to lecture on the Thirty Years' War at Manchester University." And Arthur M. Schlesinger, Jr., has named Henty as a powerful early influence: "Such knowledge as I have of ancient Egypt, the republic of Venice, India, southern Africa, the rise of the Dutch republic, the struggle for Chilean independence, the Franco-Prussian War, the Boxer Rebellion, and many other historical episodes, had its roots in Henty," he wrote. "He . . . provoked thought about history. A sturdy Tory, Henty wrote about the American Revolution from the viewpoint of the Loyalists (*True to the Old Flag*) and the Civil War from the viewpoint of the Confederates (*With Lee in Virginia*). One received a new slant on what had seemed historical verities, nor was one corrupted thereby"—a very important point, but anathema in today's climate.

To call Henty a sturdy Tory is misleading. He was in fact comparatively liberal, even politically correct according to the standards of his day. Nowhere in his books can one find, for example, the crude anti-Catholicism of Charles Kingsley, or the crude anti-Semitism of John Buchan or Hilaire Belloc, or the crude racism of any number of his contemporaries. Like many Britons who saw action in the wars of Empire, he had nothing but respect for the great fighting nations like the Zulus, the Ashantis, the Pathans and the Gurkhas. He may have dealt with the American Civil War from the Confederate point of view, but he also wrote about the Battle of the Boyne from the Irish one, and bitterly castigated "the atrocious conduct of William [III]'s army of foreign mercenaries towards the people of Ireland." A feature of every Henty book is that both sides of a given issue, however apparently questionable one of them might be, are always given due respect. Here, for example, from *Under Drake's Flag*, the author steps into the action *in propria persona* to discuss a knotty moral point:

> English boys are accustomed to think with feelings of unmitigated horror and indignation of the days of the Inquisition, and in times like these, when a general toleration of religious opinion prevails, it appears to us almost incredible that men should put others to death in the name of religion. But it is only by placing ourselves in the position of the persecutors of the middle ages that we can see that what appears to us cruelty and barbarity of the worst kind was really the result of a zeal in its way as earnest, if not as praiseworthy, as that which now impels missionaries to go with their lives in their hands to regions where little but a martyr's grave can be expected. Nowadays we believe—at least all right-minded men believe—that there is good in all creeds, and that it would be rash indeed to condemn men who act up to the best of their lights, even though those lights may not be our own.

Few people, then or now, have had a good word to say for the Spanish Inquisitors, but Henty found a way to help us understand their system of thought. Other aspects of this excerpt, too, will strike a modern reader. Do we believe, *nowadays*—as opposed to Henty's "nowadays"—that there is really good in all creeds? It would be nice to think that we do, but there's not much evidence for it, despite the sugarcoating of tolerance the schools make such an effort to deliver.

The truth is that, far from administering a simpleminded dose of imperialist rhetoric, Henty's books do indeed prompt young readers to draw their own conclusions rather than simply parrot received opinion. In *A Knight of the White Cross*, the teenaged hero, Gervase Tresham, learns in the course of his years as Knight of the Order of St. John that his Muslim enemies can be every bit as brave and noble as his Christian colleagues, and that the Turkish system, though (of course!) inferior to the Christian one, has strengths that the Christians might do well to imitate: the Turks, for example, let those of high ability rise to the top of their command, whatever the accident of their birth. The hero of *With Lee in Virginia*, Vincent Wingfield, although a slaveholder, is a humanitarian and comes close to being an abolitionist, and while the various slave characters in the novel are at first presented as childlike, as the book progresses they evolve into more responsible human beings and end up playing a very active role in the story. The treatment of the issue in fact is complex and demands a certain amount of thought and the kind of imaginative leap most schoolchildren are seldom required to make.

Henty, to be sure, was as bound and defined by the assumptions of his time as we are by ours. Whether an ancient Briton, a Carthaginian officer, a medieval knight, or a sixteenth-century Huguenot, none of Henty's heroes is ever anything but a Victorian gentleman. As one avid Henty collector has described the books, "They're always about boys 16 to 18 years old who see history taking place, who get involved in some military action, and there's always a lot of high morals talked about. The hero always married the squire's daughter and was in the landed gentry by the time he was 23."

Sometimes Dr. Arnold's creed is ludicrously out of place in the historical context into whose service it has been pressed. In *Under Drake's Flag* two young Elizabethan buccaneers face their apparently imminent death with a rather un-Elizabethan diction and philosophy:

> "Well, Ned, we have had more good fortune than we could have expected. We might have been killed on the day when we landed, and we have spent six jolly months in wandering together as hunters on

> the plain. If we must die, let us behave like Englishmen and Christians. It may be that our lives have not been as good as they should have been; but so far as we know, we have both done our duty, and it may be that, as we die for the faults of others, it may come to be considered as a balance against our own faults."
>
> "We must hope so, Tom. I think we have both done, I won't say our best, but as well as could be expected in so rough a life. We have followed the exhortations of the good chaplain and have never joined in the riotous ways of the sailors in general. We must trust that the good God will forgive us our sins, and strengthen us to go through this last trial."

Campy, yes, easy to laugh at—straight Blackadder, in fact. Henty's total lack of irony makes him absurd to modern eyes, but also refreshing; recent equivalents of this sort of action adventure, like *Indiana Jones*, tend to be smirkingly ironic as though in perpetual apology for their unsophisticated subject matter.

But Henty's books, though hokey, are not unsophisticated, or at least not in a couple of very important ways. First of all, their syntax and vocabulary demands much more of the reader than contemporary books for the same age group, that is, ages ten to fifteen. "These tactics were admirably adapted to the nature of the contest; the only thing which threatened to render them nugatory was the presence of the fierce dogs of the Spaniards." Would any modern author for the preteen market challenge his readers with such a sentence? As for subject matter, Henty assumes a breadth of historical knowledge that practically no teenager, English or American, commands today: for example, in the introduction to his *In the Reign of Terror: The Adventures of a Westminster Boy*, he writes, "My object has been rather to tell you a tale of interest than to impart historical knowledge, for the facts of the dreadful time when 'the terror' reigned supreme in France are well known to all educated lads." Today very few educated lads would be able to muster many facts about the Terror, perhaps not even its date, and as for the Ashanti campaign or the Carlist Wars—!

The failure of multiculturalism to provide American students with a truly multicultural education or worldview has been dismal, as we found out in the panicked scramble for information and enlightenment after the September 11 attacks. If we had all been reading Henty's *To Herat and Kabul* instead of *The Babysitter's Club* as children, we might have been better prepared! And how many of the people struggling to understand what they perceive as the unprecedented crimes of Osama bin Laden remember or have even heard of the Mahdi? They could do worse than to have a look at Henty's excellent *With Kitchener in the Soudan*, or John Buchan's *Greenmantle*.

The *New York Times* has reported that the study of foreign languages has declined significantly in the last forty years and that at last count, in 1998, only 8 percent of college students were enrolled in a foreign-language course. In a recent article for the *Times* magazine, Margaret Talbot wondered just what exactly the multicultural approach has achieved: "What it apparently did not do was promote the study of other languages, or indeed of other cultures. . . . It was the upbeat ethnic-festival approach, which is nice, but which also allows you to leave out a lot of groups, like those that speak difficult languages or live in rough neighborhoods of the world or don't seem to treat women particularly well."

Now, suddenly, Henty is a wallflower no more. Three publishing houses, PrestonSpeed Publications, Lost Classics Book Company and Memoria Press, have begun reissuing Henty titles for the home-school market, and home-schooling parents are buying them in quantity. They like them for several reasons: most of all for their educational value, but also for their unswerving moralism—as PrestonSpeed's press material tells us, Henty's heroes are "diligent, courageous, intelligent, and dedicated to their country and cause"—and for what the largely evangelical Christian home-schooling population sees as a congenially

Christian point of view. It is true that Henty's heroes are professed Christians, or if not actually Christian, as in the case of Hannibal's junior officer, Josephus's lieutenant, or Beric the Romanized Briton, at least some species of proto-Christian: but it should be pointed out that modern American evangelical Christianity and the Victorian muscular variety are two rather different things. High religious enthusiasm was not the norm among British Imperial army officers; General Gordon's evangelistic fervor, for example, was considered exceptional. Jan Morris has provided an amusing characterization of the religious attitude of the British officer class (to which Henty's heroes always belong at least in spirit): "Most officers considered themselves good Christians, but they did not think too deeply or too often about their religion, and when they did, their thoughts were not likely to be profound. Wolesley once wondered what heaven was like and thought 'surely there must be a United Service Club there where old Army and Navy men may meet to talk over wars by land and sea.'"

On the whole the home-schoolers' revival of Henty is a very fine thing, but they miss the mark when they try to kill two birds with one stone by making Henty serve both as history and literature. History yes; literature no. Henty books, while entertaining, are formulaic, stilted, and carelessly written—about on the level of *The Hardy Boys*, only with vastly more interesting subject matter. The fact that Henty wrote 144 books in his career should indicate their quality: they are unedited, repetitive, and sloppy; he must have dictated at a tremendous pace and done very little proofreading before the books went to press. He was a writing machine, and the finished products reflect that fact.

Yet one can understand the home-schoolers' dilemma. They reject the always controversial *The Catcher in the Rye* and its ilk, as well as the new books that boost sensitivity toward gays, native Americans, and other minority groups—a genre that cannot qualify as "literature" any more than Henty can. As Adrian Wooldridge has written in *The*

Economist, "The fact that so many people feel that they have to choose between politically correct yuckiness and Victorian imperialism surely suggests that there is a lucrative gap in the children's book market." Yes, except that there are plenty of alternatives that should already fit the bill for those who like and approve of Henty yet want real literary content. Walter Scott and James Fenimore Cooper have become hopelessly dull and dated, but what about Robert Louis Stevenson? If *Doctor Jekyll and Mr Hyde* is too rich for the home-schoolers' blood, there are always *Kidnapped* and *The Master of Ballantrae*. And what about *Lorna Doone*, *Kim*, *Great Expectations*, *A Tale of Two Cities*, *Northanger Abbey*, *The Time Machine*, *The Invisible Man*, *The Turn of the Screw*? Even old chestnuts like *The Scarlet Pimpernel* and *Beau Geste* are infinitely better books than anything Henty wrote.

Henty, like his heroes, was an eyewitness to some of the most exciting events of his time. As a journalist, he was in Paris under the Communes, with Wolesley in the Ashanti Country, and with Napier in Ethiopia; he saw the Carlist Wars in Spain, spent time with Garibaldi's army in Italy and with the Turks in Serbia, visited the California gold fields, was present at the opening of the Suez Canal, and toured India with the then–Prince of Wales (later Edward VII). His books reflect the excitement of a heady historical moment. "What theatre!" Jan Morris has remarked of the era. "The tragedy of Isandhlwana, the thrilling defence of Rorke's Drift! Gordon martyred at Khartoum! 'Dr. Livingstone I presume'! The redcoats helter-skelter from the summit of Majuba, Sir Garnet Wolseley burning the charnel-houses of Kumasi!"

It was only a century ago, yet its essence is already as defunct as that of Periclean Athens. During the decade after Henty's death, younger writers like Forster and Conrad created the new vision of empire, and it is a vision that persists today. Rightly or wrongly, the imperial ideal has been hopelessly degraded. The last war of the British Empire, the Falklands War, was a pathetic affair likened by one observer to two bald men fighting over a comb; what excitement it generated was both febrile and transient. What would a modern equivalent of Henty write about? What emotions would he attempt to awaken? What titles might he come up with? *In the Caves of Kabul? To Kuwait with Stormin' Norman*?

The home-schoolers' effort to revive Henty is both admirable and touching; let's hope it is not entirely quixotic.

Bram Stoker and Modern Myths

Upon its publication in 1897, Bram Stoker's *Dracula* was seen as nothing more than a slightly cheesy thriller, if an unusually successful one. Most such "shilling shockers" were forgotten within a year or two. But this one was different: over the course of the next century Count Dracula, the aristocratic vampire, left his natural habitat between the pages of a book and insinuated himself into the world's consciousness as few other fictional characters have ever done. Now, more than a hundred years after his appearance in print, Dracula has shed the status of "fictional character" altogether and has become an authentic modern myth.

Why has this odd and terrifying figure exerted such a hold on our collective imagination? Why does the image of the vampire both attract and repel, in apparently equal measure? If, as has been argued, *Dracula* owes its success to its reflection of specific anxieties within the culture, why then has its power continued unabated throughout more than a century of unprecedented social change? Late-Victorian anxieties and concerns were rather different from our own, yet the lure of the vampire and the persistence of his image seem as strong as ever.

Dracula's durability may in part be due to Tod Browning's 1931 film, for when most people think of the character, it is Bela Lugosi's portrayal that springs to mind. But in spite of memorable performances by Lugosi and by Dwight Frye as Renfield, the film is awkward and clunky, even laughable in parts; in terms of shocking, terrible, and gorgeous images, it cannot compare with the novel that inspired it. It is hard to believe that, on its own, it would have created such an indelible impact.

Once *Dracula* became lodged in the popular imagination, it began to accrue ever-new layers of meaning and topicality. The novel has provided rich material for every fad and fancy of twentieth-century exegesis. It has been deconstructed by critics of the Freudian, feminist, queer theory, and Marxist persuasions, and has had something significant to offer each of these fields. Today, in the age of AIDS, the exchange of blood has taken on a new meaning, and *Dracula* has taken on a new significance in its turn. For post-Victorian readers, it has been a little too easy to impose a pat "Freudian" reading on the novel, in which the vampire represents deviant, dangerous sexuality while the vampire hunters stand for sexual repression in the form of bourgeois marriage and overly spiritualized relationships. This interpretation certainly contains a large element of truth, but the novel's themes are much richer and more complex than such a reading might suggest.

Readers coming to *Dracula* for the first time should try to peel away the layers of preconception they can hardly help bringing to the novel. We should try to forget Bela Lugosi; we should try to forget easy (and anachronistic) Freudian clichés; we should put out of our minds all our received twentieth- and twenty-first-century notions of friendship and love, both heterosexual and homosexual. If we let the novel stand on its own, just as it appeared to Bram Stoker's contemporaries in the last years of the Victorian era, what exactly do we find?

We find a thriller, but one that is imagined at an unusually high level of art and constructed with the kind of craft and skill that is seldom squandered on mere potboilers. *Dracula* bears comparison, in fact, with any of the great nineteenth-century examples of the genre—

Mary Shelley's *Frankenstein* (1818), for example, or Wilkie Collins's *The Woman in White* (1860), Robert Louis Stevenson's *The Strange Case of Dr. Jekyll and Mr. Hyde* (1886), or Edgar Allan Poe's short stories. Stoker's first readers were, on the whole, enthusiastic (though the reviewer in the influential *Athenaeum* magazine gave it only a lukewarm and qualified endorsement). Anthony Hope Hawkins, author of the swashbuckling classic *The Prisoner of Zenda* (1894), wrote to Stoker, "Your vampires robbed me of sleep for nights"; Sir Arthur Conan Doyle, creator of Sherlock Holmes, one of the few fictional characters that has rivaled Count Dracula in popular appeal, thought it "the very best story of diablerie which I have read for many years. It is really wonderful how with so much exciting interest over so long a book there is never an anticlimax." Contemporary readers tended to agree; what is more, they seemed to find nothing sexually odd about *Dracula*—or if they did, they forbore to remark upon the fact, for to do so would have been to admit to a greater sexual knowingness than was considered acceptable at the time.

Like Wilkie Collins, whose novel *The Woman in White*, a runaway success, served as something of a prototype for suspense fiction for many years after its publication, Bram Stoker decided upon a modified epistolary format. *Dracula* is not a straightforward narrative but a collection of documents that, taken together, tell the tale in its entirety: journals and letters by the principal characters, transcriptions of recordings on the newfangled phonograph, newspaper clippings, even a ship's log. The story constructed by these fragments is a rather complex one, and dramatists and filmmakers, in adapting the novel, have usually felt free to alter the plot in drastic ways, dropping major characters or amalgamating them into one another, changing around the various love interests, and generally ignoring and upsetting Stoker's carefully built fictional edifice. In doing so they have sacrificed layers of meaning and radically changed Stoker's original intentions.

The novel's first narrator is Jonathan Harker, a young solicitor who travels to the wilds of Transylvania to advise a client, the mysterious Count Dracula, on the count's purchase of a decrepit abbey in England and his plans to move into it. In Harker's journal we read of his increasing unease at the sinister goings-on at the castle, and soon we discover that he is in effect being held prisoner by his frightening host. During Harker's stay at Castle Dracula he is approached by three seductive vampire maidens, but Dracula chases them away, claiming the quaking Harker as his own.

Harker manages to escape from the castle, and the scene shifts to England, where we are introduced to Mina Murray, Harker's fiancée, and her friend Lucy Westenra. Lucy, a fragile beauty, has three suitors: Dr. Jonathan Seward, the director of a mental hospital next door to Dracula's English abbey; Quincey Morris, an attractive American adventurer; and Arthur Holmwood (later Lord Godalming), the most eligible of the three and the one whose proposal she decides to accept. On a holiday by the sea, Lucy and Mina encounter a mysterious being whom we recognize as Dracula, now at large in England, and Lucy is attacked and bitten by him. Losing blood nightly, she begins to fade away; eventually she dies, becomes a vampire herself, and preys on small children.

Aided by a venerable doctor and wise man, Abraham Van Helsing, the principal characters try to undo Dracula's evil work. Harker and Mina, now married, Lucy's three suitors, and Van Helsing enter the undead Lucy's tomb and truly kill her, driving a stake through her heart and decapitating her. Soon, however, Mina herself falls prey to Dracula. In a combined effort that involves ancient wisdom, modern science, good brains, and stout hearts, the group of friends finally succeeds in chasing Dracula back to his native land, killing him, and hence freeing his soul from eternal torment as they have already freed Lucy's.

This, very briefly summarized, is the plot. Admittedly the characters are not highly developed, but their web of mutual interactions allows Stoker to explore many sorts of relationships, sexual and otherwise, that troubled his society and himself. These nuances were discarded by later simplifying dramatists and filmmakers, who in focusing almost exclusively on Dracula and on the brilliantly realized Renfield, Dracula's grisly apostle, have turned the story into one of mere horror spiced with occasional humor.

Stoker handled his many-layered plot capably and professionally, but it is in his use of descriptive prose that he showed—at least in this one novel of the thirteen he produced during his lifetime—something close to genius. Here, for example, is Jonathan Harker's first glimpse of his undead host reposing in his native earth at the Castle Dracula:

> There lay the Count, but looking as if his youth had been half renewed, for the white hair and moustache were changed to dark iron-grey; the cheeks were fuller, and the white skin seemed ruby-red underneath; the mouth was redder than ever, for on the lips were gouts of fresh blood, which trickled from the corners of the mouth and ran over the chin and neck. Even the deep, burning eyes seemed set amongst swollen flesh, for the lips and pouches underneath were bloated. It seemed as if the whole awful creature were simply gorged with blood; he lay like a filthy leech, exhausted with his repletion. . . . There was no lethal weapon at hand, but I seized a shovel which the workmen had been using to fill the cases, and lifting it high struck, with the edge downward, at the hateful face. But as I did so the head turned, and the eyes fell full upon me, with all their blaze of basilisk horror. The sight seemed to paralyse me, and the shovel turned in my hand and glanced from the face. . . .

This is only one of the more dramatic examples; there are countless passages in *Dracula* that show the author's unerring feeling for the strong word, the strong image, the fundamental shock.

Like his great peers, but unlike so many second-string horror writers, Stoker had a fine feeling for humor. In *Dracula* he uses it sparingly but to marvelous effect, making it heighten, through the rather hysterical laughter it prompts, the gruesomeness of the situation. Aside from a few crude jokes from Van Helsing (who has a punster's propensity for remarking offhandedly that he is embarked on a "grave duty" and that "the stake we play for is life and death"), almost all of *Dracula*'s humor is concentrated in the character of Renfield, Dr. Seward's bizarre patient who, the reader comes to understand, is the vampire's victim and unwilling acolyte. Renfield's diet of insects provokes laughter, however grudging, and Dr. Seward's deadpan manner of recording his patient's oddities only compounds the effect:

> When I went into the room, I told the man that a lady would like to see him; to which he simply answered: "Why?"
>
> "She is going through the house, and wants to see everyone in it," I answered. "Oh, very well," he said, "let her come in, by all means, but just wait a minute till I tidy up the place." His method of tidying was peculiar: he simply swallowed all the flies and spiders in the boxes before I could stop him. It was quite evident that he feared, or was jealous of, some interference. When he had got through his disgusting task, he said cheerfully: "Let the lady come in," and sat down on the edge of his bed with his head down, but with his eyelids raised so that he could see her as she entered.

The contrast between this maniacal behavior and the charming, erudite conversation of what we must accept as the "real" Renfield—"Lord Godalming, I had the honour of seconding your father at the Windham; I grieve to know, by your holding the title, that he is no more. . . ."—makes the madman's odd condition funnier and, in a stroke of true originality, more poignant as well.

But Stoker's descriptive gifts are not limited to the grotesque and the macabre; in *Dracula* he also paints prose landscapes of exquisite and fearsome beauty. The attentive reader will notice that the appearances of the vampire are preceded by sunsets, often almost painfully resplendent ones: "Before the sun dipped below the black mass of Kettleness, standing boldly athwart the western sky, its downward way was marked by myriad clouds of every sunset-colour—flame, purple, pink, green, violet, and all the tints of gold; with here and there masses not large, but of seemingly absolute blackness, in all sorts of shapes, as well outlined as colossal silhouettes."

Even Dracula's manifestations out of frightening nighttime fog are made mesmerizingly lovely:

> Everything is grey—except the green grass, which seems like emerald amongst it; grey earthy rock; grey clouds, tinged with the sunburst at the far edge, hang over the grey sea, into which the sand-points stretch like grey fingers. The sea is tumbling in over the shallows and the sandy flats with a roar, muffled in the sea-mists drifting inland. The horizon is lost in a grey mist. All is vastness; the clouds are piled up like giant rocks, and there is a "brool" over the sea that sounds like some presage of doom.

Stoker uses a very finely tuned version of the "pathetic fallacy" to achieve his effects, and it is this as much as anything that has given Count Dracula the indefinable attractiveness he retains in spite of all his horror: morally and physically ugly as he is, he is so consistently associated with a real, tangible, even violent beauty that the beauty ends up in some manner becoming part of him. Stoker's painterly eye, his ability to see divinity even in "the wonderfully smoky beauty of a sunset over London, with its lurid lights and inky shadows and all the marvelous tints that come on foul clouds even as on foul water," remind us that *Dracula*'s creator inhabited the world not only of Sherlock Holmes and Jack the Ripper but also of James Whistler and Claude Monet: he was a thrill-master, but he was also an aesthete.

Bram Stoker was not primarily a writer. Writing was a sideline for him, a source of extra income and a creative outlet. *Dracula* was his only truly successful book and the only one that is still widely read today. But he led an active life at the cultural and artistic vortex of London, and its story affords some interesting insights into *Dracula*.

Abraham Stoker (Bram was a nickname) was born in Ireland in 1847, only a year after the great potato blight that killed millions of Irishmen and sent many more to America. He came from a Protestant, Tory, solidly middle-class family: his father was a civil servant in the parliamentary section at Dublin Castle, the seat of the British government in Ireland, and it was expected that young Bram would probably follow him into government service. A sickly child, he eventually developed into a large, powerful man and a successful athlete. At Trinity College he excelled in debating and began to fantasize about a career as an actor. His family did not consider this an option; instead, as planned, he began work at Dublin Castle as a clerk in the Registrar of Petty Sessions. He nurtured his love of the theater, however, by taking unpaid work as a drama critic for the Dublin *Evening Mail*, a conservative newspaper that was Unionist and anti-Catholic.

Stoker was prone to hero worship. One of his first idols was Walt Whitman, whose revolutionary poetry celebrated democracy, comradeship, and love between men; his "Calamus" poems, most famously, came close to being specifically homosexual manifestos. Stoker wrote the older man emotional, revealing letters: "How sweet a thing it is for a strong healthy man with a woman's eyes and a child's wishes to feel that he can speak so to a man who can be if he wishes father, and brother and wife to his soul." Whitman responded warmly from across the Atlantic. Stoker, he later told a friend, was "a sassy youngster. What the hell did I care whether he was pertinent or impertinent? He was fresh, breezy, Irish: that was the price paid for admission—and enough: he was welcome!" Whitman's friendship, his poetry, and his passionate doctrines remained centrally important to Stoker throughout his life.

Another hero acquired at this time would permanently change the course of Stoker's career: the actor-manager Henry Irving. When Stoker first saw him on the stage, in an 1867 production of *The Rivals*, the actor was twenty-nine years old and just reaching the apex of his profession, a position he would hold until his death nearly forty years later. Irving was the heir of David Garrick and Edmund Keane, the progenitor of Laurence Olivier: the greatest stage star of his day. Irving, Stoker later commented, was "a patrician figure as real as the persons of one's dreams, and endowed with the same poetic grace."

Once established as a drama critic, Stoker felt it a personal mission to boost Irving's work and defend him from hostile reviews in other papers. The actor began to notice and appreciate the sympathetic, intelligent reviews he consistently received from the *Evening Mail*, and invited Stoker to dinner one night when he was in Dublin. They talked all night and dined again the next evening. "Soul had looked into soul!" Stoker recalled. "From that hour began a friendship as profound, as close, as lasting as can be between two men."

In 1878, Henry Irving procured the Lyceum, one of London's greatest theaters, and offered Stoker the job of acting manager, in charge of the business end of the company. Stoker accepted with alacrity, resigning his position at Dublin Castle and taking only a brief holiday to marry Florence Balcombe, a Dublin beauty who had the distinction of having also been courted by Oscar Wilde. (Wilde, along with his eccentric parents, had long been a friend of Stoker.) Florence's face was legendary: "People used to stand on chairs to look at her," the Stokers' son, Noël, recalled.

The Stokers' marriage was singularly cool from the very beginning, and this would not change over the course of their thirty-four years together. It was a situation that perhaps suited them both; as Noël Stoker also remarked, Florence was "an ornament not a woman of passion," and she seemed perfectly content to spend her evenings in the company of one of her many swains, W. S. Gilbert for example, while her husband was at the theater. Her granddaughter thought her "cursed with her great beauty and the need to maintain it. In my knowledge now, she was very anti-sex." As for Stoker, his true marriage was to Henry Irving, a selfish, devouring man who soaked up the talent, time, and devotion of his acolytes, of whom Stoker was the foremost: many readers have found an echo of Irving and Stoker in the relationship between the parasitical Dracula and his hapless victims. Except for an early sweetheart who died young, Irving had no important woman in his personal life. His work was all that mattered; as George Bernard Shaw once quipped nastily, Irving "would not have left the stage for a night to spend it with Helen of Troy."

Stoker's job, which he held until Irving's death in 1905, was a demanding one, but he managed to pursue other interests. In 1881 he published a collection of short stories called *Under the Sunset*; his first novel, *The Snake's Pass*, appeared in 1890. He would eventually produce fourteen books of fiction, including *Dracula*. He also began legal studies at the advanced age of thirty-nine and was called to the bar in 1890. Here, finally, was a profession Florence found socially acceptable, and henceforth she never referred to her husband as a theatrical manager or an author but only as a barrister.

Irving's Lyceum specialized in classical and romantic productions, with Irving himself usually in a heavyweight role, often a menacing one—Shylock, Macbeth, or Mephistopheles; his forte was the malevolent and the tormented. Though Stoker never asked Irving to play the part, it is impossible to believe that he did not have a stage version, with Irving in the lead, in mind when he wrote *Dracula*. As many critics have noted, the count's role would have been a natural one for Irving, and echoes of Irving's great performances are to be found in *Dracula*'s text. From one of *Hamlet*'s speeches, for example:

> 'Tis now the very witching time of night,
> When churchyards yawn, and hell itself breathes out
> Contagion to this world. Now could I drink hot blood
> And do such bitter business as the day
> Would quake to look on.

Shortly after the publication of *Dracula*, Stoker arranged a reading of a dramatic version at the Lyceum in order to protect the copyright but also to interest Irving in playing the role. Irving made no comment at the time; when Stoker asked him later what he thought, he replied in one dismissive word: "Dreadful!" Perhaps he thought the vampire's role too small (in the novel, the count is "on stage" for less than one-sixth of the text); perhaps he didn't want Stoker rising from his subordinate position in the partnership. In any case, he never considered taking the part. In retrospect this seems nearly as bad a mistake as his decision not to play Sherlock Holmes when Conan Doyle offered it to him. Irving's old-style romanticism was going out of fashion, and he himself was becoming something of an anachronism; either of these roles would have gone far toward reviving his career.

On October 13, 1905, an ailing Henry Irving played Thomas à Becket; after the performance he spoke to the audience, as was his custom. It was, as Stoker's biographer Barbara Belford commented, Irving's last salute "to those who had given him all he ever knew—or cared to know—of love." An hour later he died in the lobby of his hotel. There was no bequest for Stoker, no mention of him in the will. Irving, who in 1895 had become the first actor to receive a knighthood, was buried in Westminster Abbey.

With Irving's death, Bram Stoker's life lost its focus and its purpose. In failing health himself, he was not able to find another theatrical job. Instead he worked hard at journalism and fiction, but in spite of the success of *Dracula* Stoker never made much money from his writing—though his last novel, *The Lair of the White Worm* (1911), did well. Stoker died in 1912, at the age of sixty-four. His great-nephew Daniel Farson, who wrote a biography of Stoker in 1975, claimed that he died from the effects of syphilis, but subsequent analysis has not confirmed this diagnosis; it seems more likely that his symptoms were due to a series of strokes. If Stoker enjoyed love affairs with members of either sex, he did so with the utmost discretion, and in any case his preferred role was not the dashing lover but the avuncular confidant.

Florence Stoker survived her husband by twenty-five years. As executor of his estate she tried to make the most of his literary remnants, and when she discovered that the German director F. W. Murnau's 1922 silent film *Nosferatu* was largely inspired by *Dracula*, she accused the producers of copyright infringement and tried for years to get the print destroyed. Fortunately she failed in this, and *Nosferatu* remains as a major work of German expressionism. In 1930 Universal Pictures paid Florence $40,000 for the film rights to *Dracula*; since that time Count Dracula has appeared on the cinema screen more often than any other fictional character save Sherlock Holmes.

Dracula is not a psychologically knowing book, but it is very much a product of its time—a time, that is, when ideas about the nature of repression and the unconscious were not yet current but were definitely in the air. It appeared at a turning point in social and intellectual history. Between 1895 and 1900, Sigmund Freud was developing many of the major ideas that would inform twentieth-century psychology—dream interpretation, the unconscious, and repression—and in 1897, the year of *Dracula*'s publication, he began his famous program of self-analysis. His seminal text, *The Interpretation of Dreams*, appeared in 1899.

It is probably no coincidence that the 1890s and early 1900s produced a spate of brilliant proto-Freudian novels. Stevenson's *The Strange Case of Dr. Jekyll and Mr. Hyde* (1866) was one of the most striking examples. In this gruesome tale, Freud's concepts of ego, id, and superego are given nearly perfect fictional form before the ideas were current or even formulated: the respectable Dr. Henry Jekyll—the quintessential ego perfected by a vigilant superego—becomes at night a hideous and murderous monster, Mr. Hyde, who personifies all the horrid qualities we fear are lurking, repressed, in our ids. The atavistic Mr. Hyde, like Dracula (who is unusually hairy and can take the form of a wolf or a bat), inhabits the border territory between the human and the animal, a no-man's-land that seemed to cause particular anxiety to Stevenson's and Stoker's contemporaries. Another of Stevenson's tales, *The Master of Ballantrae* (1889), also deals with doubles, in this case twins, who can be seen to represent ego and id.

Oscar Wilde's *The Picture of Dorian Gray* (1891) illustrates the impossibility of complete repression. The beautiful young man Dorian Gray makes a Faustian pact by which, however depraved his behavior might become, he always retains his youthful radiance; only his portrait, which he keeps hidden away, exposes the dissipation and cruelty of his soul. H. Rider Haggard's *She* (1887) juxtaposes, like *Dracula*, images of death and sex; H. G. Wells's popular scientific fantasies like *The Time Machine* (1895) and *The Invisible Man* (1897) play with contemporary nightmares of atavism and the dual nature of man; James M. Barrie's *Peter Pan* (1904) vividly fictionalizes the male mother fixation and unwillingness to grow up.

While Stoker, in *Dracula*, does not seem to be working within a particular psychological scheme, neither does he seem unconscious of the psychological implications of his story, as Barrie does. His character Dr. Seward, after all, is medically up to the minute; he speaks of Jean-Martin Charcot, the pioneer of hypnotic suggestion under whom Freud studied during his early years, and mentions the relatively recent concept of unconscious cerebration. Stoker was a sophisticated man, no innocent, and while modern critics have tended to assume that *Dracula*'s women are meant by Stoker to be pure, its men brave and gallant, it is worth considering the possibility that Stoker was not unaware of the book's real ambiguity. Here, for example, is one of the novel's most famous scenes—rightly famous, for its graphic power is particularly intense:

> The Thing in the coffin [the undead Lucy] writhed; and a hideous, blood-curdling screech came from the opened red lips. The body

> shook and quivered and twisted in wild contortions; the sharp white teeth champed together till the lips were cut, and the mouth was smeared with a crimson foam. But Arthur never faltered. He looked like a figure of Thor as his untrembling arm rose and fell, driving deeper and deeper the mercy-bearing stake, whilst the blood from the pierced heart welled and spurted up around it. . . .
>
> And then the writhing and quivering of the body became less, and the teeth ceased to champ, and the face to quiver. Finally it lay still. The terrible task was over.

As nearly every modern reader remarks, Arthur and the vampire Lucy here enact a terrible parody of the sex act, ending in the "little death" of orgasm. If it is so obvious to us, could it have been totally hidden to Stoker? And what about Mina's frightful experience with Dracula?

> With his left hand he held both Mrs Harker's hands, keeping them away with her arms at full tension; his right hand gripped her by the back of the neck, forcing her face down on his bosom. Her white nightdress was smeared with blood, and a thin stream trickled down the man's bare breast which was shown by his torn-open dress. The attitude of the two had a terrible resemblance to a child forcing a kitten's nose into a saucer of milk to compel it to drink.

No sexually experienced adult could fail to note that Dracula and Mina are mimicking the act of fellatio. The movements are explicitly sexual, and the act is described in detail. Later, when Mina looks back on the scene, the connection is made even more clear: "When the blood began to spurt out, he took my hands in one of his, holding them tight, and with the other seized my neck and pressed my mouth to the wound, so that I must either suffocate or swallow some of the—Oh my God! my God! what have I done?" The placement of the dash, the moment at which Mina breaks off her sentence, simply cannot be accidental. Some of the what?

The only "sex acts" in the novel are vampiric; the only time we see its characters explicitly sexualized is when they become vampires. Thus when Jonathan Harker is approached by the three vampire maidens at Castle Dracula he feels in his heart "a wicked, burning desire that they would kiss me with those red lips" and watches their approach "in an agony of delightful anricipation." When one girl goes on her knees—another reference to fellatio—he finds her "deliberate voluptuousness" to be "both thrilling and repulsive."

This is definitely not the Jonathan Harker we see throughout the rest of the book, and while the latter is certainly an admirable husband to Mina, one doubts whether the passion he achieves with her ever reaches the level it might have done with this vampire girl; once he returns to England he seems somehow diminished, and certainly older. The playful, curious boy of the early journal entries is gone.

One might, of course, count the male characters' gift of blood to the ailing Lucy as a sexual act, though more a conjugal than a passionate one. Arthur says afterward that he now feels as though he and Lucy were really married, and Van Helsing is too tactful to tell him that the other men have already performed the same act, as though to do so would be to accuse Lucy of promiscuity. Seward too feels that he has achieved some sort of physical union with Lucy after giving her blood: "No man knows till he experiences it, what it is to feel his own life-blood drawn away into the veins of the woman he loves."

But it is in the character of Lucy herself that we are given the most explicit contrast between vampiric sensuality and Stoker's portrayal of the ordinary human variety. Lucy, when we first encounter her, is obviously attractive to men—she receives, after all, three marriage proposals in one day—and she is coquettish too: "Why can't they let a girl marry three men, or as many as want her, and save all this trouble?" she asks, only half-jokingly. Still, she is pure, and she is frequently dressed in white as though to emphasize this purity. Her principal attribute, constantly reiterated, is sweetness. Sitting in the Whitby churchyard Lucy is "sweetly pretty in her white lawn frock"; asleep in her room she "looks, oh, so sweet"; meeting Van Helsing and Dr. Seward she is "very sweet to the Professor (as she always is)."

But it is a girlish sweetness rather than a womanly one, and in her pliability she displays "the obedience of a child" rather than the adult decision and strength characteristic of Mina. The contrast with the undead Lucy therefore becomes all the greater: undead, "the sweetness was turned to adamantine, heartless cruelty, and the purity to voluptuous wantonness"; "the whole carnal and unspiritual appearance . . . [was] like a devilish mockery of Lucy's sweet purity."

Some feminist scholars have found Stoker's attitude to be incurably sexist. Phyllis A. Roth, for example, has written: "I would emphasize that for both the Victorians and twentieth-century readers, much of the novel's great appeal derives from its hostility toward female sexuality." This seems an overly simplistic way of looking at this not entirely simple tale. In what way, for instance, can the novel be said to be more hostile toward female than toward male sexuality? Is not the least wooden, the most genuinely passionate *human* character Mina, rather than the various conventional and interchangeable young men? Van Helsing describes her as "one of God's women, fashioned by His own hand to show us men and other women that there is a heaven where we can enter, and that its light can be here on earth."

Mina has, as Van Helsing describes it, a man's brain and a woman's heart; by contrast Lucy, who is all femininity (at least within the limited and conventional terms in which *Dracula* defines femininity), is seen to be a moral as well as a physical lightweight, something less than a whole person and therefore unable to defend herself against the monster. Lucy is capable only of extremes—sweetness or cruelty, purity or wantonness—while Mina is a more balanced human being, hence less vulnerable. If there is a moral to *Dracula*, it might be that simple goodness is not adequate to fight evil. One must bring brains and moral strength into the arena as well.

Therefore in an important sense *Dracula* can be seen as a feminist rather than an anti-feminist novel, in spite of the demonization of sexuality in general terms and the offhand, almost obligatory denigration of the "New Woman." It is Mina who laughs at the New Woman, and yet she herself could hardly be more of a New Woman if she tried: a self-supporting career woman, capable, accomplished, an equal (in fact more than equal) partner to her mate. She, the New Woman—also, by the way, married and sexually experienced—is able to defeat the vampire while the pure, sweet, and still virginal Lucy is not.

Poised as it is on the threshold between the nineteenth and twentieth centuries, *Dracula* displays the period's uneasy weighing of the relative importance of science and religion. Dracula, in the time-honored fashion of fictional monsters, is explicitly connected with hell and represents an inversion of traditional Christianity. "Dracul," in fact, is the word for "devil" in the count's native Wallachian, and one of his incarnations is a crawling lizardlike creature. The circumstance of Harker's first meeting with him, on the feast day of St. George, sets up the theme of dragon-slaying, the figurative fight between religious faith and coarse instinct, as does the peasant woman's gift to Harker of a crucifix, which, as a Protestant and a man of science, he regards with suspicion and bemusement.

Dracula is presented as a sort of Antichrist, Renfield as his St. Paul; both speak in language that consciously echoes or paraphrases the Gospels. Dracula's speech during his mock marriage ceremony with Mina is meant to be particularly shocking and still succeeds, even in our own irreligious age: "And you, their best beloved one, are now to me, flesh of my flesh; blood of my blood; kin of my kin; my bountiful wine-press for a while; and shall be later on my companion and my helper." As Antichrist, Dracula also offers his followers what Christianity claims to offer: the resurrection of the body and life everlasting.

The novel's vampire fighters are all nominal Christians, and indeed almost their last word before Quincey Morris expires and the unholy stain disappears from Mina's forehead is "a deep and earnest 'Amen,'" but simple faith has clearly not sufficed to slay this dragon: modern science, intellectual effort, and the bonds of friendship have all been needed to back it up.

As the twentieth century progressed, the religious elements of the vampire myth became less interesting to the public, and the vampire figure began to take on different attributes. The strangest and most perverse has been the transformation of the vampire from a figure of terror to a romantic outsider, a sexy, Byronic hero. Barnabas Collins of the kitschy television show *Dark Shadows* (1966–1971) was perhaps the first sympathetic vampire, but the type was perfected in Anne Rice's *Interview with the Vampire* (1976) and its sequels, which developed a new archetype, that of the self-conscious and confessional vampire. Performers and directors, most notably Frank Langella, who portrayed Dracula on Broadway in 1977, have added a decidedly sensual element to what was originally intended to be a purely terrifying monster.

Stoker's monster was not born without forebears; there was already a vampire tradition not only in folklore but in literature as well. John Polidori's *The Vampyre* had been a brisk seller in 1819, as had James Malcolm Ryder's *Varney the Vampyre: or, the Feast of Blood* (serialized 1845–1847). Joseph Sheridan Le Fanu's more recent *Carmilla* (1872) described a female vampire with lesbian leanings. Famous works by Goethe, Coleridge, and Southey had also contained vampire imagery. Dracula owes something to each of these; and something of *Dracula* has gone into every work of vampire fiction that followed it. And while the figure of the vampire has continued to evolve, sometimes in surprising ways, it is Bram Stoker that has come closest to crystallizing it, and Stoker's images that have most persistently haunted our imagination.

No Ladies' Man

*Y*ou would think that Henry James, like Virginia Woolf, must by now be one of those people about whom little if anything remains to be said. Not so, however, for in her recent book *A Private Life of Henry James: Two Women and His Art*, Lyndall Gordon has produced a remarkably entertaining and informative study, funny and moving by turns, filled with fresh material and provocative assertions. The author is an enthusiastic Jamesian without being a hero-worshipper, and she firmly rejects the image of the solitary genius that James created through the "phantasmagoria," as she skeptically calls it, of his autobiographical writings, the self-conscious mythologizing of the prefaces to the New York edition of his work, and his selective destruction of personal letters.

She is not the first reader to be annoyed by his pretensions: W. H. Auden, for one, complained that in the prefaces, "there are times when their tone of hushed reverence before the artistic mystery becomes insufferable"; James's eminent contemporaries H. G. Wells and Somerset Maugham were also quick to express their irritation at his overblown ego and his, to them, equally overblown reputation. By and large, though, James succeeded—and still succeeds—in making posterity swallow a highly edited and polished version of his life and character.

It goes without saying that James was a great writer. He was also petty, predatory, selfish, and catty. Like many imaginative artists, he could be quite blatant in the way he appropriated friends and family members as raw material for his work. Gordon contends that James carried this propensity further than most, that he had, in fact, a "terrifying will to possess the souls of certain people he had marked for 'use.'"

She takes as her subject two women who both were very close to James and who, each in her own way, seized his imagination and molded his fiction while he in turn "put his stamp on them, and made them 'Jamesian.'" The first and the more important so far as James's work was concerned was his cousin and contemporary Minny Temple, who died of tuberculosis in 1870 at the age of twenty-four. Unusually independent, beautiful, intelligent, avid for life and experience, Minny embodied what James saw as a modern and peculiarly American femininity, quickened with "intellectual grace" and "moral spontaneity." After her death she would become the model for Daisy Miller, Isabel Archer, and Milly Theale.

Minny and her three sisters had been orphaned as children and raised in a rather distant manner by an aunt and uncle. Minny was easily the most striking of the family and the most rebellious. Always questioning, searching, she possessed Isabel Archer's theoretical side as well as her charm and vitality. "Do you remember," she wrote to a friend, "my old hobby of the 'remote possibility' of the best thing, being better than a clear certainty of the second best? Well, I believe it more than ever, every day I live. Indeed I don't believe anything else."

Minny was never to be allowed to put her theories about marriage to the test. At twenty-two she developed a "deposit" in her lung and began a steady decline. Her life as an invalid was a lonely one, but in her time of trouble Minny proved as courageous as her fictional counterpart Isabel Archer. She lavished sympathy on her cousin Henry's (largely imaginary) ailments while making light of her own very real ones. Increasingly helpless, she nurtured her spirits with the fantasy of fulfilling her lifelong ambition to see Europe, where James was now traveling freely, pockets stuffed with introductions to luminaries like Minny's idol George Eliot.

Minny was too delicate and diffident to ask her cousin outright to take her to Europe. He constituted, however, her only hope of getting across the Atlantic, and she dropped the most gossamer of hints to this effect in her letters to him. He backed off; so did she. A few months later the hint was dropped again. His reaction was to collapse "into an invalidism so intractable and absorbing that it must, of necessity, exclude any need but his own." James had the power to make Minny's final months happy; he chose not to do so. It was not a very clear-cut moral decision, and it would be a mistake to blame him too much. James, to all appearances a sociable man, was in fact ruthlessly protective of his privacy, as almost every serious artist must be. Yet James would eventually reveal an awareness that in this particular case he might, perhaps, have behaved more nobly. Many years later, in *The Wings of the Dove*, the dead Milly Theale is mourned by Merton Densher, in many ways James's counterpart, who comes to care for her only after her death and deeply regrets not having married her, knowing, as he now does, that it would in any case not have been for long.

In an odd way, Minny's death seemed actually to give James a feeling of personal liberation, even of enlargement. He "tried to impress on his conscience the fact of loss, but what he actually felt was all gain. . . . In some way her death and the act of writing were linked, as though her vitality had passed to him," writes Gordon. In the decade that followed her death, James would achieve international fame, thanks in large part to the deeply American heroines Minny inspired. It was the first of his great waves of genius. The second, culminating in *The Ambassadors* and most of his best short stories, was enriched by another woman friend, the writer Constance Fenimore Woolson.

James met her in 1880 in Florence, when both were in their late thirties. The friendship developed rapidly. Florence, Woolson wrote to a friend, had swept her "pretty well off my feet! Perhaps I ought to add Henry James. He has been perfectly charming to me for the last three weeks." James was less forthcoming about the new connection, for Woolson, the quintessential bluestocking, was not someone to cast much reflected glory. When he did mention her to friends, he belittled her. Still, they became very close. As a Europeanized American from his own milieu, she provided not only fine literary material but the easy, familiar companionship so often craved by uprooted expatriates.

Woolson was a successful fiction writer with a broad popular audience, but she was also a woman of her time and knew better than to put herself forward when talking shop with the Master. "Even if a story of mine should have a large 'popular' sale," she wrote him once, "that could not alter the fact that the utmost best of my work cannot touch the hem of your first or poorest." Fully conscious of James's ego and his territorial instincts about his material and his market, she played herself down accordingly. She was an ideal companion in fact: a writer with refreshingly subversive ideas yet always gratifyingly submissive. "I do not come in as a literary woman at all, but as a sort of—of admiring aunt," she wrote, though she was only three years his senior. At the time James was sorely in need of such buildup, for the 1880s were a period of relative failure. The fertile creative period from *Daisy Miller* to *The Portrait of a Lady* had ended, and all three major novels of the decade were commercial flops. Woolson, on the other hand, was on something of a roll, and the success she achieved with her serious novels and stories for the better magazines was of a type James can only have envied.

The two writers discussed their work in detail; they also used and influenced each other in their fiction. Woolson emerges as a clear prototype for Maria Gostrey in *The Ambassadors* and for several characters in James's short stories, while she herself produced caustic portraits of her friend in *The Street of the Hyacinth* and *Miss Grief*. More significantly, Woolson, who specialized in metaphoric tales about artists, may have inspired James to appropriate and perfect the very same genre in his own great stories like "The Lesson of the Master" and "The Figure in the Carpet."

James was always an unreliable ally; in the end he proved a treacherous one. In 1887 he published an essay about his friend. Supposedly an appreciation of her work, it was really a brutal put-down. In a tone of condescension, James presented Woolson as a moderately talented writer flawed by feminine sentimentality and feminine isolation from the larger world of men, and entirely ignored Woolson's radical ideas and her ambiguous attitudes toward love and marriage. It was an influential misreading, aimed directly at Woolson's readership (he published it in *Harper's*, her own usual forum), and, in the event, it ensured her future obliteration.

In Venice in 1894 Woolson, after a minor bout with influenza, fell to her death from her bedroom window. There exists an overwhelming array of evidence (letters implicitly preparing friends for the event, precise instructions for her funeral, and so forth) to indicate that Woolson had planned her suicide carefully. But James, perhaps to exonerate himself for not having sensed her real despair, reacted hysterically, insisting that she must have been overcome by a sudden and uncontrolled "dementia." It was a position that, all evidence to the contrary, he would never abandon.

Gordon goes a little too far when she hints that James's coldness might in fact have been responsible for his friend's self-destruction. Woolson had all her life been subject to crippling depressions. She was also a realist through and through, and must always have been conscious of James's personal limitations. But it does seem clear from James's behavior that he himself felt guilty. He knew, after all, that he was emotionally inaccessible; it was a characteristic he transferred to many of his male protagonists.

James's relations with both sexes were complex. Although he had a liking for handsome young men and sought out their company whenever possible, it seems to have been more for the purpose of aesthetic than sexual gratification. His real interest in love, sex, and gender was more literary than personal. Throughout James's career—and most particularly in the cases of Minny Temple and Constance Fenimore Woolson—it was not love or even friendship he sought, but the very best fictional material.

The Wizard Behind the Curtain

Like many another children's classic, L. Frank Baum's *The Wonderful Wizard of Oz* (1900) has been eclipsed by the film it inspired. In this case, unlike so many others, the film is a great one, the equal of the book. But the MGM movie and the novel differ in fundamental ways, and it is too bad that the eccentric, attractive world Baum imagined remains unfamiliar to so many readers.

Take for example the Wicked Witch of the West as she is treated by Baum, and subsequently by the creators of the film. Baum's witch is afraid of the blustering Cowardly Lion, and even of the dark. In short she is human, with pathetic little human weaknesses and foibles, and not a figure of pure evil; Baum did not believe in pure evil. And Baum's Dorothy, having accidentally melted the witch, is not overcome by emotion and remorse as is Judy Garland's tenderhearted celluloid Dorothy. Instead she simply "drew another bucket of water and threw it over the mess. She then swept it all out the door." This pragmatic act is entirely characteristic of the unsentimental tone of the *Oz* books, their emphasis on the homely American virtues of self-reliance and practicality.

The quintessentially American quality of these tales has struck many readers. Alison Lurie has likened Oz "to an idealized version of

America in 1900, happily isolated from the rest of the world, underpopulated, and largely rural, with an expanding magic technology and what appear to be unlimited natural resources." And the values Baum unobtrusively preached to his small readers are also characteristically American, or at least they *used* to be characteristically American: egalitarianism, tolerance, suspicion of pomp and ceremony, and a deep mistrust of leaders, even democratically elected ones. As the Tin Woodman remarks of his stint as emperor of the Winkies, "Like a good many kings and emperors, I have a grand title, but very little real power, which allows me time to amuse myself in my own way." Baum often uses such little asides as a vehicle for wry commentary: the citizens of the Emerald City, for instance, are pleased by the Scarecrow's accession to the throne, "'For,' they said, 'there is not another city in all the world that is ruled by a stuffed man.' And, so far as they knew, they were quite right"—the "so far as they knew" being a brilliant comment upon rulers as a species.

For some odd reason, L. Frank Baum has never been the subject of a full-length biography. Now Katharine M. Rogers, a scholar and a lifelong Oz devotee, has introduced Baum to the general reader, and a charming figure he turns out to be. In many cases it is better simply to enjoy a writer's work and not delve too deeply into his or her private life, but Baum appears to have been one of the very few who really was exactly as one would want him to be: sweet-natured, kind, a loving husband and father. He was also reasonable and liberal, by the lights of his era, with a sardonic sense of humor that prevented his books from ever becoming cloying. His worst fault was ineptitude with money, but he was wise enough to marry a woman whose gifts complemented his. One of Baum's four sons described him as "a creative man with glorious ideas—but a poor businessman—enthusiastic—imaginative—but unreal and impractical—I always said it was a good thing that Mother managed the family finances instead of Father." "He was a very handsome man," a contemporary recalled, "but very modest and reserved. He liked to meet people, mingle with them, talk with them."

Born in 1856, Baum passed a happy, upper-middle-class childhood in and around Syracuse, New York, where his father was a prominent businessman. Baum had a passion for the stage, and after he appeared in a play at the Union Square Theater in New York his father handed over to him a string of theaters he owned upstate. Baum set about writing comedies and melodramas for them, with some success, but business troubles—not, for once, entirely his own fault—ended this venture.

In 1882 he married Maud Gage, a handsome and strong-minded woman who was, it would turn out, a perfect balance and foil for the easygoing Baum. Maud was the daughter of Matilda Joslyn Gage, an important feminist leader who helped Elizabeth Cady Stanton and Susan B. Anthony found the National Woman Suffrage Association. Under the influence of his wife and mother-in-law, Baum became an enthusiastic convert to feminism. He was "a secure man who did not worry about asserting his masculine authority," and was not bothered by the fact that Maud had the upper hand in the marriage; in fact he seemed to welcome her take-charge attitude. His feminist beliefs would have a profound effect on his fiction: nearly all of his child heroes were girls, and they are girls who rely on their own resources and not on the aid, or validation, of men. He thought men who did not support feminist aspirations "selfish, opinionated, conceited or unjust—and perhaps all four combined," as he claimed in a newspaper editorial. "The tender husband, the considerate father, the loving brother, will be found invariably championing the cause of women."

In 1888 he decided to try his fortunes in the West, and moved his family to the grim town of Aberdeen in what would eventually become South Dakota. It is the Dakota Territory and not Kansas (which he never visited) that was the inspiration for Dorothy Gale's gray, austere home. Baum's shopkeeping venture was, predictably, a failure; the bank foreclosed, and Baum then bought one of Aberdeen's newspapers, which he ran for less than two years—"until," as he commented, "the sheriff wanted the paper more than I." In 1891 the family relocated to Chicago and Baum started all over again, this time as a journalist. His first fantasy for children, *Mother Goose in Prose*, was published in 1897, and after the spectacular success of *The Wonderful Wizard of Oz* in 1900 his serious money troubles were more or less over, though he continued to mismanage his finances whenever he was given the chance and at one point even had to declare bankruptcy.

Baum wrote more than seventy children's books, some under various *noms de plume*, but except for a few outstanding tales—*Queen Zixi of Ix* (1905), for example, or *The Master Key: An Electrical Fairy Tale* (1901)—his reputation rests on the *Oz* books. Katharine Rogers is a fine interpreter of these tales; she shares Baum's aesthetic and especially his sense of humor. She devotes an unnecessary number of pages to describing the books' complicated plots, but these passages are easily skipped over and do little to mar what is essentially a strong and sympathetic portrait.

Over his writing desk, Baum hung a framed quotation from the Bible as a caveat: WHEN I WAS A CHILD I SPAKE AS A CHILD, I UNDERSTOOD AS A CHILD, I THOUGHT AS A CHILD. Baum succeeded in writing simply while never sacrificing emotional sophistication or his natural respect for every child's moral capacities. One of the things that makes his stories fascinating is their idiosyncratic attack on ancient philosophical questions, as Michael Patrick Hearn, author of *The Annotated Wizard of Oz* (1973), has pointed out. The argument between the Scarecrow and the Tin Woodman on the relative importance of head and heart, for example, echoes Plato's dialogue "Charmides": instead of resolving this unresolvable problem Baum wisely offers a compromise in which the Scarecrow and Tin Woodman vow, at the end of *The Marvelous Land of Oz*, never to part. Another timeless conundrum, the question of where exactly the soul resides, is amusingly illustrated in the person of the Tin Woodman, who started out human but kept accidentally chopping off bits of his body and having them replaced by the tinsmith until eventually he became all tin. These are real intellectual problems, as Rogers remarks, and while "It is easy to see the characters' naiveté, . . . Baum also raises doubts about definitions conventionally accepted as adequate."

Romantic love was, in Baum's opinion, an "unsatisfactory topic which children can comprehend neither in its esoteric nor exoteric meaning," and he resolved to banish it from Oz. It was a rule he honored, brilliantly, in the breach, introducing romantic love into his stories only rarely and in order to comment ironically on its silliness. As the lovelorn Gloria remarks in *The Scarecrow of Oz* (1915), "a young lady cannot decide whom she will love, or choose the most worthy. Her heart alone decides for her, and whomsoever her heart selects, she must love, whether he amounts to much or not."

The Tin Woodman of Oz (1918) contains a superb satire on romantic conventions. Years earlier, before he became tin, the Woodman loved a Munchkin girl, Nimmie Amee. She became even fonder of him in tin than in human form, since she would no longer have to cook for a man who did not eat or make the bed for one who did not sleep—a pragmatic preference which proved her, so far as the foolish Woodman is concerned, "as wise as she is beautiful."

Now, many books later, the Woodman remembers Nimmie Amee and decides that duty requires him to return and offer himself to her. He teams up with a Tin Soldier who became tin in the same way that he did and who also once loved Nimmie Amee: they decide to seek her out and see which of them she wants to marry. But when they finally find her they discover that she is already married to Chopfyt, a creature made up of the discarded body parts of the two tin men, and that after having trained her new husband to hoe the cabbages and dust the furniture to her satisfaction, she takes no further interest in her former swains. As Rogers comments, even children can understand Nimmie

Amee's "crass materialism" and the incongruity in the tin men's "resolution to marry for duty alone, their confidence about the feelings of a girl they have forgotten for years, and their blissful unawareness that their attitude is inappropriate. Adults can perceive a similarity between these absurdities and attitudes that have been seriously presented in romantic literature."

While the *Oz* books have always sold fairly well, Baum's reputation went steadily downhill after his death in 1919. His work, for some reason, began to be attacked for blandness and for what Gillian Avery once called "easy optimism." Edward Eager, himself a children's writer of genius, complained in the 1940s of the *Oz* books' "lack of literary distinction" and said that "some of [Baum's] later books really typify all one doesn't like about the America of the World War One period." And in the 1950s Baum was suspected of having been something less than a red-blooded capitalist, with Oz's utopian elements (not developed until late in the series) looking a little too socialistic for comfort.

Rereading Baum, with his gentle irony and easy rationalism, it is hard to understand these criticisms, or to attribute them to anything loftier than mere shifts in fashion. And now, in the light of twenty-first-century problems and obsessions, his lessons seem especially relevant. In Oz as in the real world, for example, war is too often based on illusory or meaningless differences, and patriotic bombast is born from base provincialism: Baum's Boolooroo in *Sky Island* "knows" that earth is uninhabitable and laughs at the ignorance of the Americans who "know nothing of Sky Island, which is the Center of the Universe and the only place anyone would care to live." Baum also promoted a respect for the point of view of others: even the most terrifying beings, such as the Wheelers in *Ozma of Oz* (1907), have some essential weakness that makes them vulnerable and which all the frightening aggression and bravado is designed to cover up. And Billina, the intelligent hen of the same novel, illustrates the importance of cultural relativism: when Dorothy expresses disgust at the hen's diet of live bugs, Billina reminds her that "Live things are much fresher and more wholesome than dead ones, and you humans eat all sorts of dead creatures."

As for the value of diversity, a lesson that today's children's authors and librarians go to sometimes painful lengths to promote, what writer teaches this better than Baum? His stories almost always involve a group of highly diverse but equal individuals, each of whom contributes something to the resolution of the plot. No one, however bizarre, is excluded. In *The Land of Oz* a highly magnified Woggle-Bug encounters the little party of heroes, which consists of a boy, a pumpkin-headed man, a live sawhorse, the Scarecrow, and the Tin Woodman. The Woggle-Bug is startled. "'But—pardon me if I seem inquisitive—are you not all rather—ahem!—rather unusual?'" To which the Scarecrow wisely replies, "'Not more so than yourself. . . . Everything in life is unusual until you get accustomed to it.'"

With the Murphys: What a Swell Party It Was

Some fifty years after meeting Gerald and Sara Murphy, a still dazzled Donald Ogden Stewart wrote: "Once upon a time there was a prince and a princess: that's exactly how a description of the Murphys should begin. They were both rich; he was handsome; she was beautiful; they had three golden children. They loved each other, they enjoyed their own company, and they had the gift of making life enchantingly pleasurable for those who were fortunate enough to be their friends."

Gerald and Sara Murphy were, to many of their contemporaries, *the* beautiful couple of the 1920s, and they left their mark on many works of art of the period: F. Scott Fitzgerald's *Tender Is the Night*, Ernest Hemingway's *Snows of Kilimanjaro*, Philip Barry's *Holiday*, Archibald MacLeish's *J.B.*, John Dos Passos's *Big Money*, and Pablo Picasso's *Woman in White*, among others. Yet the Murphys' life together was no fairy tale; in the end it came close to being a tragedy. Amanda Vaill, a skillful and compassionate writer, gives us their story in a marvelously readable biography, *Everybody Was So Young*. It is not the first telling of the tale, but it is the most important—more comprehensive than Calvin Tomkins's *Living Well Is the Best Revenge*

(1971) and more graceful than the telling by Honoria Murphy Donnelly, the Murphys' daughter, and Richard N. Billings, *Sara & Gerald: Villa America and After* (1982).

Sara Sherman Wiborg and Gerald Clery Murphy became friends as adolescents in the hothouse social world of New York in the first decade of the twentieth century. Gerald's father was proprietor of the Mark Cross Company, purveyor (as it still is) of luxury leather goods. Sara's father was an exceedingly rich industrialist, and Sara spent much of her youth at their thirty-room East Hampton mansion, The Dunes, or traveling around Europe with her parents and sisters, celebrating the coronation of George V in London, hobnobbing with the English aristocracy, and generally, Vaill writes, "living life as one of the matched pieces of her mother's luggage." She performed the role with a natural grace but chafed in it, finding an unexpected outlet for her feelings in a budding friendship with Gerald Murphy, an awkward prep-school boy five years her junior.

Sara was attracted by Gerald's reflective nature, quiet sense of humor, and habit of questioning convention. An aesthete from his earliest years, he was uncomfortable in the boardrooms and clubrooms for which he was being groomed. The grooming process was not proceeding smoothly: he flunked the Yale entrance exams three times, though he eventually matriculated there and performed respectably, creating what he later called "the likeness of popularity and success."

Gerald and Sara did not become engaged until 1915, when Sara was thirty-two years old, over the hill in those days. Although Gerald was well-off and eligible, her parents could hardly bring themselves to countenance their daughter married to someone "in trade." The senior Murphys greeted the news gloomily, not so much because they had objections to Sara as because they seemed incapable of approving of anything Gerald did: he had been, his father said, a "great disappointment" to him; Gerald's vision of life was "unsound and warped."

Considering their frigid families and what Sara called "the heavy hand of chaperonage" that had always weighed firmly upon them, it is no surprise that the young Murphys looked upon their marriage not as a tie but as the beginning of glorious freedom. "Think of a relationship that not only does not bind, but actually *so lets loose* the imagination!" Gerald wrote. The Murphys cherished a Tolstoyan ideal of husband and wife working and living side by side. But this way of life was hard to bring to fruition within their parents' sphere of influence. And so in 1921, after Gerald had served in the army's air units during World War I and had spent a stint learning landscape architecture at Harvard, the Murphys sailed for Paris with their three small children, Honoria, Baoth, and Patrick, drawn there by the favorable exchange rate, the distance from their families, and the galvanizing new artistic life of the French capital. The *belle époque* was over, and the Murphys enthusiastically entered the modern age, which they were to ornament.

Too much, perhaps, has been written about Paris in the twenties, and certainly more than enough about the Murphys' circle: still, Vaill's version is elegantly written and well worth perusing. Joyce, Mirò, Picasso, Man Ray, Stravinsky, Hemingway, Beckett, Brancusi, Léger, Balanchine, Fitzgerald, Isadora Duncan: everyone, it seemed, was in Paris, and the Murphys—generous, stylish, and hospitable—knew and entertained them all. "The Murphys were among the first Americans I ever met," Stravinsky said, "and they gave me the most agreeable impression of the United States."

Their Paris apartment was modern and unconventional, but it was at the Villa America, their house at Cap d'Antibes on the Riviera, that the Murphys came into their own and made their indelible impression on their contemporaries; it was there that they seemed most to embody the period and its aesthetic. Until their day the Côte d'Azur had been strictly a winter resort, practically deserted during the hot summer months. From 1923 the Murphys almost single-handedly made it fashionable, inviting exotics like the Fitzgeralds, the Picassos, Hemingway and his first and second wives, and Fernand Léger to their little beach of La Garoupe.

Gerald, who in the words of a friend "always became a native of wherever he was," adopted a casual wardrobe that in later years would become what amounted to a Cap d'Antibes uniform: striped sailor jersey, espadrilles, and knitted fisherman's cap. Sara was very much the striking beauty that Fitzgerald would bring to life as Nicole Diver in *Tender Is the Night*, her face "hard and lovely and pitiful," her bathing suit "pulled off her shoulders," her characteristic rope of pearls setting off her deep tan. Around them they created a perpetual aura of luxury, celebration, and fun. "Sara est très festin," Picasso remarked approvingly, as he watched her setting the picnic cloth with flowers and ivy.

Scott and Zelda Fitzgerald became particular friends of the Murphys. "We four communicate by our presence rather than by any means," Gerald told them. "Currents race between us regardless." But it was never a friendship between equals: the Fitzgeralds were younger and far less stable, and the very qualities that attracted them to the Murphys—the older couple's inherited wealth and their unthinking generosity, their glamour, and their air of settled contentment with each other and with their children—made Fitzgerald envious and defensive.

In spite of the talent and intelligence the Murphys prized, F. Scott Fitzgerald was without a doubt one of the foremost boors of American letters. Even the tolerant Gerald admitted that Scott "really had the most appalling sense of humor, sophomoric and—well, trashy." Murphy himself was all too often the butt of Fitzgerald's drunken venom. Yet never once did he grudge Fitzgerald affection, praise, financial and moral support. It was Murphy who bailed Fitzgerald out in 1939 and paid to keep his daughter at Vassar; he and Sara were among the few to show up at Fitzgerald's funeral the following year. Fitzgerald, however, proved an unreliable friend, fostering, as did Hemingway, the image of Gerald Murphy as a spoiled dilettante.

But Murphy, modest about his gifts as he was, was no dilettante. He had unexpectedly taken up painting soon after his arrival in Paris, after seeing an exhibition of work by Picasso, Derain, Gris, and Braque. "There was a shock of recognition which put me into an entirely new orbit," he later wrote. "If that's painting," he told Sara, "that's the kind of painting that I would like to do." He began to study with the futurist artist Natalia Goncharova, and, along with Sara, to help paint scenery for Diaghilev's Ballets Russes.

Murphy was an infinitely slow and meticulous painter who produced only a small output in his brief career. His surviving works formed the nucleus of a posthumous Museum of Modern Art exhibition in 1974 that John Russell in the *New York Times* called "a distinct contribution to the history of modern American painting." These works, striking and contemporary, show him to have been a sort of pop artist before Pop Art; they garnered considerable attention at the Salon des Indépendents of the 1920s and had a marked influence upon the better-known Stuart Davis, among others. *Art in America* magazine, reviewing the 1974 retrospective, judged Murphy to be "an astonishingly original, witty and prophetic painter."

The Murphys' seemingly charmed life ended abruptly, and forever, in 1929 when tuberculosis was diagnosed in their youngest son, Patrick. Gerald put away his paintbrushes, never, so far as anyone knows, to touch them again, and for the next seven years he and Sara poured all their energies into their son. They spent much of that time at a Swiss sanatorium, where they gallantly tried to keep life and hope going by creating the festive atmosphere that was their specialty.

Then in 1935, to everyone's shock, their elder son, Baoth, who had always been vigorous and healthy, suddenly developed meningitis and died. A year later Patrick lost his long battle at the age of sixteen. "Life itself has stepped in now and blundered, scarred and destroyed," Gerald wrote to Fitzgerald. "In my heart I dreaded the moment when our youth and invention would be attacked in our only vulnerable spot—the children." Fitzgerald responded, "The golden bowl is broken indeed, but it was golden."

In 1937 the Murphys returned to New York for good. From this period their marriage underwent a shift. It seems probable (though Vaill is very discreet, perhaps too much so) that Gerald's primary orientation was homosexual; but Sara had always been the most important thing in his life, their marriage paramount. Now, differences that had always existed between the two became more clearly defined, and to a certain extent they distanced themselves from one another. "You are surprised anew periodically that 'warm human relationship' should be so necessary to you and less to me," Gerald wrote to Sara. "Yet nothing is more natural under the circumstances. You believe in it (as you do in life), you are capable of it, you command it. I am less of a believer (I don't *admire* human animals as much)."

The Mark Cross Company was on the verge of bankruptcy, and in 1934 Gerald took it over at last, spending the remainder of his working years turning it back into a prosperous concern. As an elderly man he lived the life he had fled as a youth, going to an office and lunching every day at Schrafft's. He never spoke about his painting or about his dead sons. Sara threw herself into volunteer work with children.

They entertained old friends and made new ones, like Edmund Wilson, Dawn Powell, and Calvin Tomkins, who wrote a long article for the *New Yorker* about the Murphys, "Living Well Is the Best Revenge," later published in book form. (Gerald liked the article but not the title: he had never wanted revenge on anyone, he said.) Gerald died in 1964, Sara eleven years later.

Other writers, even old friends, did not treat the Murphys as kindly as Tomkins did. Hemingway's posthumous memoir, *A Moveable Feast*, called them rich "bastards." Vaill quotes portions deleted from the published book in which Hemingway nastily—and unforgivably, considering their generosity to him—commented, "They were bad luck to people but they were worse luck to themselves and they lived to have all that bad luck finally." Gerald reacted with his odd, characteristic blend of sympathy and resigned detachment: "What a strange kind of bitterness—or rather accusitoriness. . . . What shocking ethics! How well written, of course."

Main Street's Scourge

Sinclair Lewis's *Main Street* is one of those very rare novels whose appearance became a national event rather than merely a literary one. In its day everyone read *Main Street*; within months of its publication in 1920 the very title had become a synonym for provincialism and narrow-mindedness. Its obscure author quickly became one of the most famous writers in the world, a notorious scourge of polite convention and accepted pieties. As Malcolm Cowley later commented,

> Our normal book-buying public consists, perhaps, of two or three hundred thousand people. When a novel passes the latter figure, it is being purchased by families in the remoter villages, families which acquire no more than ten books in a generation. In the year 1921, if you visited the parlor of almost any boarding house, you would see a copy of "Main Street" standing between the Bible and *Ben-Hur*.

Defying the conventional wisdom that novels about small towns sell poorly, *Main Street* soared to the top of the best-seller lists and stayed there. Only a few months after its publication, sales had reached 100,000, and they continued at a high rate. It became the best-selling American novel for the entire period 1900 to 1925, and probably the most influential as well. As Ludwig Lewisohn commented, "Perhaps no novel since *Uncle Tom's Cabin* had struck so deep over so wide a surface of the national life."

One of the reasons *Main Street* made such an immediate impression was that it spoke for so many people. In 1920 the majority of native-born adult Americans had grown up in small towns or rural areas, despite the demographic shift to cities that was well under way. Most of the novel's readers had intimate knowledge of their own particular Main Streets, which were usually not so very different from that of Gopher Prairie; as Lewis writes in the novel, Gopher Prairie is not only its distinct self but "ten thousand towns from Albany to San Diego." *Main Street* told the literal truth about many thousands of American lives, and readers recognized themselves and their world. "Some hundreds of thousands read the book," Lewis later commented, "with the same masochistic pleasure that one has in sucking an aching tooth." "I lived every page of *Main Street* for fifteen years," one female reader wrote, with feeling.

It was an intensely liberating document that toppled a number of dearly held American myths: that in the Midwestern United States, and there only, was to be found God's Country; that "broad plains necessarily make broad minds, and high mountains make high purpose"; that the American small town had achieved a level of perfect and simple democracy unknown to older and more effete societies; that institutions such as "Polite Society, the Family, the Church, Sound Business, the Party, the Country, the Superior White Race" were recipes for general happiness rather than tyrannical enforcers of arbitrary norms. *Main Street* lanced the bubble of self-satisfaction that had formed around provincial American culture, and cast mockery and doubt on Middle America's creed, formulated at the beginning of the novel:

> *Main Street is the climax of civilization. That this Ford car might stand in front of the Bon Ton Store, Hannibal invaded Rome and Eras-*

mus wrote in Oxford cloisters. What Ole Jensen the grocer says to Ezra Stowbody the banker is the new law for London, Prague, and the unprofitable isles of the sea; whatever Ezra does not know and sanction, that thing is heresy, worthless for knowing and wicked to consider.

Our railway station is the final aspiration of architecture. Sam Clark's annual hardware turnover is the envy of the four counties which constitute God's Country.

Sinclair Lewis could not have written of Gopher Prairie with such a potent combination of affection and contempt, hate and love, had he not been a product of it himself. A native of Sauk Centre, Minnesota, a prairie town that had a population of some twelve hundred at the time of his birth in 1885, Lewis knew his subject intimately—too intimately, perhaps, for it was not until he revisited his hometown with his bride, a city girl like *Main Street*'s Carol Kennicott, and saw it, as though for the first time, through her alien and feminine eyes, that he was able to move ahead with the vague idea for a novel about small-town life that had been haunting his imagination for years.

As early as 1905, when he was still a college student at Yale, the germ of what was to become *Main Street* was born in him during a series of conversations with Charles Dorion, a dreamy, bookish lawyer who was dissatisfied with life in Sauk Centre but too passive to move on. In his diary Lewis recorded their talks, dubbing Dorion's disaffection "the village virus." "I shall have to write a book of how it getteth into the veins of good men & true. 'God made the country & man made the town—but the devil made the village.' Where in the city one would see a friend or go to the theatre, in Sauk Centre there is nothing to do save drink or play poker (for those who do not read much)." Later Lewis claimed that at that time he had written twenty thousand words of a novel he called *The Village Virus*, but no trace of this aborted work remains.

But the idea for *Main Street* continued to percolate over the course of the next decade, during which time he published three novels, a boys' adventure story, and a good many short stories. Then, after several years in New York as a Greenwich Village bohemian, Lewis went to visit Sauk Centre with his new wife, Gracie. He noticed Gracie's reactions to things he had always taken for granted: as, for example, when she attended a meeting of the Gradatim Club (which would become the Thanatopsis Club in *Main Street*), and they discussed their literary agenda for the following year, deciding to devote their entire course of study to the Bible.

The visit almost magically refocused his thoughts, and he suddenly knew how the novel must evolve. The Charles Dorion character, whom he had named Guy Pollock, retreated into the background and the novel's central intelligence became a woman, based in large part on Gracie: the fastidious, artistic Carol Kennicott, full of real dreams and ambitions, and just as full of silly affectations and vanities—a perfect foil for ugly, utilitarian Gopher Prairie.

In much the same way that Jane Austen, in *Northanger Abbey*, used the heroine's romantic expectations to emphasize the banality of her actual experiences, Lewis used Carol's fantasies of village life, fed by literature, to underline the crudity of the genuine article. Just arrived in her new home, for instance, she goes to the bedroom window,

> with a purely literary thought of village charm—hollyhocks and lanes and apple-cheeked cottagers. What she saw was the side of the Seventh-Day Adventist Church—a plain clapboard wall of a sour liver color; the ash-pile back of the church; an unpainted stable; and an alley in which a Ford delivery-wagon had been stranded.

It is easy to make fun of Carol's overheated imagination, but we can never really do that, for we realize that the ugliness she perceives everywhere in Gopher Prairie is not incidental but spiritual. In the entire town there are "not a dozen buildings which suggested that, in the fifty years of Gopher Prairie's existence, the citizens had realized that it was either desirable or possible to make this, their common home, amusing or attractive."

Likewise, when Carol founds a theater group in Gopher Prairie she is inspired by heady visions of sparkling Shavian wit, the experimentation of the Abbey Theatre, and the scenic magic of the great Gordon Craig; but the best that she and the town are able to come up with is a lowbrow farce called *The Girl from Kankatee*, which even she admits, after the event, turned out to be "a bad play abominably acted." Again and again Carol's hopes are shattered, and while we are often amused by her aspirations, we are never really unsympathetic to them, however ridiculous they might be. At least she tries for something better; at least she refuses to be content with utility and mediocrity.

Harry Sinclair Lewis, Midwestern America's rebellious but not unaffectionate son, was born in Sauk Centre on February 7, 1885, the third child of Dr. Edwin J. Lewis. Dr. E.J., as he was known, was transparently the model for Dr. Will Kennicott of *Main Street*. Like Will, he was solid, hardworking, utterly respectable, and uncommunicative, but with a humorous, sardonic streak. Like Will, he could be seen in a rather heroic light: making country calls four or five times a week, driving far into the frozen countryside in a sleigh, and performing surgery by candlelight on kitchen tables.

Lewis's mother died of tuberculosis when he was six, and a year later Dr. E.J. married Isabel Warner, a kind, motherly woman who soon became a pillar of the community, taking a leading role in the Gradatim Club, the Monday Musical Club, and the Order of the Eastern Star. Like Carol, she was interested in the welfare of the Scandinavian farmers in the surrounding countryside and established a rest room in Sauk Centre where farm wives and children could be comfortable while their husbands drank or did business in town.

Young Harry did not appear to be marked for success. His father reportedly informed his older brothers that they might have to look out for him: "You boys will always be able to make a living," he told them. "But poor Harry, there's nothing he can do." This changed when, as a teenager, Harry became fired with a driving ambition to attend Harvard.

He was sent for a precollege year to Oberlin Academy in Ohio, then a religiously oriented school where, for the first and last time in his life, he took a serious interest in Christianity and decided he wanted to become a missionary. Furious, Dr. E.J. laid down the law: missionary work was out, and so was the relatively freewheeling Harvard. "You must prepare for Yale or go to *No* college," he stormed.

Lewis toed the line, not without some relief, as his zeal was already waning; he would quickly develop into what he was to remain for the rest of his life, a confirmed atheist with a deep dislike for fundamentalist Christianity. Asked in the 1940s whether a lack of religious belief did not make for an unhappy life, he objected heatedly to the idea.

> If I go to a play I do not enjoy it less because I do not believe that it is divinely created and divinely conducted, that it will last forever instead of stopping at eleven, that many details of it will remain in my memory after a few months, or that it will have any particular moral effect upon me. And I enjoy life as I enjoy that play.

He was not by any definition a success at Yale. Loud, overenthusiastic, extremely provincial and unsophisticated, he was also physically unprepossessing, with his tall, gangling frame, red hair, and acne. Added to these disadvantages was the fact that he was poor, at least in comparison with most of the other Yale boys.

Lewis made a little extra money by taking a night job on the New Haven *Journal Courier* as a rewrite man. His discovery of the theater, and most particularly of George Bernard Shaw and Henrik Ibsen, who would become his prophets and heroes, changed his life. These two playwrights were revolutionary in their refusal passively to accept the status quo. They examined all the monolithic institutions of society—Marriage, the Family, Business, the Church, the State—and found them not only inadequate but arbitrary in their exercise of power. Things need not be as they were; anything could be questioned, changed, rejected.

This doubting, reforming mode was one religion Lewis could adhere to wholeheartedly, and it would dominate his career. All his major novels—*Main Street*, *Babbitt* (1922), *Arrowsmith* (1925), *Elmer Gantry* (1927)—would question his society's most basic values and assert that a better world was not only necessary but possible.

Lewis dropped out of Yale in 1906 and went to work at Upton Sinclair's utopian community, Helicon Hall. He soon found that, like so many utopias, it was a hotbed of petty feuds and jealousies, and he left after a very short stay. He then took a series of short-term jobs and returned to Yale to graduate in 1908.

After graduation, Lewis set out to be a newspaperman, an obvious career move for him. The lightning pace of the newsroom was not congenial to him, however, for he wrote best when he had the leisure to think, rewrite, and revise; he lost jobs in rapid succession. During this time, he was beginning to write fiction and to see that as his vocation. Finally, later in 1909, he moved to New York, the nation's intellectual and artistic capital.

He took an apartment in Greenwich Village and eagerly participated in the "Little Renaissance" that was in full swing there, soaking up modern art and literature as well as new ideas like Freudianism (which he instinctively rejected), and becoming a socialist. Lewis's socialism was of the gradualist Fabian variety: he followed Shaw and Wells rather than the revolutionary Marxists, and he found *Das Kapital* "dreadful," worse even than the Bible. Lewis's political views would change very little over the years. His fundamental creed, voiced succinctly in his 1935 novel *It Can't Happen Here*, was the classic liberal view that "everything that is worth while in the world has been accomplished by the free, inquiring, critical spirit and that the preservation of this spirit is more important than any social system whatsoever."

Lewis published a boys' adventure novel and, shortly afterward, his first novel for adults, *Our Mr. Wrenn*, very much under the influence of his idol H. G. Wells. At the same period—in 1912—he met his future wife, Grace Livingston Hegger, a pretty and elegant beauty editor at *Vogue*. Gracie's family had slipped down into the middle class, but she tried hard to maintain the Park Avenue lifestyle and demeanor of its earlier prosperity. She spoke with an English accent, though she had spent her entire life in America: it was hers, she claimed, by inheritance, since her parents were English. She renamed her fiancé "Hal"; Harry and Red, his usual nicknames, she found too plebeian, Sinclair too formal.

Many of Lewis's friends found Gracie unspeakably pretentious and an embarrassing social climber, and wondered why Lewis was so deeply in thrall to her. H. L. Mencken, for instance, wrote that Lewis's "inferiority complex made it simply impossible for him to stand up to her. He lived in wonder that so ravishing and brilliant a female had ever condescended to marry him." It is true that the two proved, in the end, incompatible. Lewis's inability to settle down in one place and, eventually, to stop drinking made life almost impossible for her, and Gracie's snobberies and prejudices soured Lewis. But their relationship was a close one for years, and Gracie contributed a great deal to Lewis's life and work, not least as the model for Carol Kennicott. Most important, perhaps, she shared his very real hatred for narrow-mindedness and intolerance, a hatred that was one of the driving forces of his life, and she supported him intellectually and emotionally to the best of her abilities.

Lewis was making progress in his fiction. His short stories were selling well, and when he was taken on as a regular contributor to the

Saturday Evening Post he felt justified in quitting his publishing job at George Doran and Company to become a full-time writer. His next two novels, *The Trail of the Hawk* (1915) and *The Job* (1917), were enthusiastically received, with critics laying bets that here was a major writer in embryo.

He was beginning to move in a more satirical direction, taking aim at some of the baneful aspects of contemporary life that would preoccupy him throughout his career: the cutthroat worlds of business and advertising, the evangelism racket, the American obsession with pseudo-religions like New Thought and theosophy. Lewis's disgust for the low tactics of business and the American tendency to apotheosize its "ethics" would come to full maturity in *Babbitt* but was already bearing fruit in a series of short stories about a "bunk" advertising man, Lancelot Todd, and his imaginative series of scams on the public. Fastidious *littérateurs* criticized what they considered the stories' vulgar style, but Lewis, to his credit, remained unconvinced that vulgarity was such a very undesirable quality. He was, as it turned out, creating a new way of dealing with language in literature, formulating a strong, stylized version of the American vernacular that would resonate in his readers' ears. Lewis's characters, like many characters in fiction, *are* what they speak. The high ideals of the young research physician Martin Arrowsmith struggle to break free from his limited, provincial vocabulary; the ethereal, Keatsian beauty of *Main Street*'s Erik Valborg is negated whenever he comes out with his characteristic "Yumps" and "You bets."

When America entered World War I in 1917, Lewis found his voice momentarily stilled. He was disgusted with the general outpouring of anti-German venom and disturbed by the effective limits that were put on free speech, or indeed anything that could be construed as the least bit anti-American. In 1918 one of Lewis's heroes, the labor leader Eugene Debs, was imprisoned merely for expressing his opinion that the United States ought to have stayed out of the war.

Lewis waited; three years later, in *Main Street*, he would reveal his own feelings about the surge of wartime jingoism.

The postwar mood was more cynical, more willing to question American motivations and values—more in tune with Lewis's own personality and beliefs. *Main Street* was published at what was probably the perfect moment, with more and more people—not just artists and intellectuals but ordinary Americans—coming to share his doubts. Its success was not only attributable to his particular genius but was a sign that America was ready to swallow his bitter medicine.

As an international celebrity in the 1920s, Lewis continued the peripatetic habits of his youth, dragging Gracie and their young son, Wells, around Europe—which Gracie enjoyed—and through various points west of New York, which she often did not. In France they were snubbed by their fellow expatriates in the Hemingway-Stein crowd, who scorned their provincialism. In England they were intimidated by the Bloomsbury set but made an impression, of a sort, on other literary celebrities there. Rebecca West found that after a few hours in Lewis's company she "ceased to look upon him as a human being. I could think of him only as a great natural force, like the aurora borealis." Arnold Bennett, who liked Lewis in spite of his brash, manic demeanor, provided a memorable portrait:

> Lewis has a habit of breaking into a discussion with long pieces of imaginary conversation between imaginary or real people of the place and period of the discussion. Goodish, but too long, with accents, manner and all complete. He will do this in any discussion; he will drag in a performance, usually full of oaths and blasphemy.

To Europeans and Europeanized Americans Lewis might have seemed crude, but the strength of his voice and his vision were undeniable. *Babbitt*, whose eponymous hero is an unimaginative businessman who feels, vaguely and inarticulately, that there must be more to life, was published in 1922 and made nearly as strong an impression as *Main Streeet* had. H. L. Mencken had been urging Lewis for some time to take on "the American city—not New York or Chicago but the cities of 200,000–500,000—the Baltimores and Omahas and Buffaloes and Birminghams." Lewis assured him that in *Babbitt*'s imaginary town of Zenith he had reproduced the real thing. "All our friends are in it," he told Mencken—"the Rotary Club, the popular preacher, the Chamber of Commerce, the new bungalows, the bunch of business jolliers lunching at the Athletic Club. It ought to be at least 2000% American, as well as forward-looking, right-thinking, optimistic, selling the idea of success, and go-getterish."

Babbitt was brilliant satire, but unlike *Main Street* it was more satire than novel. George Follansbee Babbitt achieves pathos but not tragedy, and Lewis's efforts to give him a soul were not entirely successful. This lack might have contributed to his decision to make his next novel, *Arrowsmith*, significantly less satirical than his two previous ones—a "straight" novel, in fact. *Arrowsmith*, the story of an idealistic doctor and medical researcher, is a powerful and emotional novel, and though it is very funny in places—Lewis did not find it easy to suppress his humor—it is essentially a serious piece of work about the assertion of personal beliefs in the face of social and financial temptations.

Arrowsmith was named winner of the 1926 Pulitzer Prize for fiction, but Lewis, true to his convictions about his country and his own role within it, refused the honor, explaining his decision to the committee thus:

> [The] terms are that the prize shall be given "for the American novel published during the year which shall best present the wholesome atmosphere of American life, and the highest standard of American manners and manhood." This phrase, if it means anything whatever,

would appear to mean that the appraisal of the novels shall be made not according to their actual literary merit but in obedience to whatever code of Good Form may chance to be popular at the moment.

Elmer Gantry, Lewis's next novel, took on a subject he had long wanted to tackle: evangelism. Elmer Gantry is a bunk preacher just as Lancelot Todd was a bunk ad man. Lewis, who had been given a tremendous amount of help in researching *Arrowsmith* by a doctor, Paul de Kruif, realized he needed the same sort of insider knowledge for *Gantry*, so he set up shop in Kansas City and started reaching out to men of the cloth of every type, entertaining them—which meant questioning them, heckling them, challenging them—at weekly lunches that came to be known as "Sinclair Lewis's Sunday School classes." Paradoxically he became very fond of these hard-drinking, fornicating, doubting, and all-too-human ministers whom he was so soon to lampoon in his novel. As his publisher Alfred Harcourt said of Lewis, he hated bunk, but it was never individuals he hated, only their bunk performances.

Lewis tended to show an affectionate magnanimity toward his fictional characters, with one important exception: the recurring character based on Gracie. The portrait of Carol Kennicott, only four years into the Lewises' marriage, is affectionate; that of Martin Arrowsmith's shallow second wife, Joyce, is less so; the portrayal of the arch-bitch Fran, in *Dodsworth* (1929), shows how badly the marriage had deteriorated.

Lewis had been drinking heavily during the writing of *Elmer Gantry*, and had had a hard time finishing the novel, the later chapters of which show the strain. Still, the book was a sensation, with heated reviews for and against, and the phrase "Elmer Gantry," like "Babbitt," entered the American language, in this case as a term to describe an on-the-make priest. His next novel, *Dodsworth*, was another success, though this time without the element of sensation.

Dodsworth was a gentler tale, about a wandering American in Europe, Lewis's contribution to the venerable novelistic tradition contrasting the Old World with the New.

Lewis and Gracie divorced in 1928, and the same year he married Dorothy Thompson, one of the most vocal and influential journalists of the century and a superstar in her own right. Dorothy had spent much of her career in Germany, and she was one of the first Americans who understood just how dangerous Hitler and the nascent Nazi movement were likely to be. Her columns in the American press expressed her anti-fascist beliefs, her fears about the German regime, and her worries about communism to an America that was trying hard to retain its comfortable isolationist position.

In 1930 Lewis became the first American to be awarded the Nobel Prize for Literature. It was not a universally popular decision. The "Paris bunch," led by Hemingway, were angry that the prize should go to a realistic writer rather than to one of the experimentalists they championed, Ezra Pound or James Joyce. Others, like Sherwood Anderson, were afraid that Lewis won because his novels, so critical of his native country, catered to the knee-jerk anti-Americanism of the European prize-givers. In Lewis's case, as in the case of many others, the Nobel proved to be a mixed blessing; while it affirmed his genius and the validity of his style, an original blend of satire and realism, it proved an artistic inhibitor. How, he wondered, could he possibly live up to the honor?

Dodsworth turned out to be the last of what are generally considered Lewis's best novels. He managed, against the odds, to quit drinking, but his talent was beginning to fade. He continued writing novels right up until his death in 1951, and some of them were quite successful, notably *Ann Vickers* (1933), the resonantly anti-fascist *It Can't Happen Here* (1935), *Cass Timberlane* (1945), and *Kingsblood Royal* (1947), a radical, ahead-of-its-time story of race relations that won *Ebony* magazine's annual prize for the book that did the most to promote interracial understanding. But his days as an influential contemporary novelist were essentially over.

Lewis and Dorothy divorced in 1942 after years of unhappiness, and Lewis spent his last years more or less alone, always looking for friendship and love but alienating nearly everyone with his tempers, his egotism, and his sporadic returns to the bottle. He died in 1951 and was buried in Sauk Centre. After years as a sort of pariah in his hometown—with *Main Street* he had made it, after all, an international laughingstock—he had been forgiven and embraced as the town's favorite native son. Sauk Centre, with all the *echt*-American commercial instincts Lewis had mocked and deplored in his fiction, had turned its most famous dissenter into a product. At the time of Lewis's death, Sauk Centre boasted a Main Street Garage, a Gopher Prairie Inn, and a brand of butter called The Pride of Main Street. In later years would come Sinclair Lewis Avenue and Original Main Street, the Sinclair Lewis Boyhood Home Museum.

One of the objections that experimental, international modernists like Hemingway had to Lewis's work was that it sometimes leaned more toward sociology than art. This quality, however, can be understood as an experiment in its own right, and a remarkably successful one. *Main Street*'s journalistic command of contemporary details helped it communicate clearly to its earliest readers, and even the fact that so much of the cultural ephemera found in its pages are now mere historical artifacts does not make its effect less immediate. Lewis was working within, and developing, a particular Anglo-American tradition rather than breaking and reinventing the rules like his contemporary, James Joyce. His immediate predecessors and models were Hamlin Garland, Theodore Dreiser, George Moore, Edith Wharton, and H. G. Wells. Lewis acknowledged Dreiser as a master without whom his own career would probably not have been possible:

> Dreiser more than any other man, marching alone, usually unappreciated, often hated, has cleared the trail from Victorian and Howellsian timidity and gentility in American fiction to honesty and boldness and passion of life. Without his pioneering, I doubt if any of us could, unless we liked to be sent to jail, seek to express life and beauty and terror.

Hamlin Garland, now nearly forgotten, was another writer whose work provided a liberating precedent for the budding realist who wanted to portray his banal surroundings as they really were.

> I had realized, in reading Balzac and Dickens, that it was possible to describe the French and English common people as one actually saw them. But it had never occurred to me that one might, without indecency, write of the people of Sauk Centre, Minnesota, as one felt about them. Our fictional tradition, you see, was that all of us in mid-Western villages were altogether noble and happy; that not one of us would exchange the neighborly bliss of living on Main Street for the heathen gaudiness of New York or Paris or Stockholm. But in Mr. Garland's *Main-Traveled Roads* I discovered that there was one man who believed mid-Western peasants sometimes were bewildered and hungry and vile—and heroic. And, given this vision, I was released; I could write of life as giving life.

Lewis spoke of fiction as "contemporary history" and blended historical and social issues smoothly into all his stories. *Main Street* is, among so many other things, an illustration of the contemporary populist concern over the exploitation of farmers by the parasitical townspeople: Thorstein Veblen had propounded theories about the rise of the country town in a 1915 book, *Imperial Germany and the Industrial Revolution*, which Lewis's novel directly addresses. The overheated patriotism that had so disgusted Lewis during World War I also finds a place in *Main Street*, in which Lewis was able, if belatedly, to express his contempt for tribal chest-beating.

With his portrayal of Carol and Will Kennicott's up-and-down marriage, Lewis added his voice to the excited cultural dialogue that was taking place on the subject of marriage and women's roles in and out of the home. Ibsen's ground-breaking play *A Doll's House* (1879) had shocked contemporary audiences with its portrayal of an apparently happy, spoiled, bourgeois wife who leaves her husband and family to learn to become a full-fledged human being. Where Ibsen's Nora Helmer is a tragic figure, Carol is earthbound and frequently ridiculous; but Carol's anguish is no less real, and the issues and circumstances that divide her from her husband are no less pressing. When Carol says, "I am trying to save my soul," we are meant to respect this statement as the literal truth.

Mencken, here as so often Lewis's greatest appreciator and critic, understood the sociological significance of the Kennicott marriage in "the disparate cultural development of the male and female, the great strangeness that lies between husband and wife when they begin to function as members of society. The men, sweating at their sordid concerns, have given the women leisure, and out of that leisure the women have fashioned disquieting discontents."

What is so brilliant about Lewis's treatment of the Kennicott marriage is that he upsets our expectations by making the frequently lumpish Will the more powerful personality of the two and often the more sympathetic as well. This was a conscious decision: in his introduction to a 1937 edition of the novel Lewis admitted that Carol is not "of as good stuff as her husband. . . . I had most painstakingly planned that she shouldn't be—that she should be just bright enough to sniff a little but not bright enough to do anything about it."

Some readers have exaggerated Carol's deficiencies, assuming that she is meant to be a complete lightweight and that the solid virtues of Will and of his friend Sam Clark constitute the most positive values on Main Street. A 1921 Broadway play adapted from the novel took this point of view and portrayed Carol as a pretentious featherhead. This is a drastic misreading, however. Will, though demonstrably a good man and endowed with both more intelligence and more humor than his wife, is severely limited as a human being. Carol, though a foolish woman in many ways, is saved by ideals and ambitions that are as noble as they are absurd. Her tragedy is not great drama but simply "the humdrum inevitable tragedy of struggle against inertia." Even silly little Erik Valborg, her minion, is validated by his hopes and dreams, and if he meets a mediocre end as a B-movie actor, then perhaps the next Erik Valborg who comes to Gopher Prairie really *will* turn out to be a Keats.

For the real enemy is not affectation, like Carol's, or mindless enthusiasm, like Erik's. It is

> An unimaginatively standardized background, a sluggishness of speech and manners, a rigid ruling of the spirit by the desire to appear respectable. It is contentment . . . the contentment of the quiet dead, who are scornful of the living for their restless walking. It is negation canonized as the one positive virtue. It is the prohibition of happiness. It is slavery self-sought and self-defended. It is dullness made God.

Main Street is very, very American, but it is not purely American. Shaw, with characteristic flippancy, spoke the truth when he said that Lewis's criticisms applied to other nations as well, but that Americans clung to the idea that they were unique in their faults. The British novelist John Galsworthy remarked, truly, that "Every country, of course, has its Main Streets." Still, a disdain for intellect (or for what we nowadays prefer to denigrate as elitism) has been particularly marked in America, perhaps because of our commitment, stated if not practiced, to egalitarian democracy: on Main Street, Lewis writes, "to be 'intellectual' or 'artistic' or, in their own word, to be 'highbrow,' is to be priggish and of dubious virtue."

More than eighty years after Lewis's novel this is still true, and it is true not only on Main Street but on Wall Street as well, and on Park

Avenue, and on Pennsylvania Avenue. This is what makes *Main Street* such a stunning achievement: while it succeeds in being "contemporary history," capturing a particular place and time, it also speaks for our own time, and it is startling to see how much of *Main Street* is still pertinent. Gopher Prairie at war is not so very unlike our own flag-waving "war on terrorism." Will Kennicott's breezy and self-defeating dismissal of legal procedure—"Whenever it comes right down to a question of defending Americanism and our constitutional rights, it's justifiable to set aside ordinary procedure"—can be read on almost any editorial page today. Gopher Prairie's commercial ethos of material "progress" at the expense of every other variety, an idea Lewis would expand and crystallize in *Babbitt*, has been refined rather than improved in our own era of no-collar workers who meditate or practice yoga before closing the Big Deal rather than smoking cigars and guzzling alcohol.

Lewis, unlike so many of his contemporaries, was never tempted to look for an answer in political dogma: he hated dictatorships and had no particular faith in the virtue or good judgment of "the people." All he really believed in was the wavering, imperfect liberal spirit: "Even if Com[monism] & Fax[cism] or both cover the world, Liberal[ism] must go on, seeming futile, preserving civilization," he wrote in his notes for *It Can't Happen Here*.

An atheist with no political illusions, two failed marriages, an unconquerable addiction to alcohol, and a moribund talent might be thought to have had every reason to give up in despair. Lewis, to his credit, did not. "It is a completely revelatory American tragedy," he said in his Nobel Prize speech, "that in our land of freedom, men like [Hamlin] Garland, who first blast the roads to freedom, become themselves the most bound." This has been true of many; it was never true of Lewis. Like Carol Kennicott, he was still reaching—though generally failing to grasp—right up to the end. His particular type of sociological fiction had gone out of fashion at the time of his death, and he continued to be undervalued for decades afterward. But in recent years we have returned to an appreciation for what he accomplished artistically. For what he was able to tell us about the American condition, in his day and ours, we can only be grateful.

William Saroyan's Unchained Ego

The promising and, in the end, horrifying career of William Saroyan is a case study in the limits of raw talent. Talent Saroyan undoubtedly possessed, and in abundance. But he refused to refine it or develop it, refused to educate or discipline himself, scorned the role of apprentice, scorned any role, in fact, but that of genius. As a result his early and meteoric success was succeeded by a long, humiliating, inevitable decline. As John Leggett points out in his grimly fascinating biography, by the time Saroyan was in his mid-thirties he was already a burnt-out case.

> He could look back on three of his impressive assaults on the entertainment world: on publishing, on Broadway theatre, and on Hollywood. For each there had been a spectacular debut, shimmering with the promise of a major discovery, followed by an overreaching, then a fizzling disappointment, a falling out with close associates, and final alienation. It was a rocket's trajectory—and a short one.

For a few years in the late 1930s and early '40s, Saroyan rode a tidal wave of literary fame. His early short stories had earned him an outsize reputation as an iconoclastic original, possibly *the* American writer of his generation. "I have read them with my eyes, ears, nose," Kay Boyle commented on first encountering the stories; Saroyan, she felt, was "terribly, marvelously good . . . more alive and funnier than anyone else." In 1939, his *annus mirabilis*, Saroyan had three plays running on Broadway simultaneously, won (and refused) a Pulitzer Prize, and reveled in the *succès fou* of his short fiction. The charming *My Name Is Aram* would be published the following year; *The Human Comedy*, novel and screenplay, would crown his triumph.

The world called Saroyan a genius, and he was only too happy to concur. What had passed for cockiness when he was young quickly revealed itself as hubris. The paranoia he had once been able to control got wildly out of hand; everyone who was not a hundred percent with him was against him. Therefore he rebuffed many talented, experienced would-be mentors: Whit Burnett of *Story* magazine; Bennett Cerf and Donald Klopfer of Random House; theatrical directors Harold Clurman and George Abbott; old Broadway hands Lawrence Langner and George Jean Nathan; the executives and writers at MGM. He conspicuously lacked both humility and, more importantly, restraint, an underrated but vital quality in literature.

Saroyan was self-destructive on an epic scale, a monster of narcissism who let his outsize ego blight and finally devour his life. Leggett relates the sorry tale with a kind of stoic determination to face the worst, but he is not entirely without sympathy for his subject: one feels that he started out a Saroyan enthusiast and was driven to disgust somewhat against his will. Saroyan had some good qualities, after all. For all his faults he was, as one friend wrote, "a dedicated pacifist, a ridiculer of the goose-step, a foe of peonage and patronage. He was impatient of dissimulation, generous and charitable . . . and was respectful of all religions." Just as whimsy and self-pity mar his good work, his bad work is usually alleviated by a lifelong, and perfectly correct, contempt for human pride and pretension.

> [H]e began to think of really comical things everywhere, the whole town, the people walking in the streets, trying to look important, but he knew, they couldn't fool him, he knew how important they were, and the way they talked, big business, and all of it pompous and fake, and it made him laugh, and he thought of the preacher at the Presbyterian church, the fake way he prayed, *O God, if it is your will*, and nobody believing in the prayers, and the important people with big automobiles, Cadillacs and Packards, speeding up and down the country, as if they had some place to go. . . .

Like J. D. Salinger, Saroyan wrote blistering excoriations of phoniness. Like Salinger too, he had very little to offer in place of phoniness except for an idealized innocence that is sometimes pretty phony in its own right.

Saroyan was born in Fresno, California, in 1908. His parents, Armenak and Takoohi Saroyan, had arrived in America three years earlier, fleeing the genocide in their native Armenia. Armenak died in 1911, leaving Takoohi unable to provide for her four children. She placed them temporarily in an orphanage and took a job as a domestic: Bill, as he was now called, was three. He spent the next five years in the orphange, until his mother was finally in a position to make a home for the family.

Bill was an unwilling schoolboy: the hatred of institutions and rules that would drive him to an emotional breakdown during his army years in World War II was already evident in early childhood. He helped support the family by selling papers and, later, working as a Postal Telegraph messenger, like his character Homer Macaulay in *The Human Comedy*. At the age of eighteen he left Fresno High School without a diploma.

In his early twenties Saroyan began to produce a stream of short stories, often two in a single day. They were remarkably original: conversational, direct, superbly colloquial. They were also sentimental, even mawkish on occasion, but this unfortunate tendency was masked, at least at this point, by the strength and assurance of Saroyan's narrative voice. It was only with time and an evident failure to mature that Saroyan's sentimentality would begin to be seen as a flaw rather than a benison. As early as 1941 Wallace Stegner was complaining that Saroyan was a complete romantic whose "conviction that love conquers all makes him difficult to argue with. One can only disagree." And in 1948 James Agee made a rather brutal but not unfair summary of Saroyan's career to that point:

> Saroyan is an entertainer of a kind overrated by some people and underrated by others—a very gifted schmalz-artist. In the schmalz-artist strength and weakness are inextricably combined—the deeply, primordially valid, and the falseness of the middle-aged little boy who dives back into the womb for pennies.
>
> The schmalz-artist requires more belief, more wishful thinking on the part of his audience, than better artists would require. Reality is as much his deadly enemy as it is the superior artist's most difficult love affair. At his best, Saroyan is a wonderfully sweet-natured, witty and beguiling kind of Christian anarchist, and so apt a lyrical magician that the magic designed for one medium still works in another. At his worst, he is one of the world's ranking contenders for brassy, self-pitying, arty mawkishness, for idealism with an eye to the main chance, for arrogant determination to tell damnably silly lies in the teeth of the truth.

But back in the 1930s Saroyan's strengths were far more evident than his faults. In 1934 Random House published a collection of the best tales under the title *The Daring Young Man on the Flying Trapeze*. It made an immediate impression on the literary world, even climbing onto the New York best-seller list—a rare achievement for a book of short stories—and Saroyan became an overnight star.

The effluence of Saroyan short stories did not slow down, and the author bombarded Random House with new material, presenting Cerf with second, third, fourth, and fifth collections. The editor, however, was dismayed by the uneven quality of the work and unwilling to publish. He urged the restless author to settle down and write a novel, but Saroyan didn't seem to have one in him, and in any case he lacked the discipline to provide a novel's structure. Cerf and Saroyan inevitably fell out, and Saroyan began what was to become a lifelong dance between various publishers, to whom, what with his creative ups and downs and his incessant demands for loans to finance his frenzied gambling sprees, he generally brought more pain than gain.

Saroyan was one of those compulsively feckless artists who kid themselves into believing that financial necessity can be a spur to creativity. This is how he justified wagering, and losing, enormous sums—sometimes tens of thousands of dollars in a single night—on feverish trips through Nevada or the Riviera. As a result he was, though one of the best-paid writers of his time, perpetually in debt to friends, family, publishers, and the IRS. Far from being a spur to creativity, poverty inspired much of his shoddiest and most careless work.

Saroyan's brief but complete conquest of the Broadway theater began with *My Heart's in the Highlands*, a gentle, appealing play he adapted from one of his short stories: it was the surprise hit of the 1939 season. It was followed later the same year by *The Time of Your Life*, which he wrote in five days (a typical gestation period for a Saroyan play). This drama, in which the audience is made privy to the hopes and dreams of the various barflies who frequent a city saloon, was a major hit: it won a Pulitzer Prize, though its author, citing his dislike for institutional patronage of the arts, turned the honor down. The play was taken at face value as an amiable, good-spirited fantasy, but for those who care to look for it there is a dark side, well verbalized by Leggett, who sees the central character of Joe the bartender as an unsavory alter ego for Saroyan himself: "a striking self-portrait of a man who sees himself as spectator and manipulator, a vessel of knowledge, wealth, and power, a benevolent despot to his dependents, a man who sees friendship as dominance."

Saroyan's Broadway success fizzled almost as quickly as it ignited. He was to write many more plays, but none ever gripped the public imagination as these first two had done. And in fiction, only *My Name Is Aram* and *The Human Comedy* would live up to the early promise. One fault, perhaps, lay with the very distinctiveness of Saroyan's voice: it was the voice of an innocent, unspoilt America, the America that would perish with World War II. The postwar world was a more complicated place than the trademark Saroyan simplicity and goodwill could encompass, but Saroyan couldn't, or wouldn't, learn any new tricks. His wife Carol (later Mrs. Walter Matthau), whom he married and divorced twice and with whom he played out an insane *folie à deux* for sixteen years, understood the routine well.

> Bill had the mentality of a matinée-idol. He was like an actor who'd made a great success of a certain role in his youth and, when he goes on to summer stock in his later years, still relies on what worked for him in the past. He plays the part they all loved him as in every play he's in, no matter what the play is, and when the old ladies come backstage, he's got the robe and ascot on. But he's ruined the entire play because he's not an ensemble player, he's a star.
>
> That's what Bill did in his writing. He always gave himself the same star part, used the same words, had the same problems. It was the world against the poet. The poet against the politician. And because he had gone on record as loving humanity, he didn't have to be nice to the people in his life.

"Didn't have to be nice" is a wild understatement. Saroyan was a world-class, king-sized, copper-bottomed Shit, with a capital S. John Leggett, like many literary biographers, seems to have an aversion to discussing his subject's vagaries in terms of mental illness, but Saroyan appears to have been, as well as a compulsive gambler and a devouring egomaniac, a clinical paranoiac. He was an appalling father who did his best to subsume his children and destroy their confidence; a domineering friend; and an impossible client to his long-suffering agent and publishers. By the time he reached old age, his enemies list was longer than Richard Nixon's and included most of the people he had once counted as his friends.

But the most bizarre part of Saroyan's story is his marriage. Carol Marcus was seventeen (or, by her own account, sixteen) when they met; Saroyan was thirty-four. She had been born illegitimately to a fifteen-year-old beauty, Rosheen, who put Carol and her younger sister into foster care until she was able to hook a rich and indulgent husband. Then the little girls, removed from their foster families and adopted by their new stepfather, were given a louche café-society education by Rosheen, with the object of handing them off as soon as possible to rich, successful (and by definition older) men.

The story of Carol's launch onto the marriage market along with her bosom buddies Oona O'Neill (later Chaplin) and Gloria Vanderbilt (later Stokowski) has been told by Carol Matthau herself in her memoir *Among the Porcupines* (1992) and by her son Aram Saroyan in *Trio* (1985). It makes horrifying reading: Carol had in effect been taught to sell herself to the highest bidder while simultaneously being spoon-fed by her mother and everybody around her an impossibly romantic notion of marriage as Undying Love. The Saroyans' relationship was hurricane-strength and mutually abusive. He tried to turn her into an old-style Armenian wife, refusing to let her see or telephone her friends; she, with entirely different ideas, spent all the money he was finding it increasingly hard to earn on bankrolling her high-octane social life and budding acting career. They drank and fought continually; when, on occasion, they separated, the sinister Rosheen would show up again in the role of Pandarus.

The Saroyans' first marriage ended when it was disclosed that Carol, as Saroyan had long suspected, was Jewish. He then cloaked his anti-Semitism in a pose of injured innocence, claimed that he could never live with someone who had deceived him on so fundamental an issue, and removed himself. Their subsequent remarriage in 1951 was brief, for Carol had by now grown up and was beginning to realize that there were other men out there, men just as famous as Saroyan but richer and infinitely easier to deal with.

The twilight of Saroyan's career was a long one, but it was prolific: he doggedly cranked out work, bad or mediocre, to the bitter end. He was not much of a novel writer, perhaps because his ego got in the way of his imagination; as Leggett says, "He lacked the heart to create characters. He resented them, and he suspected it was because the more urgent job was to recreate his own character." Nothing he wrote in his last twenty years had much success, but some of it is worth reading, if only to experience real, honest-to-God bile, for once Saroyan finally stopped being a romantic, he channeled pure anger onto the page. *Boys and Girls Together* (1963), for example, a bitter railing against Carol and her friends, who appear under only the most perfunctory of disguises, is not a particularly good book, but it is fascinating nonetheless. Other more straightforward memoirs, like *Here Comes, There Goes You Know Who* (1961), *Obituaries* (1979), or *Places Where I've Done Time* (1972) contain, between their thick strata of self-justifying bullshit, veins of honesty that make them not entirely negligible. But although the Saroyan name retained a certain luster, his readers were ever fewer and farther between. He died in 1981, creatively and spiritually bankrupt, having disinherited his children and alienated his friends.

What went wrong? "Was it loss?" Leggett asks. "Had the bright bird of his talent flown away into the war clouds of 1941? Or was it the form? Were the novel's demands for structure, character, and patience too much for his impulsive skills? Or was it the times? Had these earlier triumphs been relatively simple ones—his own youthful concept of self as a heroic, disenfranchised David taking on the Goliath of an inhibiting, misleading, establishment-ridden society?" The answer, of course, is all three. But there is also a fourth reason: a fatal limitation in talent and vision that was already present when he was at the height of his powers. As Brooks Atkinson, Saroyan's hardest and most perceptive critic, remarked, nowhere in Saroyan's plays is there a single "instance of a love that is a union and represents a surrender of self. As an egoist Mr. Saroyan may not know that such a thing exists but as an artist he ought to take it on faith." Only Saroyan's self was real to him: the rest of the world he saw, and portrayed, as a series of caricatures.

The Dishonorable Schoolboy

Novelists who achieve a cult status write, by definition, for a narrow and usually specialist readership, and while their books are not for everyone, they attract certain passionate partisans. One cult figure, the English novelist, journalist, and television writer Simon Raven (1927–2001), did not reach a mass audience or even attain a very broad readership among the upper middle class and the intelligentsia; but then, he never exerted himself very far to do so. "I've always written for a small audience consisting of people like myself," he remarked, "who are well-educated, worldly, skeptical and snobbish (meaning that they rank good taste over bad). And who believe that nothing and nobody is special."

"People like myself": there are few of them left, for Raven was one of a breed that was dying in his youth and is now all but extinct. Not that well-educated, worldly, skeptical, and snobbish people have entirely disappeared, only that Raven's own type is no longer to be seen: his was not an earnest agnosticism but a robust eighteenth-century paganism. A civilized man should, he believed, "reject both enthusiasms and faiths, if only because of the ridiculous postures, whether mental or physical, which they require." This philosophy was allied with a deep contempt for the egalitarian moral code of post–World War II

England with its namby-pamby unwillingness to offend. He himself suffered from no such diffidence.

Raven's offensiveness did not grow from bile or melancholy but from extreme high spirits. From earliest youth he reveled in the role of outrageous provocateur and exuded what one of his school contemporaries, Gerald Priestland, recalled as a "Luciferian aura." "Brilliant when he could be bothered, handsomely copper-headed but with a world-weary slouch and drawl, [he] moved through Charterhouse trailing an odour of brimstone." Noël Annan felt him to be one of the rare "liberators" some of us are lucky enough to encounter during our lives: "Simon was one of those very assured undergraduates who by their example liberate their contemporaries from the shackles of family, school or class."

Raven was the author of thirty-four books (as well as many radio and television plays, essays, and reviews), but his reputation today rests almost entirely on his ten-volume *roman-fleuve*, *Alms for Oblivion* (1964–1976). His undertaking has inevitably been compared with Anthony Powell's *A Dance to the Music of Time*, dealing as it does with the same social milieu (but a generation younger), and touching on the same themes of time and mutability.

> I wanted to look at the upper-middle-class scene since the war, and in particular my generation's part in it. We had spent our early years as privileged members of a privileged class. How were we faring in the Age of the Common Man? How *ought* we to be faring?. . . Would the high-minded lot stoop to conquer?. . . And what about their unscrupulous confrères? No Queensberry rules for them, so they had a flying start. But Fate has a way of bitching things up just when you least expect it.

Many of *Alms for Oblivion*'s protagonists attended the same public school, served in the same regiment (the dashing and aristocratic Earl Hamilton's Light Dragoons), and read Classics or History in a more or less desultory manner at the same Cambridge college (Lancaster, a thinly disguised version of King's). The novels, which, unlike Powell's, jump back and forth in time, take the characters from school (*Fielding Gray*, 1967) to the army (*Sound the Retreat*, 1971, and *The Sabre Squadron*, 1966), the "corridors of power" (*The Rich Pay Late*, 1964, and *Friends in Low Places*, 1965), scenes of international intrigue (*The Judas Boy*, 1968), student unrest during the sixties (*Places Where They Sing*, 1970), the movie business and an excursion into American Philistia (*Come Like Shadows*, 1972), and finally to nemesis and impending age (*Bring Forth the Body*, 1974, and *The Survivors*, 1976).

English *romans-fleuve* of the last century have tended to be elegiac, for obvious reasons. The horror of World War I, the breakdown of traditional society during the interwar years, and its complete reinvention during the postwar period were deeply traumatic to the upper middle class from whose ranks so many serious novelists came. Siegfried Sassoon's and Ford Madox Ford's novel sequences record that trauma with bleak eloquence. *A Dance to the Music of Time* subtly, and Evelyn Waugh's *Sword of Honour* rather less subtly, lamented the end of what their authors perceived as a stable social order. Simon Raven tried, intermittently, to be elegiac too, for he bitterly regretted the decay of the ritualistic, male-oriented society in which he grew up and to whose institutions—public school, army, cricket, university—he was romantically attached.

But Raven was a little too cynical to pull off an affecting elegy. He was the Petronius of his generation, a cold-blooded satirist whose characters were compilations of various appetites and ambitions rather than living beings: if his novels were to be represented graphically, they would perhaps constitute a crude, cartoonish, somewhat pornographic decorative frieze rather than having the Poussinesque melancholy of Powell's elegant books. And the resemblance to Petronius extends to the personal as well as the literary, with Tacitus's description of the author of the *Satyricon* perfectly applicable to the unregenerate Raven: "By his dissolute life he had become as famous as other men by a life of energy, and he was regarded as no ordinary profligate, but as an accomplished voluptuary. His feckless freedom of speech, being regarded as frankness, procured him popularity."

Simon Raven occasionally wrote about his life, most notably in *Shadows on the Grass* (1981), a memoir which has the dubious distinction of being, in the opinion of E. W. Swanton, "the filthiest book on cricket" ever written. ("Can I quote you on that, Jim?" Raven asked eagerly.) But even more delightful is Michael Barber's *The Captain: The Life and Times of Simon Raven* (1996), a wonderfully hilarious biography which is, rather sadly, better than anything Raven himself ever wrote. But since the persistence of the Raven cult is due more to Raven's personality than to his gifts, which were beguiling but minor, this is acceptable, and Barber more than does his subject justice. His affection for the disreputable writer is obvious, and it is impossible for his reader not to share it, for Raven, for all his vaunted snobbery, intolerance, and amorality, was essentially a sweet man.

Simon Arthur Noël Raven was the grandson of a Victorian industrialist who had made a fortune in the manufacture of socks. His father, Arthur, lived off this fortune and frittered it away over the course of his life until there was very little left for Simon and his two younger siblings. Raven describes his childhood as "middle-class, for which read respectable, prying, puritanical, penny-pinching, joyless."

His intelligence and precocious facility with the classical languages was evident very early, and he won the top scholarship to Charterhouse, where his academic success continued. Raven never ceased to be grateful for his classical education, which imparted not only a tremendous verbal facility, thanks to constant exercises in translation, but a comprehensive and multilayered worldview. The upper layer, a schoolmaster's version of Hellenism that was propagated in the public schools, Raven described in the following manner:

> First, the truth must be sought honestly and with intelligence on every level, and must be prized above convenience and even perhaps above freedom itself, because it is not made by man but exists independently of him. . . . One comes at the truth by logic, patience, and fairmindedness. From which it follows, by extension, that one should always be *moderate*. . . . With moderation comes tolerance. . . . Being free meant that you were not '*servile*,' i.e. that subject to the general good you did not have to do anything against your will and must not, as a point of honor, do anything for monetary gain. . . . Pericles . . . expressed stern views about women: They should be heard of, he said, neither for good nor ill. . . . [T]he Greeks strongly disapproved of inflated pride. . . . They took the view that anyone who became too pleased with himself or thought himself too clever would be punished by the gods with disgrace and ruin. (From *The Decline of the Gentleman*, 1961)

This simplified and sanitized Hellenism was developed for the purpose of civilizing crass public schoolboys, and designed to harmonize with Christianity: the Greeks were presented as proto-Christians, lacking only the knowledge of Christ to make them perfect. But there were layers beneath layers, and to those with sufficient intellect and curiosity the classical authors also delivered an unsanitized, definitely un- and anti-Christian message, entirely subversive of public school values; Raven sucked this up greedily.

> Here was Horace, openly boasting of how he ran away from a battle. Tacitus, quietly equating enthusiasm with stupidity. Thucydides, grimly announcing that the only law of human affairs was 'Necessity.' Lucretius, recommending regular one-night stands as a way of securing immunity from passion, which was simply the unwholesome and ridiculous product of suppressed or thwarted lust. Catullus, advocating sex with women or sex with boys, whichever you fancy at the time, because there is no such thing as right or wrong in this context. . . . *All*

of them insistent that you take what pleasure you can from this world because only superstitious fools believe in the existence of the next.

Both versions of Hellenism were to mold his character. He remained, from school days on, doggedly pagan, "ready," as he put it, "to back Greek reason against 'revealed truth' any day of the week." In all his novels he honored Greek themes—the irresistible forces of Retribution and Necessity are often given a central position, and he did not underestimate the power of the Furies—and understood that the gods must be placated; but he had little use for God the Father or His putative son: "Christ asked for everything he got," remarks Captain Detterling, one of the many characters in *Alms for Oblivion* who tend to serve as mouthpieces for the author's own thoughts. The best Raven was ever to say of Christianity was that Anglicanism at any rate is "a quiet and decent superstition, as they go, offering a wide choice in decoration and no poisonous enthusiasms."

Raven was a brilliant schoolboy but in no way a model one, for he took the advice of Lucretius and Catullus rather more literally than his masters would have liked. Sexually he had catholic tastes, no inhibitions whatever, and scant respect for the moral code imposed by the school. He made countless conquests among the other boys and enjoyed "a number of experiences," as he later boasted, "far more erotic (and poetic) than the perfunctory grabbing and snatching and jerking depicted on Greek vases." Raven's school adventures are related in *Fielding Gray*, the most autobiographical novel in *Alms for Oblivion*, but X-rated as the novel is, the reality seems to have been even more so. In the end even the tolerance of Charterhouse's long-suffering headmaster was exhausted, and Raven, though he had won his First XI Cricket colors and a scholarship to King's, was expelled.

For a few weeks, he said, he felt "like Adam and Eve did when they had to do a proper day's work." Like his alter ego Fielding Gray, he had hoped and expected to become "a wining and dining don. A witty, worldly, *comfortable* don." Would Cambridge still have him? He was now to learn one of the most important lessons of his life: "I got a commission, joined clubs and took up my place at King's as if nothing had happened. People just giggled when they learnt I'd been sacked for 'the usual thing.' . . . One trembled in fear of the last trump and all that sounded was a wet fart."

With his compulsory term of military service impending, Raven joined the Parachute Regiment and was soon shipped to Bangalore as an officer cadet. In this capacity Raven set the pattern for his later behavior as an officer in the regular army: "He had this romantic, Edwardian view of what being a subaltern entailed," said Raven's Charterhouse and army friend James Prior (later Lord Prior, longtime cabinet minister under Margaret Thatcher and the model for *Alms for Oblivion*'s opportunistic Peter Morrison). "It was vital to look the part—carry a swagger stick and wear kid gloves. . . . You were there to lead your platoon over the top in the event of a fight. Otherwise, it was a case of 'Carry on, sergeant.'"

But it was 1947 and the Raj was winding up its business in undignified haste: "One got a crash course in the sudden fall of Imperial greatness," Raven remarked. It was a richly symbolic historical moment at which Raven was given a ringside seat, and the novel it produced, *Sound the Retreat*, is the finest volume of *Alms for Oblivion*: full of irony, compassion (a rare quality in Raven's work), and featuring the strongest and most memorable character in the sequence, the colorful Muslim officer Gilzai Khan.

Raven duly took his place at King's in 1948. The postwar climate was anti-elitist and leveling, rife with progressive dogma, and King's was particularly "pink" in shade; one might have thought that Raven, with his rapidly hardening conservative attitudes, would have rebelled. Yet as he acknowledged, the college's very pinkness presented distinct advantages to himself: "Nobody minded what you did in bed or what you said about God, a very civilized attitude in 1948."

Raven was undiscriminating in his sexual tastes, and Cambridge offered these more scope than Charterhouse had done: one disgruntled Newnham girl was overheard saying, "I'm not going to bed with Simon ever again. One day it's Boris, then a choral scholar, then it's me, then it's back to Boris again. No!" Raven was a promiscuous bisexual who on balance favored boys and young men over women: he admitted to Michael Barber that he "never really cared for straight fucking because you can't see your willy." Nevertheless he managed to knock up a recent graduate, Susan Kilner.

This was a potential disaster, for he prized his independence above everything else. (Two of his early novels, *Doctors Wear Scarlet*, 1960, and *Close of Play*, 1962, feature characters who take this desperate need for personal independence to violent extremes.) So, as Raven remembers it, "I said, 'Right ho, I'll marry you. That'll keep your family happy. But I won't live with you—ever.' Very caddish of me, I agree. But I knew, you see, that if ever there were a born bachelor, it was me. And Susan accepted this. She was a brick." Although he kept in touch with Susan and their son, Adam, for the rest of his life, and would eventually foot the bill for Adam's education, they did not seriously impinge on his resolutely single life.

At the end of his undergraduate career Raven was awarded the studentship (that is, graduate fellowship) he coveted. But extended scholarly endeavor turned out, perhaps not surprisingly, to go against his nature. "Scholarship was one thing, drudgery another. I very soon concluded that nothing would induce me to read, let alone make notes on, hundreds and hundreds of *very, very, very* boring books."

How then to make a living? Raven was by now earning a small income reviewing books for the *Listener*, under the aegis of the legendary J. R. Ackerley, but his first novel had been rejected, business ("money-grubbing") was beyond the social pale, and schoolmastering was impossible, "because I was on every blacklist in existence." He ended up joining the regular army with back-dated seniority, attaching himself to the smart King's Own Shropshire Light Infantry.

Raven spent three years in the army, serving in Germany (his experiences there would go into *The Sabre Squadron*) and in Kenya against the Mau Mau (a conflict which, fictionalized, became the backdrop for his first novel, *The Feathers of* Death, 1959). He looked at the British army, even in its decline, in a highly romantic light: "although there was more in him of Alcibiades than Achilles," comments Barber, "he retained a sentimental attachment to the Homeric ideal."

It became rapidly apparent that he was far too lazy to make a decent field commander. "I loved the Army as an institution and loathed every single thing it required me to do," he later said. A brother officer remembers that "Captain Raven settled down to organize his life, believing that ability to delegate authority was the true mark of a leader of men. He speedily delegated 100% of his." His most significant achievements were to effect an improvement in the food, and to set up "a rough and ready knocking shop" for the men. A middle-class man trying to lead an upper-class life, he ran up massive debts and had to leave the army hurriedly: he would later recreate his ejection from the cozy regiment into a cold world in his 1959 novel *Brother Cain*.

"And so, at the age of thirty," Raven wrote in *The Decline of the Gentleman* (1961), "I had successively disgraced myself with three fine institutions, each of which had made me free of its full and rich resources, had trained me with skill and patience, and had shown me nothing but forbearance and charity when I failed in trust." He now fell back on his last resource: writing. "For in a literary career there was one unfailing advantage: No degree whatever of moral or social disgrace could disqualify one from practice—and indeed a bad character, if suitably tricked out for presentation, might win one helpful publicity."

He embarked on a rackety, hand-to-mouth Grub Street life, described fairly faithfully in the early career of Tom Llewellyn, the unwashed intellectual in *Alms for Oblivion.* He enjoyed some success, but his weakness for gambling, drinking, and overeating quickly took control of his life, and physical deterioration followed apace. J. R. Ackerley provides a memorable portrait of the prematurely aging Raven:

> A disaster has happened to him, I fear [Ackerley informed E. M. Forster]; he has got plump. His one-time crowning glory, that abundant Titian hair, crinkles thinly and gingerly now above a fat pink face, with creases of fat about the eyes. . . . Suede boots, and a loose, short, shapeless, not very clean camel-hair coat—or wd it be called duffle? He looked like the kind of person who asks for a light in the Long Bar of the Trocadero and to whom one replies with only a regretful mutter as one edges away. . . . He has his intelligence still, and indeed his charm and warmth of manner, but I did not accompany him to his homosexual club.

Raven seemed set on a course of complete self-destruction, but salvation now appeared in the guise of his publisher, Anthony Blond. "This is the last hand-out you get," Blond told him. "Leave London, or leave my employ." Blond offered his feckless client generous terms: if he would move at least fifty miles from London, Blond would pay him a steady £15 and settle the following bills: dentist, tailor, nightly dinner at a restaurant and, within reason, wine merchant. Raven obeyed without a moment's hesitation, moving to Deal, in Kent, where his brother Myles was teaching at a preparatory school. He was, to his own surprise, immediately happy.

The removal from London revealed a surprising side to Raven's character: the steady worker. The rake who lived for pleasure disappeared and was replaced by a worker bee of extremely regular habits. He would write all morning, read in the afternoons, dine at a nearby hotel, and spend the evening at the local pub with Myles and his schoolmaster friends. Under this regimen he produced a huge quantity of work.

His motto was "Art for art's sake, money for God's sake," and not all of his large output was of the highest quality. He took on the daunting task of producing a second *roman-fleuve* for instance, *The First-Born of Egypt*, only for financial reasons. It was a continuation, of sorts, of *Alms for Oblivion*, but Raven had long since run out of ideas and material and was excruciatingly bored during the writing process ("How can I go on with this?" he frequently asked himself. "Please God, let me win a football pool"); the boredom shows, badly, in the final product. But somewhere along the way Raven had acquired a professional attitude, and his television plays, notably the BBC adaptation of Trollope's *Palliser* novels and other adaptations of books by Iris Murdoch, Nancy Mitford, and Aldous Huxley, were very fine indeed. He possessed in fact a natural gift for adaptation, a technical skill he likened to translating in and out of Latin.

In middle age he preferred, by his own admission, "a good dinner to a good fuck." When in funds he enjoyed treating his friends to expensive meals, paying the bill with a flourish: when out of them he never economized *too* radically. A friend remembers him, in dire straits, saying "Well, dear, I'm going to be hellish mean. I'm not going to take anyone out to dinner." "What about you?" said the friend. "Are you going to go on taking yourself out to dinner?" "Oh yes, dear, I'm not going to be *miserly*."

Raven spent his last years in Sutton's Hospital, an almshouse for impoverished old gentlemen, long connected with Charterhouse, which gave precedence to "decrepit or old Captaynes either at Sea or Land" and "Souldiers maymed or ympotent." It was hard to get a place there, and although at this point Raven was certainly "ympotent," he was neither decrepit nor maimed. But he managed to talk his way in, and so ended his days contentedly enough, in yet another all-male club.

Although he readily and even happily admitted to being no gentleman, Raven revered the gentleman as an ideal and mourned his passing, for the modern age, he believed, had rejected the gentleman and everything he represented. "Gentlemen can now only behave as such, or be tolerated as such, in circumstances that are manifestly contrived or unreal," he asserted in *The Decline of the Gentleman*: in anachronistically hierarchical institutions, that is, like the military.

He illustrates this contention in the career of Peter Morrison, one of the protagonists of *Alms for Oblivion*. Morrison has all the trappings of the gentleman, certainly. The eldest son of an old East Anglia family, Morrison inherits substantial estates, distinguishes himself in the Indian army at the time of independence, enjoys a happy and monogamous marriage, and serves for many years as a Conservative M.P., eventually becoming minister of commerce. Yet he is subtly, without even knowing it himself, a hypocrite and an opportunist, and always manages to further his own interests while leaving his "honour"—a flexible term in his case, as in most of ours—intact. "Oh, he likes to do the right thing, observes Detterling; ". . . to be seen to do the right thing, and even to believe it himself, if he possibly can. But he's got a lot of shit in his tanks."

Morrison's antipode is the Machiavellian journalist and politician Somerset Lloyd-James (thought by many readers to resemble Raven's former schoolfellow Lord Rees-Mogg). Lloyd-James also comes from a "good" family and has received a gentleman's education, but unlike Morrison he feels no obligation to uphold the gentleman's creed: he is openly unscrupulous and grasping, relishing the brute struggle for power and influence. A practicing Catholic, he habitually resorts to Jesuitical casuistry in dubious justification of whatever shady deal he might have in mind at the moment.

In their early thirties the two men compete for the Conservative candidacy for the Parliamentary seat of Bishop's Cross. Morrison is in every way the superior candidate—*apparently*: three years previously, during the Suez crisis, he had resigned from Parliament because, while he disapproved of the government's actions, he didn't want to show a lack of support for the army, to which he remained loyal. It was a complicated matter of personal conscience, in other words, surely commendable, showing rare delicacy in a politician. But while Morrison congratulates himself, others can see behind the façade of high principle. Fielding Gray castigates Morrison as "a pompous, self-satisfied prig. All this prate about duty and honour and loyalty, and not a row of beans to show for it." Sir Edwin Turbot, a Whitehall power broker, opines that "Lloyd-James is pretty foul, I grant you that. But he does things. He doesn't sit around moaning about his honour." And the political grandee Lord Canteloupe, one of Raven's finest and most robust creations, frankly prefers working with a "howling shit" like Lloyd-James: "For the great thing about shits," he reflects, "was that they got on with it (provided the price was right) and didn't ask damn silly questions."

Idealism and realism are at war throughout *Alms for Oblivion*, with Raven reserving all the heavy artillery for use against idealism. ("Idealists are far more dangerous than criminals," says the mathematician Daniel Mond, the only character in *Alms for Oblivion* who can be said to represent the Good. "Criminals stop when they've got what they wanted. Idealists never stop because they can never attain their ideal.") Lord Canteloupe, the personification of appetite and greed, is the series' great realist, for better and for worse. He makes his first appearance in *Friends in Low Places*: having turned the grounds of his Stately Home into a profitable theme park, in the manner of the Duke of Bedford, he receives an offer to advise the government on a project for morally uplifting public entertainment. His ideas on the subject are worth quoting:

> "Now what about this? Government-sponsored caravan sites for holidays. Make a filthy mess of some well-known beauty spot—they'll love that—and then publish a lot of balls about The People

> enjoying its Rights in the Countryside, that kind of blab. Jam the bloody caravans as close together as possible—you know how they love being crowded—make a song and dance about being good neighbors, give a prize for the best behaved family, and perhaps throw in compulsory P.T."

Lord Canteloupe is manifestly *not* a gentleman: he is an aristocrat, a class for which Raven shows little mercy. "Whereas the gentleman always seeks to deserve his position," Raven observed, "the aristocrat, disdainful and insouciant, is quite happy just to exploit it." A rare (and refreshing) bird among conservative English authors of the last century, Raven displayed no romantic nostalgia for an aristocracy in picturesque decline.

Alms for Oblivion contains quite a number of selfish aristocrats, like Canteloupe, and pseudo-gentlemen, like Morrison: what it does *not* contain are very many *real* gentlemen. In fact these are so thin on the ground that one is tempted to wonder whether in Raven's scheme of things the genuine article actually exists or is, instead, merely an intellectual abstraction. A few characters fit the bill in the moral sense, but none of them, significantly, is an *English* gentleman in the traditional sense: Daniel Mond, a Jew; the Muslim Gilzai Khan; Tom Llewellyn, of lowly Welsh origins; Piero, a teenaged Italian prostitute. Fielding Gray, who claims to live by the code of officer and gentleman, is far too tainted a character to qualify as the latter.

Raven's *Weltanschauung*—what one friend called his "Regency, cynical, materialistic outlook"—made for some fine comedy, but its limitations became evident when something more was called for—real emotion or strength. He always maintained that his classical education had inoculated him against love. He was probably right, but the resulting immunity did not always work to his advantage. The lack of love harms his writing: all his books share a tiresome coarseness and a tendency to sentiment. No one in all the enormous cast of *Alms for*

Oblivion is the least bit emotionally affecting, except for the gallant and witty Gilzai Khan. As for the female characters, they are all of one type, the slavering nymphomaniac: Raven's was a man's world, and he could see women only as unwelcome intruders.

At one point in the sequence Raven has Fielding Gray articulate his professional creed.

> "I never said I was an artist. I am an entertainer. . . . I arrange words in pleasing patterns in order to make money. I try to give good value—to see that my patterns are well wrought—but I do not delude myself by inflating the nature of my function. I try to be neat, intelligent and lucid: let others be 'creative' or 'inspired.'

Is this how Raven saw his own writerly task? For the philosophy is spurious, of course: entertainers, if they are any good, must also be artists, and a lack of creativity or inspiration is just as fatal to their results as it would be to a more artistic (*un*entertaining?) writer. Raven too often makes the reader feel that he is simply setting up some formal and hypothetical situation and then inserting his characters into it.

Michael Barber compared Raven's work with a ball at Versailles: "all that pomp and glitter and finery while the chamber pots overflow in every corner." Raven's fascination with smut for its own sake is undoubtedly entertaining, but in the end it contributed to the work's one-dimensionality. His friend Christopher Moorson thought the novels were like a weird combination of Henty and Huysmans. "Reading these," he observed to Anthony Blond, "is like eating your way through a cake which is made of chestnuts, and covered with layers of cream and treacle." To which Blond replied: "Yes, *and* covered with shit, my dear."

Index

Account of Corsica (Boswell), 46
Ackerley, J. R., 226; on Simon Raven, 228
Agee, James: on William Saroyan, 213
All the Year Round, 136, 138
Alms for Oblivion (Raven), 220, 224, 228, 229, 230, 231, 232, 233
Ambassadors, The (James): 173; and Constance Fenimore Woolson, 174
American culture: provincialism of, 192; self-satisfaction of, 192
Among the Porcupines (Matthau), 216
Andersen, Hans Christian, x, 80; background of, 81, 82; death of, 86; and fairy tales, 84; influence of, 86; literary career of, 83; as outsider, 84; personal life, 85; schooling of, 83; traits of, 85; writing of, 84, 85
Annan, Noël: on Simon Raven, 220
Annotated Wizard of Oz, The (Hearn), 180
Ann Vickers (Lewis), 203
Antonina: or the Fall of Rome (Collins), 134
Armadale (Collins), 127, 139
Arrowsmith (Lewis), 197, 201, 202
Arvin, Newton, 98
Atkinson, Brooks: on William Saroyan, 218
Auchinleck, Lord, 44
Austen family: Cassandra, 72, 74; Charles, 72: Francis, 72; George, 72; Henry, 72, 79; James, 72
Austen, Jane, ix, 79, 194; appeal of, 66; assessment of, 66, 67, 68, 69; background of, 72; celebrity of, 73; family of, 72; and film adaptations, 65, 71; genius of, 75; and irony, 69, 70; kindness of, 77; letters of, 71, 72, 73, 74, 75, 76, 78; novels, themes of, 75, 76; sentiment, dislike of, 76; wit of, 77, 78; writing, as private activity, 72, 73

Babbitt (Lewis), 197, 199, 200–201, 208
Barber, Michael, 222, 226, 233
Basil (Collins), 135
Baum, L. Frank, 177, 178; background of, 179; career of, 179, 180; cultural relativism, importance of, 182–183; diversity, value of, 183; as feminist, 179; marriage of, 179; and

Baum, L. Frank (*cont.*)
philosophical questions, 180, 181; reputation of, 182; and romantic love, 181
Baum, Maud, 179
Beauties of Sterne, The (Sterne), 23
Beckett, Samuel, 24, 186
Bennett, Arnold: on Sinclair Lewis, 200
Bentley, Richard, 134
Bentley's Miscellany, 134
Besant, Walter, 141
Big Money (Dos Passos), 184
Billings, Richard N., 185
Birch, Jane, 8, 14
Blind Love (Collins), 141
Blithedale Romance, The (Hawthorne), 99, 101
Blond, Anthony, 228, 233
Booth, Wayne, 32
Boswell, Euphemia, 43
Boswell, James, xi, 20; background of, 44, 45; death of, 48; image of, 36, 37; and Samuel Johnson, 39, 40; law career of, 45; and mental illness, 43, 44; reputation, as artist, 42; and Rousseau, visit to, 39; on Laurence Sterne, 30; technique of, 38, 40, 41; traits of, 37, 38; writings of, 40, 46, 47, 48
Boswell, John, 43
Boswell's Presumptuous Task: The Making of the Life of Dr. Johnson (Sisman), 40
Boys and Girls Together (Saroyan), 217
Bring Forth the Body (Raven), 221
Brook Farm, 101
Brookfield, Jane, 115, 120
Brother Cain (Raven), 227
Browning, Tod, 153
Buchan, John, 145, 149
Burckhardt, Sigurd, 34, 35
Burke, Edmund, 58, 60, 61, 62
Burney, Fanny, 66, 73
Byron: Child of Passion, Fool of Fame (Eisler), 90
Byron: The Flawed Angel (Grosskurth), 90
Byron: Life and Legend (MacCarthy), 90
Byron, Lord, xi, 48; appeal of, 96; background of, 94; celebrity, thirst for, 88, 89; empathy, gift for, 95; fascination with, 90; and homosexual relations, 90, 91, 92, 93; as libertine, 88; mood swings of, 94–95; and John Murray II, correspondence between, 90; paradoxical character of, 94; personality of, 94; poems of, 96, 97; public image of, 88, 91; on Richard Brinsley Sheridan, 49, 62; as symbol, 87; women, relations with, 91, 92
By Sheer Pluck: A Tale of the Ashanti War (Henty), 143

Calvino, Italo: on Laurence Sterne, 24
Captain: The Life and Times of Simon Raven, The (Barber), 222
Carlyle, Thomas, 48; on William Thackeray, 123
Carmichael-Smyth, Henry, 108, 109
Carmilla (Le Fanu), 170
Cass Timberland (Lewis), 203
Catcher in the Rye, The (Salinger), 150
Catherine (Thackeray), 113
Cerf, Bennett, 211, 213–214
Chalandritsanos, Lukas, 93
Chapman, R. W., 71
Charles I, 7, 10
Charles II, 5, 10, 16
Chesterton, G. K.: on William Thackeray, 118–119

Children's literature, 143, 144, 151
Close of Play (Raven), 226
Collin, Edvard, 84, 85, 86
Collin, Jonas, 82
Collins, Charles Allston, 132, 134
Collins, Harriet, 133, 134
Collins, Wilkie, 155; and Balzac, 129; bohemian lifestyle of, 125, 126; death of, 141; and Dickens, friendship with, 129, 134, 135; egotism of, 127; as father, 127; humor, use of, 137; kindness of, 142; law, study of, 133; marriage, dislike of, 126; and modern detective novel, 128; moral vision of, 131; as nonconformist, 133; painting, study of, 132; as playwright, 140; pleasure, love of, 125; and political interests, 141; schooling of, 133; writing, description of, 128, 129
Collins, William, 131, 132, 133
Come Like Shadows (Raven), 221
Cooper, James Fenimore, 151
Cornhill (magazine), 122, 138, 139
Covent Garden Theater (London), 55, 56
Cowley, Malcolm: on *Main Street*, 191
Critic, The (Sheridan), 49, 50, 57, 58
Cromwell, Oliver, 6, 8
Cumberland, Richard, 49

Daisy Miller (James), 174
Dance to the Music of Time, A (Powell), 220, 221
The Daring Young Man on the Flying Trapeze (Saroyan), 213
Dark Shadows (tv show), 170
Dash for Khartoum: A Tale of the Nile Expedition, A (Henty), 143
Davis, Stuart: and Gerald Murphy, influence on, 188
Dead Secret, The (Collins), 135
Decline of the Gentleman, The (Raven), 223, 224, 227, 230
Denis Duval (Thackeray), 122
Diary (Pepys), 3, 4, 7, 9, 10, 12, 16, 17; importance of, 5; popularity of, 19
Dickens, Charles, 23, 48, 66, 138, 139; and *Bentley's Miscellany*, 134; and Wilkie Collins, friendship with, 129, 134, 135; death of, 136, 140; and William Thackeray, 105
Doctors Wear Scarlet (Raven), 226
Dodsworth (Lewis), 202, 203
Doll's House, A (Ibsen), 206
Donnelly, Honoria Murphy, 185
Don Juan (Byron), 89, 96
Dracula (film), 153
Dracula (Stoker), 158, 159, 162, 163; *Athenaeum*, review in, 155; description of, 164, 165, 166, 167, 168; as feminist novel, 169; film rights to, 164; format of, 155; humor in, 157, 158; meanings of, 154; as modern myth, 153; moral of, 168; and *Nosferatu*, 164; plot of, 156, 157; and popular imagination, 153, 154; sexuality, attitude toward, 168; success of, 153; traditional Christianity, as inversion of, 169, 170; vampire, figure of, 170; and vampire tradition, 170
Draper, Elizabeth, 32
Dreiser, Theodore, 204, 205
Drury Lane Theater (London), 56, 63
Duenna, The (Sheridan), 49, 56
Duncannon, Harriet, 61, 62, 63

Edgeworth, Maria, 66, 73
Edleston, John, 91
Eisler, Benita, 88, 90
Elmer Gantry (Lewis), 197, 202

Emma (Austen), 68, 73
"Emperor's New Clothes, The," 80, 85
Evelyn, John, 3
Eventyr, Fortale for Born, Forste Hefte (*Fairy Tales, Told for Children, First Volume*) (Andersen), 83
Everybody Was So Young (Vaill), 184
Evil Genius, The (Collins), 141

Fairy tales, 83
Fanshawe (Hawthorne), 100
Feathers of Death, The (Raven), 227
Fielding Gray (Raven), 221, 224
Fielding, Joseph, 66
"Fir Tree, The," 80, 85
First-Born of Egypt, The (Raven), 229
Fitzgerald, Edward, 61
Fitzgerald, F. Scott, 184, 186, 187, 188, 189
Fitzgerald, Zelda, 187
Fitzherbert, Maria, 59
Forster, E. M., 23, 65, 66
Forster, John, 130, 131, 134
Fourmantel, Catherine, 29, 32
Fox, Charles James, 49, 58, 59, 62
Frankenstein (Shelley), 155
Friends in Low Places (Raven), 221, 231–232
Fuller, Margaret, 98, 101

Gage, Matilda Joslyn, 179
Gage, Maud. *See* Maud Baum
Garland, Hamlin, 204, 205, 208
Garrick, David, 29, 56, 161
George IV (Prince of Wales), 58, 59, 63
Gibbon, Edward, 37, 60
Goncharova, Natalia, 188
Gordon, George. *See* Lord Byron
Gordon, Lyndall, 171, 172, 175
Graves, Caroline, 125, 126, 136
Great Hoggarty Diamond, The (Thackeray), 116
Greenmantle (Buchan), 149
Grimm, Jacob and Wilhelm, 83
Grosskurth, Phyllis, 90
Guiccioli, Teresa, 91, 92, 94

Hastings, Warren, 59, 60
Hawthorne (Wineapple), 104
Hawthorne, Nathaniel: as artist, 100; background of, 100; at Brook Farm, 101; career of, 102; character of, 99; on Civil War, 103; contrarian, reputation as, 103; Liverpool, consulship to, 103; and money worries, 102; negativity of, 98; as outsider, 103; short stories of, 100, 101
Heart and Science (Collins), 141
Hegger, Grace Livingston. *See* Grace Lewis
Heine, Heinrich, 85, 87
Hemingway, Ernest, 184, 186, 187, 189, 190, 203; on Sinclair Lewis, 204
Henty, G. A., 143; and Christian home-schooling market, 149, 150, 152; evenhandedness of, 146; historical knowledge, breadth of, 148; influence of, 144, 145; irony, lack of, 148; as journalist, 151; writing, descriptions of, 145, 146, 147, 150
Here Comes, There Goes You Know Who (Saroyan), 217
Herold, J. Christopher, 74
Hide and Seek (Collins), 135
History of Henry Esmond, The (Thackeray), 121
Hobhouse, John Cam, 91, 93, 96
Holiday (Barry), 184
Honan, Park, 68

House of the Seven Gables, The (Hawthorne), 102
Household Words (magazine), 135, 136, 138
Huckleberry Finn (Twain): as racist, x
Hughes-Hallett, Penelope, 71
Hugo, Victor, 87
Human Comedy, The (Saroyan), 211, 212, 215
Hunt, Leigh, 96
Hunt, Marianne, 89

Ibsen, Henrik, 196, 197, 206
Imperial Germany and the Industrial Revolution (Veblen), 205
Indian Captive (Lenski), 144
In the Reign of Terror: The Adventures of a Westminster Boy (Henty), 148
Interpretation of Dreams, The (Freud), 164
Interview with the Vampire (Rice), 170
Invisible Man, The (Wells), 165
Irving, Henry, xi; death of, 163; and Bram Stoker, friendship with, 160, 161, 162
It Can't Happen Here (Lewis), 198, 203, 208

James II, 5, 10, 18
James, Henry, x, 66, 98; coldness of, 175; ego of, 171, 174; reputation of, 171; Minny Temple, relationship with, 172, 173, 176; Constance Fenimore Woolson, friendship with, 173, 174, 175, 176; work of, 172
Jefferson, Thomas: on Laurence Sterne, 33
Job, The (Lewis), 199
Johnson, Samuel, 27, 37, 38, 42, 43, 48; and James Boswell, 39, 40; death of, 47
Journal of a Tour to the Hebrides, The (Boswell), 46, 48
Joyce, James, 23, 66, 203, 204
Judas Boy, The (Raven), 221

King of Inventors, The (Peters), 131
Kingsblood Royal (Lewis), 203
Knight, Edward Austen, 72
Knight, Fanny, 69, 78
Knight of the White Cross, A (Henty), 144, 147
Kundera, Milan: on Laurence Sterne, 24

Lair of the White Worm, The (Stoker), 163
Lamb, Lady Caroline, 91, 92
Land of Oz, The (Baum), 183
Laurence Sterne: A Life (Ross), 24
Le Faye, Deirdre, 71
Léger, Fernand, 186, 187
Leggett, John, 210, 211, 214, 215, 217
Leigh, Augusta, 91, 92
Lenski, Lois, 144
Lewis, Edwin J., 195
Lewis, Grace ("Gracie"), 194, 198, 202; divorce of, 203
Lewis, Isabel, 195
Lewis, Sinclair, xi, 191, 205, 209; as atheist, 196; background of, 192, 195; career of, 198, 199; as celebrity, 200; death of, 204; divorce of, 203, 204; Theodore Dreiser, influence of, 204, 205; drinking of, 198, 202; education of, 196, 197; fundamental Christianity, dislike of, 196; Hamlin Garland, influence of, 205; in Greenwich Village, 197; at Helicon Hall, 197; inferiority complex of, 198; liberalism, belief in, 208; marriages

Lewis, Sinclair (*cont.*)
of, 198, 203; and Nobel Prize for Literature, 203; novels, themes of, 197, 198, 199; Pulitzer Prize, refusal of, 201–202; socialism of, 197; theater, discovery of, 196–197; travels of, 200; and *The Village Virus*, 193; on women's roles, 206; writings of, objections to, 204
Life of James Boswell, A (Martin), 42
Life of Johnson (Boswell), 40, 41, 44, 46, 47; popularity of, 48
Lighthouse, The (Collins), 135
Linley, Eliza. *See* Eliza Sheridan
"Little Claus and Big Claus," 83
"Little Mermaid, The," 80, 85
Lives of the Poets (Johnson), 47
Living Well Is the Best Revenge (Tomkins), 184–185
London Journal (Boswell), 40, 42
Longfellow, Henry Wadsworth, 99, 100
Lord Sandwich. *See* Edward Montagu
Luck of Barry Lyndon, The (Thackeray), 116
Lumley, Elizabeth. *See* Elizabeth Sterne

MacCarthy, Fiona, 90, 92, 93, 95
Macaulay, Thomas Babington, 36, 37
Main Street (Lewis), 197, 201, 204; discussion of, 205, 206, 207; influence of, 192; as national event, 191; origins of, 193, 194, 195; pertinence of, 208; success of, 191, 200; and wartime jingoism, 200, 205
Main-Traveled Roads (Garland), 205
Malone, Edmund, 37, 44, 47, 48
Mansfield Park (Austen), 70, 73
Marble Faun, The (Hawthorne), 102, 103
Marchant de St. Michel, Elizabeth. *See* Elizabeth Pepys
Marcus, Carol. *See* Carol Matthau
Martin, Peter, 42, 45
Marvelous Land of Oz, The (Baum), 180
Master of Ballantrae, The (Stevenson), 141, 165
Master Key: An Electrical Fairy Tale, The (Baum), 180
Mathews, Thomas, 53, 54
Matthau, Carol, 215, 216, 217
Memoirs of Miss Sidney Biddulph (Frances Sheridan), 51
Mencken, H. L., 198, 201, 206
Millbanke, Annabella, 91, 92
Miss Grief (Woolson), 174
Montagu, Edward, 6, 8, 9, 11, 15; death of, 17
Montagu, Elizabeth, 32
Montaigne, 3, 4
Moonstone, The (Collins), 125, 127, 128; description of, 139, 140; imitations of, 140
Morris, Jan, 151, 159
Mosses from an Old Manse (Hawthorne), 102
Mother Goose in Prose (Baum), 180
Moveable Feast, A (Hemingway), 189
Multiculturalism: failure of, 149
Murphy, Gerald, 184, 190; background of, 185; at Côte d'Azur, 186, 187; death of, 189; marriage of, 186, 189; in New York, 189; paintings of, 188; in Paris, 186; at Villa America, 186; and Sara Sherman Wiborg, 185
Murphy, Patrick, 188
Murphy, Sara, 184, 188; background of, 185; at Côte d'Azur, 186, 187; death of, 189; marriage of, 186, 189; and

Gerald Murphy, 185; in New York, 189; in Paris, 186
My Heart's in the Highlands (Saroyan), 214
My Name Is Aram (Saroyan), 211, 215

National Woman Suffrage Association, 179
"Naughty Boy, The," 84
Newcomes, The (Thackeray), 121, 122
"Nightingale, The," 85
No Name (Collins), 126, 127, 129, 131, 138, 139
Northanger Abbey (Austen), 70, 73, 75, 78, 194
Nosferatu (film), 164

Oates, Joyce Carol: on Jane Austen, 67, 68, 69
Obituaries (Saroyan), 217
Ogle, Esther Jane ("Hecca"). *See* Esther Sheridan
Our Mr. Wrenn (Lewis), 198
Our Old Home (Hawthorne), 103
Ozma of Oz (Baum), 182
Ozymandias (Shelley), 90

Peabody, Elizabeth, 99, 101
Peabody, Sophia, 101
Pendennis (Thackeray), 109
Pepys, Elizabeth, 8, 12, 15, 16; death of, 17; temper of, 13
Pepys, Samuel, 3; on adultery, 16, 19; affairs of, 14, 15, 17; death of, 18; career of, 16, 17, 18; education of, 6; as Everyman, 4; imprisonment of, 18; on monarchy, 10; playgoing of, 11; Puritanism, admiration for, 7; and Royal Navy, 17, 18; social progress of, 11; wife, relationship with, 13; Restoration London, 5; as self-made man, 6
Persuasion (Austen), 68, 73, 75
Peter Pan (Barrie), 165
Peters, Catherine, 108, 123, 131, 142
Picasso, Pablo, 184, 186, 187
Picture of Dorian Gray, The (Wilde), 165
Pierce, Franklin, 99, 100, 103
Pilgrimage of Childe Harold, The (Byron), 92, 96
Pitt, William (the Younger), 56, 58, 62
Pizarro (Sheridan), 62
Places Where I've Done Time (Saroyan), 217
Places Where They Sing (Raven), 221
Poe, Edgar Allan, 99, 128, 155
Political Romance, A, or The History of a Good Warm Watch-Coat (Sterne), 28
Portrait of a Lady, The (James), 174
Powell, Anthony, 220, 221
Pride and Prejudice (Austen), 66, 68, 69, 73
"Princess and the Pea, The," 83
Private Life of Henry James: Two Women and His Art, A (Gordon), 171
Punch (magazine), 116, 136

Queen Zixi of Ix (Baum), 180
Quennell, Peter, 94

Rambles Beyond Railways (Collins), 134
Raven, Arthur, 222
Raven, Myles, 228
Raven, Simon: adaptation, gift for, 229; aristocracy, disdain for, 232; background of, 222; childhood of, 222; cult status of, 219, 222; education of, 222, 223, 224, 226; emotion, lack of, 232, 233; female

Raven, Simon (*cont.*)
characters, portrayal of, 233; gentleman, as ideal, 229–230; Greek themes, admirer of, 223, 224; and idealism, 231; last years of, 229; literary career of, 226, 227, 228, 229; military service of, 225, 227; and one-dimensionality, 233; as pagan, 219, 224; and *Palliser* novels, 229; self-destruction of, 228; sexuality of, 224, 226; television plays of, 229; writings of, 221, 222, 232, 233
Redskin and Cowboy (Henty), 143
Reynolds, Joshua, 30, 37, 63
Richardson, Samuel, 20, 21, 51, 66
Rich Pay Late, The (Raven), 221
Rivals, The (Sheridan), 54, 55
Rogers, Katharine M., 178, 180

Sabre Squadron, The (Raven), 221, 227
Samuel Pepys: The Unequalled Self (Tomalin), 5, 19
Sara & Gerald: Villa America and After (Donnelly and Billings), 185
Saroyan, Aram, 216
Saroyan, Carol. *See* Carol Matthau
Saroyan, William, anti-Semitism of, 217; background of, 212; on Broadway, 214, 215; career of, 210, 211, 217, 218; debts of, 214; as egoist, 218; gambling sprees of, 214, 215; marriage of, 216, 217; paranoia of, 211, 216; personality of, 215–216; publishers, relationships with, 214; Pulitzer Prize, refusal of, 214; as self-destructive, 211; short stories of, 212–213; success of, 213
Scarecrow of Oz, The (Baum), 181
Scarlet Letter, The (Hawthorne), x, 98–99, 102
School for Scandal (Sheridan), 49, 56, 59; impact of, 57
Scott, Walter, 66, 151
Sense and Sensibility (Austen), 68, 70, 75
Sentimental Journey Through France and Italy, A (Sterne), 22, 33, 34
Seven Stories (Hawthorne), 100
Shadows on the Grass (Raven), 222
Shaw, George Bernard, 162, 196, 197, 207
Shawe, Isabella Gethin. *See* Isabella Thackeray
She (Haggard), 165
Shelley, Percy Bysshe, 88, 90, 97
Sheridan, Charles, 51, 53, 62
Sheridan, Eliza, 53, 61
Sheridan, Esther, 61, 62
Sheridan, Richard Brinsley, xi, 49, 64; affairs of, 61; and American War of Independence, 55, 56; background of, 50, 51, 52, 53; death of, 63; and French Revolution, 60, 61; and Drury Lane Theater, 56, 63; Warren Hastings, trial of, 59, 60; imprisonment of, 63; Irish identity of, 50, 56; marriages of, 53, 54, 61, 62; as orator, 59; political career of, 58, 62, 63; politics of, 61; Prince of Wales, relationship with, 58, 59, 63
Sinclair Lewis Avenue and Original Main Street (Sauk Centre, Minnesota), 204
Sinclair Lewis Boyhood Home (Sauk Centre, Minnesota), 204
Sisman, Adam, 40, 43, 44, 46, 48
Sky Island (Baum), 182
Smock Alley Theater (Dublin), 51
Snake's Pass, The (Stoker), 162
"Snow Queen, The," 80, 85

Snows of Kilimanjaro (Hemingway), 184
Sound the Retreat (Raven), 221, 225
Stanier-Clarke, James, 78
"Steadfast Tin Soldier, The," 85
Stegner, Wallace: on William Saroyan, 213
Stephen, Laura, 123
Stephen, Leslie, 123
Sterne, Elizabeth, 26, 29
Sterne, Jaques, 26, 27
Sterne, Laurence, 20, 34; admirers of, 23; background of, 24, 25; celebrity of, 30; as commercial writer, 31; death of, 33; ecclesiastical career of, 26, 28; education of, 26; infidelities of, 28, 29; influences on, 24; as journalist, 27; marriage of, 26, 27; on marriage, 27; private life of, 32; and Romanticism, 23
Sterne, Lydia, 27
Sterne, Richard, 25
Sterne, Roger, 24, 25
Stevenson, Robert Louis, 13, 18, 141, 151, 155, 164, 165; on Samuel Pepys, 3–4
Stoker, Bram, xi, 153, 155, 158, 170; background of, 160; death of, 163; as drama critic, 160; and humor, 157; Henry Irving, friendship with, 160, 161, 162; law, study of, 162; marriage of, 161; painterly eye of, 159; schooling of, 160; and Walt Whitman, 160
Stoker, Florence, 161, 164
Stoker, Noël, 161
Strange Case of Dr. Jekyll and Mr. Hyde, The (Stevenson), 141, 151, 155, 164
Street of the Hyacinth, The (Woolson), 174
Stuart, Charles, 8, 9
Survivors, The (Raven), 221
Swift, Jonathan, 22, 50
Sword of Honour (Waugh), 221

Tale of Two Cities, A (Dickens), 136
Tale of the Western Plains, A (Henty), 143
Taylor, D. J., 106, 108, 123
Temple, Minny: and Henry James, relationship with, 172, 173, 176
Tender Is the Night (Fitzgerald), 184, 187
Thackeray, Anne ("Anny"), 113, 114, 123
Thackeray, Harriet Marian ("Minny"), 113, 115, 116, 123
Thackeray, Isabella, 111, 112; mental illness of, 113, 114
Thackeray, William Makepeace, xi, 23, 48; background of, 108; and *Cornhill*, founding of, 122; death of, 122, 123; and Charles Dickens, 105; gambling of, 110; and gentlemanly detachment, 106, 107; health of, 120; marriage of, 112, 113; money worries of, 115, 116; passion, lack of, 107, 108; professional career of, 110, 111; and *Punch*, 116; schooling of, 109; struggles of, 115; theater, obsession with, 109; in United States, 121; university career of, 110; writing style of, 106, 107
Thackeray: A Writer's Life (Peters), 108
Thompson, Dorothy, 203, 204
Thrale, Hester, 27, 47
"Thumbelina," 84
Tiger of Mysore: A Story of the War with Tippoo Sahib, The (Henty), 143
Time Machine, The (Wells), 165
Time of Your Life, The (Saroyan), 214

"Tinderbox, The," 83, 84
Tin Woodman of Oz, The (Baum), 181
To Herat and Kabul (Henty), 149
Tomalin, Claire, 5, 7, 9, 12
Tomkins, Calvin, 184, 189
Trail of the Hawk, The (Lewis), 199
"Traveling Companion, The," 84
Trio (Aram Saroyan), 216
Tristram Shandy (Sterne), 23; 22, 28, 29, 32; bawdiness of, 20, 23, 31; and Benny Hill, 21; humor of, 21; interpretations of, 34, 35; and Monty Python, 21; popularity of, 20; as shocking, 30; and West End sex farces, 21
Twice-Told Tales (Hawthorne), 100

"Ugly Duckling, The," 81, 85
Under Drake's Flag (Henty), 146, 147, 148
Under the Sunset (Stoker), 162

Vaill, Amanda, 184, 186, 189
Vampyre, The (Polidori), 170
Vanity Fair (Thackeray), xi, 106, 107, 109, 113, 116; description of, 117, 118, 119; serialization of, 117; wit of, 123–124
Varney the Vampyre: or, the Feast of Blood (Ryder), 170
Virginians, The (Thackeray), 122

Walpole, Horace, 37, 53
Warner, Isabel. *See* Isabel Lewis
Watsons, The (Austen), 77
Wells, H. G., 165, 171, 197, 198, 204
West, Rebecca: on Sinclair Lewis, 200
Wiborg, Sara Sherman. *See* Sara Murphy
Wilkes, John, 33, 40
Willet, Deb, 16, 17
Wings of the Dove, The (James), 173
With Buller in Natal (Henty), 143
With Clive in India (Henty), 145
With Kitchener in the Soudan (Henty), 149
With Lee in Virginia (Henty), 145, 147
Woman in White (Picasso), 184
Woman in White, The (Collins), 125, 127, 130, 139, 155; description of, 136, 137; popularity of, 138
Wonderful Wizard of Oz, The (Baum), 177, 178, 180; inspiration for, 179; lessons of, 182; utopian elements of, 182
Woolf, Virginia, 23, 66
Woolson, Constance Fenimore: and Henry James, friendship with, 173, 176; suicide of, 175
Wordsworth, William, 48, 97

Yellowplush Papers, The (Thackeray), 109, 112, 113
Young Carthaginian, The (Henty), 145

A NOTE ON THE AUTHOR

Brooke Allen grew up in New York City and studied at the University of Virginia and Columbia University, where she received a Ph.D. She then worked in the theatre for some years and with wildlife conservation organizations, and as managing editor of *Grand Street* and *Common Knowledge*, both literary quarterlies. Ms. Allen's criticism has appeared frequently in the *New York Times Book Review*, the *Atlantic Monthly*, *The New Criterion*, the *Hudson Review*, and the *New Leader*, among other publications. Her first collection of criticism, *Twentieth-Century Attitudes*, was widely praised. She lives in Brooklyn with her husband, the photographer Peter Aaron, and two daughters.